Service
Etiquette

Service Etiquette

BY
REAR ADMIRAL BRUCE McCANDLESS, U.S.N. (RET.)
CAPTAIN BROOKS J. HARRAL, U.S.N.
ORETHA D. SWARTZ

FOREWORD BY
VICE ADMIRAL ROBERT B. PIRIE, U.S.N.

*correct
social usage
for service men
on official
and unofficial
occasions*

UNITED STATES NAVAL INSTITUTE, ANNAPOLIS, MARYLAND

Printed in the U.S.A.

BY GEORGE BANTA CO., INC., MENASHA, WISCONSIN

Foreword

John Paul Jones, example *par excellence* of the fighting man, is famous for his undying words, "I have not yet begun to fight!" But no less worthy of remembrance by his successors is his letter defining the requirements for a naval officer and a gentleman.

"It is by no means enough that an officer of the Navy should be a capable mariner," he wrote. "He must be that, of course; but also a great deal more. He should be as well a gentleman of liberal education, refined manners, punctilious courtesy, and the nicest sense of personal honor."

That last sentence points up a naval tradition that is inextricably a part of the training and character of those who follow the sea. It sums up neatly the goals of our Service Academies: *liberal education, refined manners, punctilious courtesy, the nicest sense of personal honor.*

Naval officers have always been called upon to represent their Nation at home and abroad, officially and personally. They must navigate the shoals and deeps of good society anywhere in the world as skillfully and surely as they handle a ship in formation or combat.

Service Etiquette has been written to give the young officer the benefit of the social experience of generations of officers and their ladies; in the social sense, "rules of the nautical road."

Much of the information in this book is presented generally—Jones's "liberal education." Much is presented as the usage of good society—Jones's "refined manners." Some of it goes to matters of tiny detail—"punctilious courtesy." And all the behavior discussed herein must stem from "the nicest sense of personal honor."

For "the great deal more" that John Paul Jones required, an officer must have a firm base in integrity of character. Manners must reflect that integrity and show the officer as a wise leader fully aware and deeply considerate of others.

Out of my own many years in the Naval Service, I commend to you *Service Etiquette,* whose one objective is to provide that knowledge of correct social and official behavior that, complementing professional knowledge, effects the finished product described by John Paul Jones: "An officer and a gentleman."

Robert B. Pirie
Vice Admiral, U. S. Navy

Washington, D. C.
1 November 1958

Introduction

This book is written for officers of all ages in the Armed Forces of the United States. It is specifically written for the young officer—the Midshipmen and Cadets at the Service Academies, the young men in the various branches of the Reserve Officers Training Corps and the Officer Candidate Schools. The aim of this book is to reach all officers at all bases and stations —wherever an American Serviceman may be.

This book is the first text of its kind to be written exclusively for Service officers. To you, an officer, the question may arise as to the necessity for such a work—a book of good manners and etiquette for an officer and gentleman. The authors find several valid reasons for compiling such a work. First, they know that the American Service officer is the best goodwill ambassador of his country—both at home and abroad. The American officer is judged not only by his military ability in the Services, but by his manners in his social as well as his official life. He is judged by his courtesy and consideration of others as well as the way he holds his fork at a formal dinner. Secondly, they know that the American officer must acquire tact in his social and official relations between the Services and people of all Nations.

What is etiquette? According to Webster, the word *etiquette* means: "The forms required by good breeding, social conventions, or prescribed by authority, to be observed in social or official life; the rules of decorum."

Good manners are the rules of the game of life. They are the rules which you observe in your daily living with your fellow men. Good manners are not just a way of holding your fork or the proper words spoken in an introduction or the correct way to go through a receiving line.

Although the tools of etiquette are important to know at all times, there is more to being a well-bred man than the mechanics of good manners. Good manners also means kindness to others, respect for the other man's feelings, an acknowledgment of right and wrong, an awareness of someone —*anyone*—whom you meet in a hallway, on the street, or at a party. Good manners is the consideration you grant someone as a person—not because he is important or is of high rank, but because he is a human being. Your manners never should be a veneer for show only—rather, they are the mirror of yourself.

Some men, however, seem to think that etiquette applies only to the game of society and easy living, that the word denotes effeminate qualities in an individual. While it is true that too-dandified manners or a fawning or "greasy" approach to life are abhorrent to most men, it is equally true that a shouted oath does not confirm administrative ability, and that uncouth manners do not prove manliness.

Since Midshipmen and Cadets are appointed to the various Service Academies from all walks of life, the authors feel that this book is of particular value to them. And since there is a close correlation between the young men in training at the Service Academies—with the differences mainly those of Service regulations and traditions—then what a Midshipman at the Naval Academy can expect through his four years at the Academy, and thereafter, is generally what any young man in the other Service Academies can expect in his social and everyday life.

Here is a brief résumé of what a Midshipman at the Naval Academy will meet in his social life, commencing with his Plebe year and progressing through his Youngster or Third Class year, Second Class year, and the all-important First Class year. The good manners which he should know before, during, and after attending the Naval Academy are fully explained in the following chapters of this book.

Fourth Class Year. A Plebe can expect limited social opportunities during his first year at the Naval Academy. This first year is an indoctrination period in the highly specialized Naval training which sets the pattern for his remaining years as a Midshipman.

Early in the year, each Plebe will meet a sponsor who will be an officer or professor on duty in the Severn River Naval Command, who will invite him to his quarters or home for dinner or some specified social occasion.

A Plebe "drags" only during authorized leave periods—mainly at Christmas, end of the semester, and in the spring. He may drag at football games held away from the Academy (the Army-Navy game), but not at home games. The highlight of his social year is the Farewell Ball, which is held at the conclusion of June Week and which heralds the end of Plebe Year.

All Plebes are required to attend the Sunday Informals, to which young ladies in the Washington, D.C., Baltimore, and Annapolis areas are invited. The Plebe is taught how to be properly introduced to young ladies and how to go through the receiving line, as well as the functions of a stag line. If he is not an accomplished dancer, dancing instruction is available.

Third Class Year. A Youngster will have increased opportunities to attend social functions and will drag frequently. He will attend various hops and entertainments at the Academy, and may drag to football games held at home as well as away.

A Youngster will attend social functions while on the annual Midshipmen Cruise, when he is taught how to conduct himself while in foreign ports and countries. Many NROTC students at various colleges throughout the country are also on the cruise and take part in these social functions.

West Point Cadets are annually invited to participate in the amphibious operations held for this class during summer months.

Second Class Year. A Second Classman attends many social functions during all leave periods and on two weekend liberties. He drags to hops and entertainments at the Academy, and the highlight of his year is the Ring Dance, which is preceded by a formal dinner. He will continue the practice of going through the receiving lines at official functions, and by this time should be adept in greeting hosts and hostesses and other guests.

During Aviation Summer, when members of the class are on air tours of various Naval Air Stations throughout the country, he attends social functions which widen his circle of friends.

First Class Year. A Midshipman comes into his own during First Class year. Other than attending the regular hops and entertainments, there are First Class hops and the participation in After Dinner Speaking, at which occasion he is taught the fine points in speaking fluently after dinners or banquets.

First Classmen are invited to dinner in the homes of Executive Department officers, with the Battalion and Company officers entertaining them at small or large dinners. All members of the First Class are invited in groups to dinner in the quarters of the Commandant of Midshipmen at some time during the academic year.

A member of this class attends many social functions on cruises, both at home and in foreign ports. He eats in the wardroom aboard ship and is "accepted" in Officers' Country.

June Week and graduation are the climax of the First Classman's life. With his parents and drag, he will attend the Superintendent's Garden Party. Graduation Day is the most important day of his four years at the Academy. Now he is entering a new life in the Service of his choice; perhaps he is also entering the wide sea of matrimony. Now, he is on his own.

To you, the prospective new officer—the Midshipmen of the United States Naval Academy and NROTC Units, the Cadets at the Military Academy, the Air Force Academy, the Coast Guard Academy, and the Merchant Marine Academy—it is to you that this book is dedicated.

Acknowledgments

Grateful acknowledgments of the authors are extended to those individuals whose kind cooperation has made the preparation of this book possible. Special acknowledgments are also made for valuable aid in compiling the material, to various branches of the Armed Services and to officials of state and civilian organizations.

Much of the material on calling cards, invitations, seating arrangements and toasts has been taken from the Navy's official book on *Social Usage and Protocol,* with the permission of the Director of Naval Intelligence, Rear Admiral Laurence E. Frost. This handbook has been issued for a number of years by the Office of Naval Intelligence for the guidance of naval officers serving at United States Embassies abroad. Miss Ruth Nelson Tarrant, the daughter and grand-daughter of well-known flag officers, and herself a lieutenant commander in the Naval Reserve, has been responsible for compiling this official publication which is used by all admirals' staffs as a protocol reference.

Considerable material on life in the wardroom has been taken from the Navy's guidebook, *The Wardroom,* compiled for officers of the Amphibious Force, U. S. Atlantic Fleet, under the direction of Vice Admiral F. G. Fahrion.

Thanks are particularly extended to the following officers of the Administrative and Executive Departments, U. S. Naval Academy (whose official rank and/or duty may have changed since publication of this book), for assistance in checking the facts:

Captain Allen M. Shinn, Commandant of Midshipmen; Captain James Lloyd Abbot, Jr., Commander David L. G. King, Commander Walter D. McCord, Jr., Commander Isaac C. Kidd, Jr. and Lieut. Commander Alan N. Davidson.

Sincere thanks are rendered to Brigadier General Robert M. Stillman, former Commandant of Cadets, U. S. Air Force Academy; Brigadier General R. D. Salmon, Commandant, U. S. Marine Corps Schools, and Major Young A. Tucker, U. S. Military Academy.

Also to Captain Fred D. Bennett, Senior Chaplain, Naval Academy Chapel; Captain A. C. J. Sabalot (retired), former Naval Attaché to France; Colonel C. W. Harrison, head, Historical Branch, G-3 (Marine Corps); Colonel J. L. Mueller, Lieut. Colonel C. H. Welch and Major John Greenwood (Marine Corps); Major John Schlegl (Air Force), and Commander Winston L. Adair.

Also to Mr. Bernard Baruch, Jr., for information concerning the Naval

Reserve officer; Mr. Clement E. Conger, Deputy Chief of Protocol, Department of State; Mr. John P. English of the U. S. Golf Association; Mr. R. W. Gieves of Gieves, Ltd.; Mr. H. E. Harding and Mr. Frank Overcarsh of the American Express Company; Mr. Duncan Hines and Mr. Roy L. Park, president of the Duncan Hines Institute; Mr. A. J. Keenan of A. G. Spalding and Brothers; Dean Howard Bagnall Meek, School of Hotel Administration, Cornell University, and Mr. Wesley M. Oler, Director of Public Relations, General Motors Export Corporation.

Our appreciation is extended to the officers and instructors of the Department of English, History, and Government, U. S. Naval Academy; the Chairmen and members of the Naval Academy Hop Committees, 1956-58; the Hostesses, Bancroft Hall, U. S. Naval Academy, and the Dean of Women at Wellesley College.

In addition, thanks are extended to the following for their advice: Rear Admiral and Mrs. Arthur A. Ageton, Mrs. Harry A. Baldridge, Mrs. Walter F. Boone, Mrs. Charles Buchanan, Mrs. Robert B. Carney, Professor Allen Blow Cook, Mrs. Alan N. Davidson, Mrs. John H. Davidson, Admiral and Mrs. Laurence T. DuBose, Mrs. Frank W. Fenno, Mrs. Frank Jack Fletcher, Professor William W. Jeffries, Mrs. Robert T. S. Keith, Mrs. Isaac C. Kidd, Jr., Mrs. Ruthven E. Libby, Mrs. John S. McCain, Jr., Captain John G. McCutcheon, Commander Robert K. Moxon, Medical Corps, Mrs. Albert G. Mumma, Major General and Mrs. Donald R. Ostrander, Mrs. Allen M. Shinn, Mrs. Morton Sunderland, Mrs. Joseph K. Taussig, Jr., Mrs. J. M. P. Wright, and Captain and Mrs. John D. Zimmerman.

Contents

SECTION VII
ON YOUR OWN

SECTION VIII
STRICTLY SERVICE

SECTION IX
PERSONAL MATTERS IN EVERYDAY LIFE

Service
Etiquette

SECTION I

EVERYDAY GOOD MANNERS—IN UNIFORM AND OUT

Good breeding is the result of much good sense, some good nature, and a little self-denial for the sake of others, and with view to obtain the same indulgence from them.

—Chesterfield

CHAPTER 1

In Uniform — and Out

GOOD GROOMING

A good first appearance depends to a great extent upon your personal grooming. A Midshipman or Cadet is trained during his years at the Academies to take care of his gear and his person—and this training should be observed for the rest of his life.

A first appearance may be one of the most important events of your life. It is impossible to foresee which day, which hour, may be that most important event, or what casual meeting may lead to your being accepted—or refused—by a person of value to your career.

It is important that you keep your uniform, cap cover, and gloves in neat and clean condition; your shoes must be shined, and your linens fresh and in good repair. Your civilian clothes should be conservative—not too gaudy or extreme in color and design.

Good grooming means clean finger nails—well trimmed but not blunt; the use of deodorants, regular baths and shaves. Dental care is of the utmost importance to both your health and appearance. A bad breath is extremely unpleasant. There is no excuse for dandruff.

Such habits as chewing gum, scratching your head or nose, cleaning your finger nails, or combing your hair in public are *not* conducive to making a good appearance in the Services—or in any walk of life.

ON TIME!

One of the most valuable habits which you can acquire is that of being on time. All officers are trained to be punctual in their official duties—and this habit should not be laid aside in your daily or social life. It is said that promptness and responsibility go hand in hand—therefore a habitual lack of punctuality must be considered irresponsibility.

At official or state occasions, you are expected to be on time. When royalty, or very high ranking officers or dignitaries of state, are guests at a luncheon or dinner, you must arrive before they do. But you will not leave before they do.

While you are not expected to be late at a dinner party, neither should you arrive *before* the hour named in the invitation and catch your hosts unprepared.

There are times in your social living, when you are late through no fault

3

of your own—when the plane is late, when the car has a flat tire, or when fog closes in and your boat cannot leave the ship.

When you are unavoidably late at a dinner and the guests have already gone into the dining room, you should go directly to the hostess and briefly apologize, then take your seat at the table. For reasons of her own, the hostess may not be able to wait too long for late comers.

When a woman is late, she should also briefly apologize to the hostess at the table. If she is your dinner partner, you should rise and assist with her chair. All other men guests at the table should not feel the necessity of rising to their feet—which would further embarrass the late guest and also inconvenience the other seated women guests. The host will rise to his feet, and remain standing until the woman guest is seated.

While a woman is usually excused for keeping you waiting, you yourself must always be on time and never keep her waiting.

You should never deliberately be late at a party in order not to be the first guest to arrive. This is inconsiderate to the hosts and does *not* show ultra-sophistication on your part.

At an afternoon tea or cocktail party or reception, you may arrive at any time after the first hour named in the invitation but not later than about a half hour before the last hour indicated in the invitation.

When you are a guest at a family dinner, be on time. Older children may join the family group at the table, and they are invariably hungry and impatient to be fed. Most hosts feed small children early and have them squared away before guests arrive. In this case, the dinner hour is usually a little later than usual.

Of course, a host and hostess are *never* late.

TIME TO GO?

There are no set regulations that will tell you exactly when it's time to leave after a party, but many a weary host and hostess wish there were. The aim of any host is to insure that guests enjoy the occasion—but sometimes a guest exceeds his host's hospitality.

In the Services, officers of high rank are frequently the busiest persons on the base or station. Other than their official responsibilities, senior officers have many social, community, and station obligations. Sometimes, such an officer and his wife make only a token appearance at a reception, tea, or cocktail party.

If you are a junior officer at an official or social function, you do not leave until *after* the guest of honor or the high ranking guest departs. This VIP may leave within thirty minutes after a dinner, and then you may also leave.

Customarily, the high ranking guest will stay from thirty to forty-five minutes after dinner, and should stay no longer than an hour afterwards.

If you are the high ranking guest, always remember that no one can properly leave until you do—and another guest may have a real reason to leave on time. Altogether, when nothing has been planned afterwards, the time involved at a formal dinner is between three and three and a half hours.

When to leave after an official luncheon is determined by the station duty of the host and his guests, and upon the time schedule and what is planned for the visiting dignitary. Customarily, guests stay about half an hour after luncheon. Altogether, the time involved is about an hour and a half.

At an afternoon reception, at-home, cocktail party, or a tea, you should stay no less than twenty minutes—but you should not stay later than an hour before the probable dinner hour of your hosts.

At an evening reception, etc., you will probably stay about forty-five minutes, but you will possibly stay longer at a smaller reception or cocktail party—say an hour or an hour and a half.

A young couple making a call on a senior couple usually stay fifteen to twenty minutes. Although the husband or wife—or bachelor officer—must not be obvious in watching the time—watch it one must. A senior officer and his wife will have many other callers, and there are many demands on their time.

A Midshipman or Cadet should not form the habit of calling at all hours and staying for hours. If the host and/or hostess invites you to their quarters or home and insist that you stay on for TV, badminton, tennis, etc., then you may feel free to do so. When you call unannounced, and stay too long, you may be upsetting plans made by your host and hostess. Thirty minutes are long enough to stay, customarily.

At any party, do *not* be the last person to leave.

HATS ON—AND OFF

In uniform, it is a custom of the Service that you do not raise your cap when greeting a man or woman in passing out-of-doors. Instead, you give a hand salute. When greeting and passing a woman, you may accompany the hand salute with a slight bow—but the bow is not necessary. You do *not* uncover when you are introduced to a woman out-of-doors, and you may salute again when leaving.

Indoors, you generally take off your cap as you would when in civilian dress. However, although a civilian generally does not remove his hat in an elevator unless leaving his hat on would make him conspicuous, the military man should apply the rule in reverse: he should remove his cap in an elevator unless removing it would make him conspicuous.

Aboard ship, junior officers should uncover when passing through the captain's or admiral's country, except when in evening dress uniform or wearing sword.

Officers should remove their caps on entering sick bay when patients are in evidence and when passing through messing compartments.

In civilian dress, it is easy for an officer to forget to take off his hat as custom demands in civilian life, so make a habit of not forgetting. You take off your hat when you stop to talk, or are introduced, to a woman out-of-doors, and leave it off unless the weather is bad.

You must take off your hat in a place of worship, except in Orthodox Jewish synagogues and in some conservative synagogues; you take it off whenever you pray or witness a religious ceremony, including a burial or outdoor wedding, or a dedication.

You remove your hat indoors except in stores, lobbies, corridors, and in such public buildings as a railroad station, post office, bank, etc. Your hat is safer on your head in a crowded elevator than when held in front of you, but you should take it off in hotel or apartment elevators.

Inside an office building leave your hat on—but take it off when entering an office. If you stop to ask directions of the receptionist, you should touch your hat. Touching your hat means touching the crown of a soft hat or the brim of a stiff one.

Your hat may be lifted momentarily when saying *hello, goodbye, thank you, excuse me,* etc. You grasp the front crown of a soft hat or the brim of a stiff one, then lift it slightly up and forward as you bow your head or smile.

A young man lifts his hat to an older man, and a man of any age lifts his hat in respect to a dignitary or an elderly gentleman. An abbreviated hat tip, something of an informal salute, is always a friendly gesture from one man to another.

You may check your hat before entering a public or club dining room, and it may be checked in a theater or placed in the rack under your seat.

BOWING

You should return any bow directed to you—on the street, in a bus, or across the room. When you are being introduced to a woman, you may bow slightly while shaking hands.

A bow is a slight inclination of your body from the waist up, feet together. A deep bow expresses great respect. A too-deep bow is strictly a Continental custom and is not customary in the United States.

When you are seated at the table and it is awkward or impossible to arise without disturbing others around you, you may half-rise and give a slight bow. But do not remain seated and bow, unless to someone junior to you. Whenever you bow, do not give the effect of bobbing your head.

SALUTING IN CIVVIES

As all officers know, when you are in uniform you salute whenever the national anthem is played, when the flag is passing in parade or in a review, and when the flag is hoisted or lowered.

Out of uniform, you (and any male civilian) will stand at attention, remove your hat with your right hand, place the hat over your heart—but no higher than shoulder level—or if you are uncovered, then you will stand at attention.

When you are with a woman, she should stand quietly as she faces the flag and/or the direction of the music.

If wearing a hat or a cap, as you step on the quarterdeck, you face aft and salute the national ensign and then salute the officer-of-the-deck. On leaving a ship, the procedure is reversed.

GLOVES

Gloves are worn out-of-doors upon certain occasions whenever a hat is worn. When in uniform, you will wear or carry gray gloves with blue service, and when wearing your overcoat. If you should be introduced outdoors, you may remove your right glove—if you have time. It is better to shake hands with your gloves on than to keep a person waiting—and you need not apologize for leaving them on.

Remove your gloves indoors except when you are ushering at a wedding or funeral, attending a formal dance, or have official guard duty. When you are introduced to someone during any of these occasions you do not take off your glove.

At a formal function, such as a reception, you should take off your right white glove when going through the receiving line, and hold it in your left hand. Replace the glove when you are through the line.

YOUR HANDS, AND HANDSHAKE

You will shake hands upon being introduced or saying goodbye to other men—the senior makes the first move. It is unforgivable not to accept a proffered hand. You wait until a woman offers her hand before extending yours. If you are seated, rise to your feet when introduced to anyone, and upon the departure of anyone. Women do not rise when being introduced to you.

A good handshake is at elbow level. You should avoid a handclasp that crushes or is too limp. Do not hold another's hand too long, or pump it up and down. A slight bow usually accompanies a handshake.

As mentioned elsewhere, you remove your right glove before shaking hands with anyone—if you have time. And of course, when shaking hands, you always look the person you are greeting in the eye.

Kissing a woman's hand is not a customary social gesture in the United

States—you should wait until you have foreign duty for this Continental custom. If, however, you do want to kiss a woman's hand, take her hand lightly in yours, then with a slight bow over her hand, touch your lips to the back of her hand. It is not correct to kiss the hand of an unmarried woman unless she is of age.

When women shake hands, a younger woman customarily waits for an older or high ranking woman to extend her hand in greeting first. The younger woman will rise when introduced to the wife of a senior officer or a much older woman, and will remain standing until that woman is seated. A woman need not rise for an introduction to a contemporary.

Your hands should be in your lap when you are not eating at the dining table. Avoid awkward positions with your hands at all times—such as locking them behind your head, thrusting them in your civvy pockets in unattractive bulges, or standing with clasped hands behind your back or pressed together steeplewise in front.

To stroke your chin, pick at your ears or head, or to drum on a table or chair shows a lack of poise. When you are walking or standing, your hands should be in a relaxed position at your sides.

Midshipmen and Cadets do not hold hands or link arms with girls in public; any ostentatious show of affection indicates a lack of tact and proper breeding.

When dancing, your left or leading hand should hold the woman's lightly and naturally. Your right or holding hand should be placed firmly yet easily just above her waist.

When you wish to help a woman down from a bus or train, etc., extend your hand to her, palm up. Don't put your hand under her arm—that is steering.

YOUR ARMS

You should offer a woman your arm only to give assistance when needed, or as an escort at a formal dinner, or as an usher at a wedding. You never grasp or take hold of the woman's arm—unless an accident is to be avoided. She will take your arm—you do not take hers.

You do not offer your arm in the daytime unless a woman needs help over rough ground, in a crowd, or when you assist an elderly or invalid man or woman.

When you offer your right arm at a formal dinner, bend your arm slightly at the elbow with your forearm parallel to the floor. Your partner will hold your arm lightly, but not hang onto it. When ushering at a wedding, a woman customarily takes the usher's right arm. A man does not take an usher's arm at a wedding unless he is elderly or an invalid.

ON YOUR FEET

You should stand whenever a woman enters a room, and should remain standing until she sits down. You again rise to your feet upon her departure from the room.

However, common sense will dictate how long you should remain standing when a woman thoughtlessly continues to stand and keeps all the men on their feet. When a woman prefers to remain standing with a group, you may return to your own group and sit down.

You are not expected to rise to your feet every time a hostess re-enters or leaves a room. And you need not rise to your feet at a business or organization meeting when a woman arrives late and disturbs the business proceedings. You stand when an elderly or high ranking man enters the room.

You stand up—not jump up—for introductions, greetings, farewells, and whenever a person wants to pass in front of you at the movies, football game—or any place where someone must pass in front of you and you do not want your feet stepped on.

When a woman, senior officer, dignitary, or elderly person comes to your table in a restaurant, you should rise to your feet. When it is very difficult to stand at a crowded table, a half-standing gesture is better than upsetting something on the table or annoying others.

It is not necessary in this modern age of equality among the sexes to give your seat in a bus or subway to a strange woman—unless you choose to. When a woman, or man, is elderly, disabled, burdened, or obviously tired, you may want to give her, or him, your seat. But a man is frequently far more weary and needs a seat on a bus much more than a woman returning home from the movies.

When you rise to leave a party, and after you say "goodbye" do not continue in conversation or otherwise dawdle and delay. Just—*go*.

WALKING OUTDOORS

When walking with a woman outdoors, you walk on the curb side or on her left side if there is no curb. The place of honor is always on the right. When walking with two women, you may walk between them only when crossing the street or if both ladies are elderly or are in poor health and may need assistance. When abroad, ascertain and follow the local custom.

When walking with men, the junior always walks on the *left* of the senior—except that when they are pacing to and fro, positions are not exchanged. When two or more men in uniform are walking together, they keep in step, with the senior setting the pace.

When passing a senior approaching from the opposite direction, you salute well in advance. When overtaking a senior, you pass to the left if possible (otherwise to the right), salute and say, "By your leave, Sir." just before coming abreast.

You should open all doors for women to pass through. If you are escorting a woman, you first hold the door open, then follow her through and close the door behind you. If she gets to the door first and opens it, do not make an issue of it but hold the door for her to pass through.

You may start a revolving door for a woman or a male senior to pass through. You may precede a woman through any door that opens onto a dark street or leads down steep stairs.

A junior officer, or younger man, opens a door for his senior. Junior officers stand aside for seniors to pass through doors, then follow.

WHO GOES FIRST?

When you are with a woman, she does—except:

- When your assistance is needed, such as when she is stepping down from a bus or train.
- When there is no waiter to precede you to a table in a restaurant, or no usher at the theater or movies.
- In a crowd, when you will clear the way.

COURTESY IN BOATS, CARS, AND AIRCRAFT

The procedure for getting in and out of a boat, car, or aircraft is similar: normally, the senior officer will enter last, and the junior will enter first. This procedure may be reversed in entering a car at a left-hand curb. Then the senior may enter first, in order that he may sit to the right without stumbling over juniors who are seated to the left. Seniors are always accorded the most desirable seats.

In a boat, the junior officer sits forward, with the senior sitting aft. In a car, the junior sits on the left, the senior on the right. In cases of full cars, the senior officers sit in the back seat and the juniors sit in the front.

In getting out of the boat, car, or aircraft, the order is reversed: the senior officer disembarks first, and the junior last. However, if a car draws up to a left-hand curb, it may be more appropriate for the junior to disembark first. In an aircraft, if the senior officer is engaged in flying the plane, the disembarkation procedure applies only among the passengers.

When you travel aboard the personal aircraft of a high-ranking senior— for example, the aircraft of a general officer—unless instructed otherwise, you should be aboard in a designated seat before the senior arrives at the aircraft. You should also remain in your seat until after he leaves the plane at its destination.

In civilian life, it is customary for a younger man to follow an older man into any vehicle—boat, car or aircraft—and to sit where you will least inconvenience him.

When accompanying women in a car, you should be the first to get out. You should hold the car door open, assist the woman out, then close the door. You should be the last person to get in the car and you should close the door. On official or formal occasions the woman is customarily seated at your right.

When you are driving the car, you should, if possible, get out, walk around the car and open the door for any women or older person. If it is not possible for you to get out, you may excuse yourself and reach across and open the door for your guest.

When you are the driver and a doorman opens the car door, the woman will get out first. When you are passengers in a car or taxi and not in city traffic, you get out first—even if she is closer to the door than you—and then you walk around the car and open the door for her. In traffic, whoever is closest to the door on the safe side gets out first.

MANNERS AT THE WHEEL

Any Service man who has not driven for some time—for instance, a naval officer who has been at sea for many months, a Midshipman or Cadet, should be slow to get behind the wheel of a car and "step on it." Without realizing it, his judgment behind the wheel may be off—regardless of the fact that he is a qualified driver with his driver's license in perfect order.

When driving a car be considerate of others on the road. It is inconsiderate to stop suddenly in the middle of the street to pick up a friend or to talk with him when it is just as easy to pull over to the curb. It is extremely dangerous to make a game of passing other cars at a high rate of speed—even though you are in a hurry to get some place.

On dates, it is good manners to go to the door of your date's house and properly call for the young lady rather than blasting the night or day by blowing the horn. Too loud and too long horn blowing is ear-shattering to others as well as conspicuously bad manners on your part.

RIDING IN TAXIS

When escorting a woman, you should give the directions to the driver and pay the taxi fare. If you are not accompanying her to her destination, ask the driver what the amount will be and pay him, not the woman. You also pay the driver's tip along with his charge.

When you share a taxi with a woman member of the Armed Forces or a business woman, she will usually wish to pay for her share of the fare. If she gets out first, she will pay her share to that point, plus her share of the tip. If she shows no inclination to pay for her share, there is nothing for you to do as a gentleman but pay it.

You do not ask a woman unknown to you to share a taxi, but if you have a slight acquaintance and if she is going your way, you may offer to share the taxi. In case of bad weather or at a rush hour, a strange woman may ask if she can share your taxi—and you may accept or refuse as the occasion demands. When you have an important schedule to keep, you should drive there first.

Two or more men may share a taxi fare. If one man insists upon paying, you may agree and say, "Next time it's mine." Then try to be sure that there is a next time.

Taxi tips vary, but in large cities the tip is usually fifteen cents up to seventy cents fare, and from fifteen to twenty-five cents for meter readings up to $1.00. From there on the tip is about twenty per cent of the fare. You usually tip fifteen per cent for a very long fare.

SEATING A WOMAN

You will assist a woman with her chair when she sits down at the dining table, and when she rises. The chair is pulled back as she steps into place from the right, then you push the chair under her as she bends to sit down.

When she rises from the table—she usually does this to the right of her chair—you should draw the chair back without jerking it.

HOLDING COATS

When you help a woman with her coat, hold the coat right side up with the armholes at a comfortable height for her to slip her arms into. Do not muss her hair.

A woman usually does not check her coat in a restaurant or the theater. The coat may be laid across a vacant chair at the table, or across the back of her chair at the table or in the theater. You should see that the coat does not trail on the floor. A stole may be folded and laid across a chair, or chair back.

You may check your own coat and hat after entering a hotel, but before going into the dining room. These articles may also be checked at the theater, but time may be saved if you take them with you. You generally place your hat on the rack under the seat.

SENDING FLOWERS

When sending flowers to a woman, choose them to fit her type as well as the occasion on which they will be worn or displayed. Try to find out what she is wearing, and send flowers that are appropriate. You would send chrysanthemums to a woman attending a football game, and gardenias or an orchid when she's attending a dance. Flowers are pinned on a costume as they are grown—heads up.

A very short woman may not care for a very large corsage, but she would like a small corsage or nosegay to pin on her gloves or evening bag. A bouquet of flowers may be sent to a hostess by a guest of honor for the party given for him or as thanks for a favor received or party attended.

It is not advisable to send potted plants to a hostess whose husband has orders as she may be moving. In such a case, the plants and your money may be wasted.

CHANCE ENCOUNTERS

You do not pay for the lunch or dinner of a chance encounter with a woman. If you should happen to run into an acquaintance at a restaurant or lunch counter, you do not need to pay his or her bill—unless you want to. When you chance to meet a man or woman at a bus stop, or decide to share a taxi, you usually pay only your share of the charges.

If you must speak to a woman who is a stranger, or hand her something —such as returning an object she dropped on the sidewalk—you may touch her arm lightly when you catch up with her, to get her attention; then you turn away as soon as you have accomplished your mission.

When you give your seat to a woman in a bus, subway or train, you may touch your hat when you rise to your feet, but you need not say anything. When a man gives his seat to the woman you are escorting, you should touch your hat when acknowledging his courtesy.

You must avoid calling out a woman's name in public in loud tones, even when you are surprised and delighted at the encounter.

SMOKING

Although smoking appears to have become a worldwide habit, there are many people who do not smoke and others who are allergic to smoke in any form. A habitual or chain-smoker frequently is unwittingly offensive to a non-smoker, so you should be careful to observe the following rules:

- Never smoke out-of-doors when in uniform except when seated at an athletic contest or other types of outdoor activities.
- Do not take a lighted cigarette to the dining table, onto a dance floor, or into a church, theater, museum or other public place.
- Always observe the non-smoking regulations in public places.
- Never smoke at, or while taking part in, a formal or official occasion such as a wedding, reception, etc.

- Never use a saucer, dish, or plate at the dining table for an ash tray. Cigarettes are usually offered at the dining table—but when they are not, you must assume that your hostess does not wish any smoking at the table.
- Never smoke cigars during a meal, though you may do so after the women have left the table. Do not smoke cigars in the living room unless you have obtained the hostess's permission first.
- Do not spill ashes on the floor, flip ashes into a wastepaper basket, or lay a lighted cigarette on a table.
- Never take offense when someone asks you not to smoke in his or her presence.
- And, of course, you do not smoke in Navy boats.

Always offer a cigarette to a woman, or others near you, before taking one yourself. You strike and hold a match or a lighter for a woman, and also offer the light to others before lighting your own cigarette. Be careful to hold the light high enough so that a person does not have to bend over it. At a party, a man would light his hostess's cigarette before his wife's.

There is no need to cross a room and offer a cigarette to a woman, or to go entirely around a room and offer cigarettes to everyone. Cigarettes are customarily placed in convenient containers throughout a room. You may offer cigarettes to as many as you conveniently can.

When a person does not smoke, you do not need to keep offering him cigarettes. If he does smoke, but does not care for one at the moment, you may offer a cigarette later.

You may smoke during intermissions at the theater. If your woman guest does not care to smoke, she may remain in her seat while you go to the lobby. If she cares for a smoke, and you don't smoke, you should accompany her to the lobby.

CIGARS AND PIPES

There is an old-fashioned rule—now observed only by elderly or very sedate persons—which decreed that a man should never smoke a pipe or cigar in an automobile with a woman. It is customary today for both men and women to smoke cigarettes in automobiles, with men smoking anything they choose. It is important, however, that you do not light up without first asking other persons in the automobile, "Do you mind if I smoke?"

A considerate smoker doesn't blow smoke in another person's face. And you always take your cigarette, cigar, or pipe out of your mouth before lifting your hat, bowing, greeting others, or when you talk.

Men who smoke cigars and pipes should always be sure that an ash tray is large enough to accommodate all the ashes. A chewed cigar or ashes

from a pipe should not be left in other people's homes—and are not attractive in your own.

SOUNDING OFF

There is an old Service rule: "Never volunteer information." If you don't give free information about someone or something, you can't be quoted. Gossip is not confined to the opposite sex—a study of military history through the ages forces one to the conclusion that there would be no Mata Haris if Service men didn't talk.

A young officer should learn early in his career not to discuss carelessly military subjects of a classified nature. You should never speak critically of your seniors.

It is poor manners for an officer of any age to discuss such subjects as personal business or women at the officers' mess table, or in the wardroom. If you *must* discuss these, do so elsewhere—and discreetly. Always remember that your business ceases to be personal if made public.

Everyone at some time in his life has been bored to distraction by the conversationalist who drones on and on. But—are *you* sometimes guilty of being a bore by going overboard on a subject that interests you greatly? When you suspect that you are becoming long-winded—and you may detect this by observing the reactions of those around you—then change the subject and let someone else talk while you listen.

In reverse, there are times when you are exhausted beyond endurance by a monologue, and the only way to break the spell is to interject a remark at the end of a sentence or when the bore needs a fresh breath. A favorite phrase is, "Oh, that reminds me—!"

When you unintentionally interrupt a speaker, you should say, "I'm sorry," or "I'm sorry, but I thought you had finished." You should try not to interrupt a speaker, and you should pay him the attention that you hope he pays you.

EXHIBITIONISM

Exhibitionism means drawing attention to yourself in a public place. This is accomplished by shouting, whistling, clowning, loud laughter, booing, or doing something foolish or unusual. A person of good breeding does not care to make himself, or his friends, conspicuous in a public place—or any place.

You should not make a public display of your emotions or affections. Kissing in public is frowned upon in the Services, except in cases of farewell when the separation is expected to be a long one. It is a better custom to shake hands in greeting and farewell with women as well as with men, although some women insist upon kissing when meeting—other women as

well as men. Kissing and holding hands should be considered a private rather than a public demonstration.

One example of exhibitionism is the couple on the dance floor who execute too-intricate steps or who hold each other in exaggerated positions. No couple should monopolize the dance floor.

Although everyone enjoys talking about friends and acquaintances of high rank or position, with interesting or amusing anecdotes related, you can overdo it.

Another form of showing self-importance is the over-use of foreign words and phrases. Although an occasional foreign expression can be very appropriate in good English conversation, too many such expressions can become tiresome to the average person who does not speak that particular foreign language.

When you use foreign phrases, be sure that you are proficient in their usage and pronunciation—you may be among linguists who are really adept!

APOLOGIES

No one likes to apologize, but apologies are in order when:

- You are late at a luncheon or dinner party—or any social occasion such as a reception where the receiving line has already broken up. Then you go directly to the hostess and briefly apologize.
- The host and hostess have waited for your arrival at a luncheon or dinner party, but have not gone into the dining room. Then you apologize and tell them why you were late—and the reason must be excellent!
- You fail to keep an appointment. You should telephone or write a brief note, explaining your failure to keep the appointment—and again, the reason must be a good one.
- You cannot grant a request. In this case you must not only give your regrets, but if possible add some explanation, such as, "I'm sorry, but due to the great sentimental value attached to the object, I can't lend it for the exhibition, etc., etc."
- You break or damage something. You must attempt to replace the article exactly, but if you cannot, then send flowers with your calling card. You should, of course, state on the card that you are sorry concerning the mishap.
- You step or pass in front of someone, or bump into them. In such cases you say "Please excuse me," or "I beg your pardon," or "I'm sorry."
- You have caused harm, or have hurt someone needlessly, or through

carelessness. In this case you must do more than apologize—you must ask the other person's forgiveness.

SOCIAL OBLIGATIONS

A bachelor officer, or a young married couple, cannot be expected to repay the hospitality of an established or older married couple. The young couple may repay their host's hospitality in their own way—at a small cocktail party, informal lunch or dinner, or by performing some small act or favor that is sincere and without ostentation.

As a general rule, when you accept someone's hospitality, you are expected to reciprocate in some fashion. The perennial guest will eventually wear out his welcome by always being a guest, but never a host. No one wants the young couple to repay an expensive dinner party with the same kind of party, dollar for dollar. But the genuineness of the juniors' desire to repay, and their attempt to be pleasant and loyal, is all-important. As the younger couple advances in seniority and rank through the years, they in turn will extend hospitality to junior officers and young couples.

After small parties, a bachelor officer or any guest may telephone or write their hosts and say how much he enjoyed their hospitality. If the occasion was a special one, flowers may be sent to the hostess with a brief and sincere note of thanks written on an enclosed calling card. Flowers are not necessary, but the note, or perhaps a telephone call, is.

However, you do not phone thanks after large parties since innumerable calls would keep the hostess on the telephone by the hour. In such cases, a sincere expression of thanks at the time of leaving the party is generally sufficient.

All social invitations should be answered promptly. Thank-you notes should be written within forty-eight hours after the occasion. A thank-you note will take only a few minutes of your time—but this small courtesy is invaluable in matters of manners and good-will.

MORAL OBLIGATIONS

You must always remember that the word—or signature—of a gentleman is his bond. Therefore, think twice before you make promises. Signed to a check your signature means that you stand good for the amount indicated. Signed to the endorsement at the end of an examination it means that you subscribe to the work submitted and that it is your work. Signed to a letter it means that the ideas expressed are your own.

It is of the utmost importance that men in the Services be honest and direct in all their dealings. Juniors can avoid a great deal of embarrassment by giving a complete but to-the-point answer in replies to questions put by their seniors.

If you are the junior and do not know or cannot give a complete or correct answer, then you should answer *only as much of the question as you can without evasion or giving misinformation.* An honest "I don't know, Sir, but I will find out and let you know," is a better answer than an indirect one that gives minsinformation on which your senior may be basing an important decision. An evasive answer might seriously affect your Service reputation.

FINANCIAL OBLIGATIONS

It is mandatory that all members of the Services discharge their acknowledged and just financial obligations. As a member of a Service you remain a citizen and, as such, you have continuing obligations to obey certain civil statutes and to carry out any civil-court orders, decrees, or judgments to which you are a party. You cannot use your Service status as a pretext for evading your financial obligations.

This doesn't mean that you must pay unjust claims just to avoid unpleasant publicity. You are protected by the fact that your commanding officer must make a careful investigation into the justness of any claim you disavow. But be sure you are in the right before you put your commanding officer to that trouble.

However, commanding officers are not supposed to act as agents for claimants in business transactions or claim collections. Usually the CO only makes sure that the claimant's communication reaches the officer or man concerned and that a prompt reply is made. But a commanding officer cannot tolerate actions of irresponsibility, gross carelessness, neglect, or dishonesty in the financial dealings of his personnel. If he is certain that the officer is negligent or careless in regard to his personal finances, he will make an entry on the officer's fitness report and, if the circumstances warrant such action, he will necessarily recommend trial by court marital.

If you are assigned to a job involving the custody of funds—such as mess treasurer—you should make careful check to insure that you get all that you sign for when you take over. If you should be a member of an auditing board, be sure that what you certify as on hand is actually present. Never be careless in making audits and taking inventories. The fact that someone else may have signed does not mean that you can sign blindly and assume that all is well. Usually, the junior signs first, at the bottom of the page.

Officers should never lend money to, or have any financial dealings with enlisted personnel. Navy Regulations are definite in directing you not to make such loans. If someone asks for a loan, you must decline and inform him that Navy Regulations prohibit your doing so. If his case is a deserving one, he should have no trouble in getting a loan from the ship's Welfare Fund or the Navy Relief Society. While there is no similar regulation pro-

hibiting financial dealings with officers—there should be. It is better to avoid such dealings.

OFFICIAL MANNERS

As every young officer knows, when a junior reports to the office of a senior, he announces himself either through the orderly or by knocking. He waits until told to enter, then uncovers and holds his cap in his right hand, by the visor, then he goes up to the officer or within a few paces of the officer's desk. He precedes his report or request by announcing, "Ensign John Doe, Sir." When the business has been terminated, he leaves promptly.

If you are the junior officer, you will call the senior by his title and name, "Captain Jones" etc., rather than by the impersonal "Sir." On board ship or in any naval organization there is only one "Captain" (the regularly assigned commanding officer) and only one "Commander" (the regularly assigned executive officer) who are addressed as "Captain" and "Commander" without adding their name. Other captains and commanders are addressed by rank and name.

You should always be careful not to obtrude your greeting upon your senior. For instance, if the senior is engaged in conversation, working on a chart, or concentrating on some problem, he might be distracted by the necessity of replying to the greeting.

Always remember that a senior sends his *compliments* to a junior; the junior sends his *respects*. In written correspondence the senior may "call" attention, but the junior may only "invite" it.

YOUR SERVICE COMMUNITY

The Armed Services are friendly Services. No matter where you go on active duty, there will be a serviceman near you who is in or about your own age group and financial circumstances. It's difficult to be lonely in the Service, whether you are at sea or ashore.

Most Service communities are also friendly—however, a few Service people make themselves undesirable in a town or community due to their lack of consideration for the other fellow's feelings as well as his possessions. Perhaps this lack of responsibility stems from the fact that Service people are not in one place very long and thus grow careless in caring for another's property.

You should take care of the other person's property with as much—or more—respect as your own . . . and this is taking for granted that you *do* take care of your own things. When you are in quarters, or rent a house or apartment, you should not abuse it. Don't leave dirt and trash lying around, or generally wreck the place—you will not be welcome back nor will you leave a favorable impression of your Service.

It is thoughtless to borrow the other person's property and not return it—

no matter whether this is a book, a golf club, or a pound of coffee. You must always return what you borrow—and develop the habit of not borrowing.

A wise man will try to fit into a new community rather than attempt to change it. You should always be thoughtful of your neighbors. It is extremely unwise to walk into a commercial house and say, "That can be bought at the Exchange for a third of your price!"

THE SEA OF MATRIMONY

All men like to think that they are the head of their house—as they should be. However, a man should be a partner in a home—not its dictator. Good manners in marriage mean loyalty to and respect for the other partner—but this loyalty and respect should be earned, not demanded.

A man and his wife should share the responsibility in the management of the family finances, with the wife fully understanding the limitations of a paycheck and the obligations which must be met each month. Since an officer is gone from home during much of his career, it is necessary that someone carry on the family's financial obligations and keep an accurate account of the family expenditures during his sea duty.

A young wife may have had little experience in financial matters before marriage—and a young husband may have had almost as little financial experience himself. It is important that a young couple work together as a team in sharing the household responsibilities—unless one is incompetent. But what appears to be incompetence may only be inexperience.

A partnership in marriage includes a sound evaluation of each other's responsibilities: a man with his busy career and its problems and worries; a woman with a house to clean, food to cook, and children to care for when these are small. Sometimes a woman even combines these household activities with a career, or a part-time career, with little or no household help.

A husband often lends a hand—and the wife will do the same—in jobs frequently considered the specific chore of the other. But a man should not be *required* to do a woman's work any more than a woman should be expected to do a man's work or to contribute too much as a bread winner. It is important that neither the husband nor the wife hold their extra work as a mental club over the other.

A partnership in marriage means that both partners say "we" instead of "I" and "our" instead of "my." But this does not mean that a partner cannot have any liberty of thought or action. Partnership and domination do not go hand-in-hand.

A happy household is one where both the man and woman have a certain money allowance for their own personal use—with no strings attached whatsoever.

A happier household and a stronger partnership may be worked out when:

A husband does not:

- Give orders (you should confine orders to your professional career).
- Drop ashes from cigarettes, cigars, or a pipe on the floor or furniture.
- Bring someone home for a meal without advance notice.
- Interrupt his wife's story—or anyone else's.
- Forget to compliment his wife when she merits it.
- Criticize his wife's appearance, or anything else about her, in front of others.
- Compare his wife's cooking unfavorably with another's.
- Toss a hat or coat on the chair or sofa, or forget to hang up his gear.
- Leave a razor lying around uncleaned, drop a wet towel on the bathroom floor, or leave the toothpaste uncapped.

A wife does not:

- Act "bossy" or nag.
- Gossip or tell personal, official, or business affairs to others.
- Be late.
- Dress slovenly—such as wearing a robe instead of a housedress, or pin curlers or face cream during hours when these can be avoided.
- Interrupt her husband's story.
- Forget to compliment him when he deserves it.
- Talk *too* much about the baby, at parties or elsewhere.
- Visit her mother too often, or have too many in-laws as houseguests (a woman old enough to marry is old enough to maintain her own home).
- Be jealous of her husband's time, classmates, or longtime friends.
- Decide abruptly when to leave a party or any social function (she should consult her husband first).

As partners, a man and wife should never belittle each other. Any family dissension should be discussed in private—but *not* before the children or a servant. It should be a matter of personal pride for both a man and his wife to be as neat and as attractive and as mentally stimulating after marriage as before.

CHAPTER 2

Service and Civilian Dress

An abbreviated uniform chart has been worked out for the convenience of officers in the Naval Service. However, a more fully described discussion of civilian dress is necessary to make the distinctions between "black tie" and "white tie" and when such dress is worn. There is a more general description of the civilian dress needed by officers for everyday living out of uniform:

SERVICE DRESS:

Abbreviated Uniform Chart

UNIFORM		COAT-TROUSERS	SHIRT	TIE	COLLAR	GLOVES	MEDALS/RIBBONS
Official Functions as designated							
Full Dress	B	B Service	Plain	4-hand	TD	W	Lg Med-Swd
Full Dress	W	W Service	—	—	—	W	Lg Med-Swd
Black tie							
Dinner Dress	B	B Service	Stiff	BB	TD	G	Rib
Dinner Dress	W	W Service	—	—	—	W	Rib
Dinner Dress	MJ	MJ BS	Stiff	BB	TD	W	MinMed-Cum'bund
White tie							
Evening Dress	B	ED ED	Stiff	WB	W	W	Min Med-W'coat
Evening Dress	W	W Service	—	—	—	W	Min Med
Evening Dress	MJ	MJ ED	Stiff	BB	W	W	Min Med-W'coat

NOTE:

B—Blue	MJ—Mess Jacket	Min Med—Miniature medals
W—White	BS—Blue Service	Lg Med-Swd—large medals, sword
G—Gray	ED—Evening Dress	Rib—ribbons
BB—Black Bow	4-hand—four-in-hand	W'coat—waistcoat
WB—White Bow	TD—turn down	

NOTE: *With overcoat*, wear gray gloves.

The senior officer who prescribes the uniform of the day will also prescribe the gloves as a part of the uniform; gray gloves are usually prescribed with blue service. *Cap covers:* (a) whenever the uniform is modified by Alpha, wear blue cap covers; (b) whenever the uniform is modified by Bravo, wear white cap covers. Miniature medals are worn on the left breast.

NOTE: The local uniform regulations differ in various parts of the country, according to climate and locale. The change from whites to blues differs in various sections, according to the season. Details of all uniforms will be found in the *U. S. Navy Uniform Regulations.*

CIVILIAN DRESS: FORMAL

Black Tie

"Black tie" means your dinner jacket or tuxedo. The term "tuxedo" came about in the 1890's when the dinner jacket was introduced into the United States from England and was first worn at the Tuxedo Club.

This is the favorite form of men's evening dress and is worn at almost any formal occasion—receptions, weddings, theater or opera, dances, dinners, etc. "Black tie" is not properly worn on Sundays or before six o'clock in the evening. The following items of dress may be worn:

Jacket—Of black or midnight-blue worsted (or material of good quality) for winter or cold weather wear; in summer, white linen or tropical worsted, dacron, etc. The black jacket may be worn in the summer time—but it is hot. Nowadays, the new plaid dinner jacket is coming into use.

Trousers—Material matches the coat, with single stripe of matching colored braid or satin. Trousers are without cuffs. (Black trousers are worn with white jacket.)

Waistcoat—Is not worn with a double-breasted jacket; with single-breasted jacket, the waistcoat will be of plain, ribbed, or self-figured silk. Instead of a waistcoat, a *cummerbund* or a stiffened type of sash, may be worn.

Shirt—Either stiff-bosomed or the much more popular (and comfortable) attached fold collar with pleated or plain soft bosom. White is customary.

Tie—Black or midnight blue bow.

Socks—Black or dark blue to match trousers, in silk or any good material.

Shoes—Black patent leather.

Hat—Not necessary, but a black or dark blue homburg in winter, and a Panama in summer.

Gloves—Gray mocha, nylon, chamois, or buck.

Topcoat—Black, oxford gray, dark blue wool, etc., with or without velvet collar.

Accessories—White linen handkerchief; white silk scarf; studs and cuff links.

White Tie

"White tie" means full dress evening wear, or "tailcoat." Tails are not worn often except by men in the diplomatic service, senior officers, or at a very formal wedding, dinner, etc. When you need civilian tails for a special occasion, a good rental service will furnish them for the occasion.

Like dinner jackets, tails should never be worn before six o'clock, or on Sunday. Also, tails are not worn in the summer. Properly, the tailcoat should hang just below the knee in back. Here are the necessary items:

Tailcoat—Black or midnight blue worsted; peaked lapels, faced in satin or grosgrain.

Waistcoat—White piqué, single or double-breasted, with self-covered buttons, or fastened with separate studs which should match shirt studs.

Trousers—To match the coat. Double stripes of black or blue satin, faille, or braid; without cuffs.

Shirt—White linen or piqué with detachable white wing collar, and stiff, single cuffs; starched white piqué bosom or plain linen.

Tie—White piqué bow, butterfly, or straight club shape.

Socks—Matching color to tails, in silk or good material.

Shoes—Black patent leather pumps with or without grosgrain bows, or oxfords without toe caps.

Hat—Collapsible opera hat or high silk hat.

Topcoat—Same as for black tie, uniform overcoat, or cape.

Gloves—White mocha, nylon, chamois, or doeskin of the button type. Do not wear the old fashioned white kid gloves once worn for dancing.

Accessories—White suspenders; white linen handkerchief; white or red carnation for left buttonhole, or a small white gardenia, lily-of-the-valley, etc., at a wedding; white silk scarf; studs and matching cuff links. You do not wear a boutonniere if you're wearing decorations or when you are in uniform tails.

DECORATIONS

The wearing of decorations, medals, badges, and ribbons is in accordance with the instructions issued by the Bureau of Naval Personnel. Such instructions are available to all officers on active duty at any station or base.

The regulations concerning the wearing of such decorations by retired officers, as well as civilians with authority to wear them, states that: "Decorations, medals, badges, and ribbons shall not be worn on overcoats, nor with civilian clothes, except that on appropriate occasions miniature medals complete with authorized appurtenances (except the Medal of Honor) may be worn with civilian evening dress.

"Miniature replicas of ribbons or decorations, medals, and badges (except the Medal of Honor) made in the form of lapel buttons, may be worn on civilian clothes. The ribbon of the Medal of Honor, made up in rosette form, may be worn on civilian clothes."

RETIRED OFFICER'S DRESS

Although most officers retired from the Services wear civilian dress at various official and social occasions, there are occasions when the uniform may be worn—such as a military wedding or an official reception when all other officers will be in uniform.

The number of years of retirement has nothing to do with the retired officer's decision to wear—or not to wear—his uniform: the elements of good taste and propriety are the key to his decision.

FORMAL DAYTIME CLOTHES

Formal daytime clothes—the *cutaway* or *sack coat*—are mainly worn at diplomatic or governmental affairs. A man taking part in a formal day-time wedding party, or a pallbearer at a large funeral, also wears such dress. When called upon to take part in such a formal function, you will want to know just what to wear.

Cutaway—Worn less frequently than the tailcoat, may also be rented. It is of black or oxford gray worsted, cashmere, or cheviot, with peaked lapels with plain edges; bone or self-covered buttons.

Waistcoat—Single or double-breasted, will match the coat, or may be of pearl gray or buff doeskin; in summer, white or tan linen.

Trousers—Black and gray stripes, or black and white striped worsted or chevoit, cuffless. Stripes may be close together or up to one inch apart.

Shirt—White, with plain or pleated bosom. You may have a fold collar and double cuffs, or wing collar and stiff cuffs.

Socks—Black or gray, in any good material.

Shoes—Black calf oxfords.

Tie—Gray, black, or silver-gray silk; plain, figured, or striped. An ascot is usually worn with wing collar at weddings; at funerals, the tie is always a black four-in-hand with fold collar. For other occasions, either a four-in-hand or bow may be worn with either a wing or fold collar.

Outer clothes—Gray mocha gloves; black, blue, oxford gray, or any conservative colored topcoat; black silk hat.

Accessories—White or gray scarf; white linen handkerchief; gray or black and white suspenders; white or red carnation (no boutonnieres are worn at funerals or with officer's uniform); matching studs and cuff links. Spats (infrequently worn) are optional at weddings but are never worn at funerals; they should be gray felt or doeskin in winter; white or tan linen to match waistcoat, in summer.

The sack coat is interchangeable with the cutaway, but is slightly less formal. When it is needed, it can be obtained from a good rental service.

Sack Coat—Is single-breasted, of black or oxford gray worsted.
Waistcoat—Matches the sack coat.
Trousers—Same as for cutaway.
Shirt—White, with fold collar, stiff cuffs.
Tie—Four-in-hand, or black or black-and-gray silk. Sometimes a bow tie is worn.
Hat—Black homburg or derby.
Shoes, socks gloves, topcoat and *accessories* are the same as with a cutaway—except that spats are never worn.

Concerning certain accessories, boutonnieres other than white or red carnations may be worn at various occasions. Corn flowers and small white gardenias are sometimes used, and a groom at a wedding occasionally wears an orange blossom or a small sprig of lily-of-the-valley. Such flowers are always worn in the left buttonhole of a suit and are *never* worn when you are in unform.

A handkerchief placed in the breast pocket of your suit is entirely for show. It must, of course, be clean and folded, and only an inch or two shows. When you use a colored handkerchief in your breast pocket, it must blend with the colors in your tie.

A dress handkerchief is white linen and can be initialed with a single letter or with all your initials. For evening use, the initials are white, gray, or black, but other colors are correct for daytime use.

CIVILIAN DRESS: INFORMAL

Any officer faces a distinct problem in the matter of his clothes. This is because he must possess two wardrobes—naval and civilian—and, somehow, they must be paid for. Since uniforms are a necessity, they are purchased first.

When an officer of average financial circumstances purchases his uniform wardrobe and maintains it in the high state of excellence in which it should be kept, usually there is only a modest amount left over in the clothes budget. It is important, therefore, that unless he is a rare and fortunate individual with no financial problems, he purchase a conservative civilian wardrobe which can be worn for many occasions and seasons.

The best clothes are always those of good quality, subdued color, and the best possible tailoring. Such colors as gray, blue-gray, dark blue, or tans and browns, are best. Tweed sports jackets in moderate-toned greens, browns, blues, and gray mixtures are always in good taste. The same conservative overtone is important in all other items of dress—such as socks, ties, shirts, etc.

However, if you must display a flamboyant streak, it should be confined to such items as sports shirts, bathing trunks, pajamas, and even then it is possible to go too far. Although it is true that more color is used in men's clothing today than ever before, it is wise to purchase shirts and ties, particularly, with care.

In the long run, cheap clothes are the most expensive because they do not last as long and must be replaced earlier than expected. It is wise, therefore, that when you buy your first civilian wardrobe after graduating from the Academy, or when you first start out "on your own," you don't succumb to the extremes in color and style, "gambler fashion."

It is well to remember that what is good taste in one part of the country may be poor taste in other parts. The bright and unusual sports shirts and slacks which are so familiar in Hawaii or southern and western states, may not look the same in more conservative—and cooler—northern and New England states—or vice versa.

Although it is difficult to state any rule for wearing or buying clothes—particularly when you are transferred from one coast to another—appropriate dress is usually the conservative type of clothes which are good taste any place. It is also well to note that dress in foreign countries is generally on the conservative side, and a "loudly" dressed American is not a good representative of the Service.

The question often arises as to the clothes needed for a young officer's civilian wardrobe. There is no set formula, but the following suggestions are offered as helpful hints and are based on the consensus of a cross-section of officers who have learned through actual experience—oftentimes the hard way.

MINIMUM CLOTHING LIST

This list is considered a minimum to meet most occasions, and is arranged in the order of suggested purchase—or when you are acquiring your wardrobe piecemeal:

1. *A conservative suit.* One such suit will be adequate at first, but you should plan on getting two as soon as the financial situation permits. One or both suits should be suitable for wearing after six o'clock when semi-formal conditions are to be met. One of the suits must definitely be of a dark color. (The dark blue business suit is traditional.)

2. *A sports jacket.* This jacket will probably be the most useful and the most worn item in your wardrobe. You should be sure to get a good one that will not shrink despite many cleanings, and you must keep an eye out as to the color, choosing one that can be worn with almost any color slacks. Here, also, one coat is adequate, but plan on getting a second one later.

3. *Slacks.* At least two pairs of slacks are necessary, preferably of solid

colors and of good quality. Grey flannel slacks are standard any where in the world and if of good material will wear very well. On the other hand, you can run through several pairs of cheap slacks much quicker than you will run through two pairs of good ones.

4. *Topcoat.* If you find that you cannot afford a topcoat in the early stages, you can always use your officer's raincoat without the insignia. But making the raincoat "double in brass" reduces its longevity, and you should plan on getting a topcoat in the near future. Unless you expect to be stationed in very cold climates for all your tours, stick to the type topcoat that has a zipper lining. They are much more practical than getting an overcoat.

5. *Summer clothes.* It may develop that you will need summer suits and slacks immediately. Therefore, you will have to use your own discretion as to how many you should buy. Eventually you will need one or two summer suits—or odd jackets and trousers—in order to round out your wardrobe; but don't be blinded initially into sinking too much money into this type of clothes. Duties involving winter clothes will surely turn up eventually.

6. *Dinner jacket.* This should be the last item on your list, for you may have the least use for it. (This dinner jacket is a good item to put on your Christmas list for your parents to give you!) Actually, the need for a dinner jacket is increasing each year. Of course, you can wear your uniform with black bow tie and be properly dressed for the occasion. But if you know that you are going to be the only military person at a particular affair, you may develop a reluctance to being dressed differently from all the others.

Your list should also include shirts, both colored and white, striped or checked, depending on your taste. And neckties, suitable socks (but watch out for the too-gay variety), sports shirts, walking shorts, etc. A pair of loafers is always a good buy. Frequently, items like this are received as gifts. However, since they don't involve a considerable outlay of cash, they should pose no particular problem.

WHEN TO WEAR WHAT

After you have made a start at accumulating your civilian clothes, the question arises of when to wear what. The clothes discussed here mainly pertain to those localities where conservative dress is preferred for all functions except the most casual. Although there seems to be a trend toward more informality in men's dress, there are only certain times when sports jackets should be worn.

The latitude that exists today permits almost anything to be worn until six P.M. Sports jackets and sports shirts are often worn to such afternoon affairs as cocktail parties—particularly if the section of the country in which you are stationed condones this practice. However, a good rule to follow is: If you are going to an afternoon affair that you know is not formal and your partner or wife is not wearing a cocktail dress, you are correct in wearing your sports jacket, preferably with a white shirt.

At most cocktail parties, you will find a varied assortment of dress among the men folk, but the predominant dress will usually be that of a conservative suit for the practical reason that you may want to take your date or your wife out to dinner afterwards.

If you are asked for dinner and the dress is not specified—for example, "black tie"—you should assume that you will wear a conservative suit. Innovations such as the fancy waistcoat or vest are usually *not* worn at this time. That sort of dress would be strictly for affairs before six P.M.

When the dress is specified in the invitation—such as "black tie"—you are expected to wear a dinner jacket. There is one point that should be kept in mind about the "black tie" specification: if it is prescribed, you have no alternative but to wear a dinner jacket or the corresponding uniform.

Extremely formal affairs, such as debutante balls and embassy receptions, customarily call for full dress. This fact will be spelled out for you by the hour of the affair or else on the invitation itself. For debutante balls starting after nine P.M., you are expected to wear full dress—that is, "white tie and tails," or your full dress midshipman uniform or evening dress officer uniform.

A practical rule to remember is: If you have any doubt about what to wear you may call the house of your hostess and ask. It is much better to do this than to be sorry when you get there.

SECTION II

THE SOCIAL SIDE OF LIFE

CHAPTERS

CHAPTER 3

Hops and Dances

Young men in training at the Service Academies, or at the Officer Candidate Schools—or, for that matter, any young officer anywhere—will find that the etiquette observed at the Academy hops* and the college dances will generally be the same at any dance or ball. The earlier the correct etiquette at a dance is learned, the easier it will be for you to attend with complete poise and confidence any debutante ball or embassy dance.

The new Plebe classes at the Academies are made up of young men from all walks of life. Many have had previous college or preparatory school training, and have escorted young ladies to fraternity or class dances. Others, directly out of a small town high school, may not have had the opportunity of learning what to do at formal dances, or how to greet those in the receiving line.

A Midshipman or Cadet should be well versed in such courtesies before graduation and going into a Service that may take him all over the world and into various social situations.

THE NAVAL ACADEMY HOP

Since most Academy hops are formal, the uniform will be prescribed—usually evening dress uniform. A "drag"† will also wear formal dress, of long or ballerina length.

As a Midshipman (or Cadet) you will wear white gloves throughout the hop, except when assisting your young lady with punch and cakes served during intermission, or when smoking. When going down the receiving line, you will take off your right glove and hold it in your left hand.

Smoking is permitted in authorized areas only. You do not go out-of-doors for a smoke or a walk; this is against regulations. The only time you are allowed to leave the ballroom while the dance is in progress is at the "special dances" during June Week.

A hostess will always be on hand at the hop. Sometimes she will receive, or assist in receiving, guests. She will always be ready to help the couples in any way possible. The hostess is escorted to and from the hop by a member

* Hop is a Service Academy word for dance.
† "Drag" is a Service Academy word for the young lady guest or "date" of a Midshipman or Cadet.

of the Hop Committee. Such escort duties enable a Midshipman to learn how to escort and to converse with women older than himself.

HOP TIME

It is important that Midshipmen be on time at hops, which normally start at 9:15 P.M. Underclassmen may arrive no later than 9:45, but First Classmen may attend and leave when they wish—after staying a reasonable length of time. Promptness is stressed in attending hops—you may be placed on report, if late. It is wise to inform your "drag" of the necessity of being on time.

When you arrive at the hop, you will wait while your young lady takes her coat to the coatroom. Maids are available at all hops to assist with coats. They will have needles, thread, etc., for any emergency.

Plebes do not drag until the Farewell Ball, the final dance of the year, held during June Week, on graduation eve.

Underclassmen will not leave the dance floor until the hop is over, at midnight. When the National Anthem is played, you will stand at attention and your "drag" will stand quietly at your side.

First Classmen have an hour to take their young ladies home after the hop; Second Classmen have fifty minutes and Third Classmen have forty minutes.

RECEIVING LINES AT HOPS

It is a courtesy—and therefore mandatory—that you go through the receiving line at all hops. This is good training for future events and is similar to receiving lines at dances, balls, receptions, etc., any place.

The receiving line customarily forms near the entrance to the ballroom, and standing first in line is the escort of the receiving lady. At the Naval Academy, he is the chairman or a First Class member of the Hop Committee; she will be the wife of an officer on active duty in the yard or station, or a hostess.

The escort of the receiving lady always keeps his hands at his sides, or at his back, so that guests will *not* shake hands with him. It is his duty to announce the names of guests to the receiving lady at his side. She will offer her hand *first* to each guest and greet everyone in a gracious and friendly manner. She customarily wears gloves while in the receiving line, and girls being received usually leave their gloves on. As a guest, you will remove your right glove and hold it in your left hand.

At Naval Academy hops, the husband of the lady receiving does not stand in the receiving line, but he usually attends later in the evening. At other Academies—such as at the Military Academy and the Air Force Academy—he will stand in line.

Procedure

The receiving line at the Naval Academy is composed of an escort and receiving lady, with the escort standing first in line. He does *not* shake hands; she does—and offers her hand *first*.

The steps in going through the receiving line are:

1. When the Midshipman, or Cadet, and his young lady approach the line, he will be on the side of the girl toward the receiving line. In this way he can more easily give their names to the escort and she can then step ahead. She does not hold his arm.

2. The Midshipman, or Cadet, gives the girl's *last* name only to the escort.

3. When the girl steps ahead of the Midshipman, or Cadet, the escort turns to the receiving lady and says the *receiving lady's name first:* "Mrs. Brown, Miss Smith."

4. The receiving lady will shake hands with the girl and say something similar to, "Good evening, it's so nice to see you." The girl may answer, "Good evening, Mrs. Brown," or "Good evening, it's nice to be here."

5. After the escort presents the girl to the receiving lady, he turns to you (a Midshipman or Cadet), and you give your last name: "Midshipman Jones."* You do not fail to give your name, regardless of how well you know the escort. If a guest does not state his name, the escort may say, "Your name, please?"

6. The escort will then present you to the receiving lady: "Mrs. Brown, Midshipman Jones." She will probably speak to you in the same way as with your young lady, and you may answer in the same way or say, "How do you do, Mrs. Brown?" or simply, "How do you do?"

7. When the husband of the lady receiving stands in the line you would greet him in this manner: "Good evening, Sir," or, "Good evening, General Davis." It is always correct to say, "How do you do, Sir?"

8. You may bow slightly when you shake hands, you should look at the person addressed—escort, receiving lady, etc.—and not attempt a conversation.

9. The line does not form again at the end of the hop. It is always courteous, however, to thank the lady (and officer) receiving, and the hostess, and say "goodbye."

* A Midshipman or West Point Cadet is introduced or addressed as "Mister" at social or official occasions, except at certain military, state, or social occasions, a Midshipman or Cadet is introduced or addressed by his title for purposes of identification, or designation. At the United States Air Force Academy, Cadets are introduced (or will give their names) as "Cadet Doe," etc., but are addressed thereafter as "Mr. Doe."

DUTIES OF THE RECEIVING LADY'S ESCORT

The escort always calls for the receiving lady. He usually is entertained at dinner by her and her husband before the hop. It is a tradition at the Naval Academy that the Superintendent's wife receives at the Christmas Hop, and members of the First Class Hop Committee and their young ladies are dinner guests in the Superintendent's House before going on to the hop.

During June Week, First Classmen do not act as escorts; Second Classmen will escort the receiving lady, and members of the Third Class escort the hostesses. While you are on escort duty, you do not invite a young lady to be your guest at the occasion.

INFORMALS

Saturday and Sunday afternoon informal hops are frequently held during the academic year. There are no receiving lines, but hostesses are always on hand to greet guests. Girls wear afternoon-type dresses—but not sports attire that is suitable, perhaps, only for a sail on the Severn. Couples improperly attired will not be admitted to the informal.

PLEBE INFORMALS

The Plebe informal hops at the Naval Academy are a means of introducing the members of the Plebe Class to young ladies in the community and from nearby colleges. The informals serve as an instructional period when Plebes are taught how to go through the receiving line and how to get acquainted with girls they do not know. They are told how to ask for a dance: "May I have this dance?", or, "Will you dance with me?"

The girls cannot be met outside Dahlgren Hall by the Plebes, and must arrive unescorted. They are met at the entrance of the Hall by members of the Hop Committee, who introduce themselves and then take the girls to the door of the coatroom.

The girls are then taken onto the dance floor and introduced to the Plebes: "Miss Smith, Midshipman Jones." The girls will probably say, "Hello," rather than "How do you do," but they are on their own. The Plebes then takes the girl through the receiving line, when one is formed. Plebes are encouraged to cut in and introduce themselves. Punch is served during intermission, which presents further opportunities to become acquainted.

Plebes are required to attend the informals, with a certain number selected from each company. They are also represented on the Hop Committee. There are always more Plebes than girls, and the stag line is longer than at other hops. For the Plebe learning to dance, the stag line serves as an observation post—but you cannot remain there throughout the hop.

Girls must be 16 years of age, or older, to have their names placed on the invitation list for Plebe informals. The list is compiled by an officer at the Academy designated to do so, and is made up mainly from lists of girls selected by the heads of girls' schools in Washington, D.C. and Baltimore area. The girls are often Service juniors, but not necessarily so. All girls must be invited in order to attend these informals.

CARD OR PROGRAM HOPS

The advantage of the card or program dance is that you and your young lady will have the opportunity of meeting and dancing with others. Before the hop, you place the names of friends on your young lady's program— and in turn, they place her name on theirs.

A blank card at a program hop might be embarrassing to your date unless it is mutually understood that you are retaining all the dances for yourself—which is not the purpose of program hops.

You must always remember that when you have allowed your name to be placed in a girl's dance program, you *must* fulfill your commitments.

CUTTING IN

During any hop, program or otherwise, unless the tune being played has been designated a "no break," a midshipman may cut in on another couple provided he is already acquainted with the young lady, or such a close personal friend of her partner that he may expect to be introduced. He accomplishes this operation by tapping the man on his shoulder and saying, "May I cut in?" or just, "Cut, please."

It should be pointed out that the Fourth Class Informal Dances at the Naval Academy operate on a different set of rules. At Plebe dances the young ladies have been invited as guests of the entire class. Thus, any Plebe, as a host, is expected to cut in on and introduce himself to any young lady present. On the other hand, at hops for upperclassmen, the young ladies are guests of individual midshipmen and no man may cut in without an introduction—unless of course he is already acquainted with the girl.

If one of your shipmates has drawn a "brick" as a blind date, the gentlemanly thing to do is cut in on him. This will not only "spell" him a bit, but will give him the opportunity to line up somebody to cut in on you— which he is absolutely obligated to do. When someone cuts in on you it is improper to cut right back. If you want to dance with the girl again, wait until someone else cuts in on him—or arrange for it if you're in a hurry!

When you are the one who cuts in you must return the young lady to her escort after the end of that one dance. Since hops are usually very large affairs, it is wise for couples to have a pre-arranged place of meeting following a cut-in. Signs numbered from 1 to 24 are frequently placed along the balcony railing of Dahlgren Hall to facilitate rendezvous.

INTERMISSIONS

Fruit punch and cakes are served during intermission, and smoking is permitted. You may have the minor problem of finding your young lady if she was dancing with another when intermission was called.

If you should pass her, you may extend your arm and tell her partner that you will take over, which will release him to find his own young lady. If something unexpected happens to the escort of the lady with whom you have had that dance and he has not reclaimed her, *then it is your duty*—and your date's—to stand by until he appears.

SPECIAL HOPS

Special hops are held at the various Academies, such as the Christmas Hop held at the Naval Academy. Then, toys are brought by each couple to be given to underprivileged children. Another special hop is the Brigade Cotillion held in Philadelphia following the Army-Navy game.

If you have not already invited your own guest at the latter hop, the Philadelphia Cotillion Committee invites a large number of young ladies between the ages of 17 and 22 to serve as hostesses. They are customarily distinguished by their pastel colored gowns with blue and gold sashes. You may, of course, take your own "drag."

Although the Cotillion is considered formal, girls from a distance may wear cocktail-style dresses—but suits or sports attire is not worn. The Superintendent of the Academy and the Commandant of Midshipmen, and their wives, usually receives guests—and you should go through the receiving line.

CONDUCT AT HOPS

Midshipmen and Cadets are expected to conduct themselves as gentle-men at all times—on or off the dance floor. Displays of affection on the dance floor are not tolerated, and Hop Committee members will ask those who violate courtesies to leave the hop. Members of the Hop Committee are distinguished by their gold aiguillettes; they have the authority to enforce regulations.

Since it is your duty to make your "drag" as happy and to give her as enjoyable an evening as possible, you will not leave her sitting alone, or embarrass her with boisterous conduct. *Never* leave her in mid-floor. If an occasion arises when you must leave, you should leave her with a group before excusing yourself. If you are not adept at certain steps, such as in the more intricate dances, you may suggest "waiting this one out."

When you complete a dance with a girl who is not your guest, take her back to her escort or to her party, and thank her.

Since the general tone of the hop is formal, rather formal dancing is expected. A contemporary dance is permitted, but not in the too-strenuous form that demands a wide area for the performance.

It is inconsiderate to remain talking in groups on the dance floor. If you want to talk, rather than dance, you should move to the side of the floor.

DANCE INSTRUCTION

Learning how to dance is required at the Academies, with classes for the Plebes and Upper Classmen held on Sunday afternoons at the Naval Academy. Midshipmen pay for their own instruction, with a professional instructor in charge. Advanced classes are also available.

Instruction covers problems of etiquette as well as dance steps. You are taught the way your left or leading hand should hold your "drag's" hand lightly and naturally, with your right or holding arm placed firmly yet loosely just above her waist. Exaggerated positions make for bad manners as well as bad dancers.

DEBUTANTE BALLS

In metropolitan cities throughout the country, debutantes make their bows to society in large groups at Cotillions and Assemblies. Such balls are usually held for benefit of various charity organizations, with the girls' fathers making contributions to charities in lieu of the greater expense of private debuts.

Dinners honoring individual debutantes are customarily held before the balls. Daughters, or daughters of close friends and relatives, will be honored by their parents or sponsors at afternoon tea dances, which are usually held in exclusive clubs or hotel ballrooms.

Each girl attending a formal debutante ball will subscribe for two or three partners—or many more. Debutantes wear long white dresses and white gloves for their presentation. Midshipmen, Cadets, and young bachelor officers are often invited to become dancing partners at a ball, or to attend as "stags." Officers will wear evening dress uniform or "white tie." Midshipmen and Cadets wear evening dress uniform.

Partners of the debutante, as well as her close relatives and friends, will send flowers to the girl before the ball, with one corsage or bouquet selected to be worn. The other flowers will be used as a background at the place the debutante will be presented.

A buffet supper is served after midnight, and the ball is over in the early morning hours. No line is formed at the conclusion of the affair, but guests are expected to thank the debutante's parents or sponsors. If a dinner, at which you were a guest, was held before the ball, then you will thank the host and hostess of that dinner, also.

Since each cotillion has various customs and traditions, it is important that you learn the ground rules in advance, from the person who sent you the invitation.

THE FORMAL DANCE

A formal dance may be held in a large room or club, usually starting about ten o'clock, with dancing getting underway an hour later. For a very formal affair, a carpet may run from the curb to the front entrance, with an awning overhead. Guests are announced at formal and semi-formal dances.

The hostess and the guest of honor—say, a debutante—will be standing near the entrance to the ballroom, where they greet guests. The host usually stands in the receiving line during the early part of the evening, but will leave the line before the hostess and the guest of honor do, so that he can mix with the guests. The receiving line usually breaks up after three-quarters of an hour.

There will be a stag line, with an extra man for each nine or ten girls. If you are invited as a "stag," your duty is to see that the girls receive the proper attention and never lack for dancing partners.

A buffet supper is served after midnight, with no announcement made concerning its serving. The hostess usually initiates the movement of a few guests toward the buffet table, and other guests follow.

When you attend as a "stag," you may ask any unattached woman to have supper with you. You may fill both your plates, and sit wherever you like. Usually, small tables are arranged for a few guests to sit at each. At a large dance, the food may be served directly to guests seated at small tables.

DUTY DANCES

"Duty" dances are those that good manners require you to have with certain women at a private dance, or dinner dance. Such duty dances are those with your hostess, the guest of honor, and any feminine member of the hostess's family.

If you attended a dinner before the dance or ball, then you will also dance with the hostess and the guest of honor at that occasion. You have a certain duty (but it is not required) to dance also with the two women who sat at your left and right at the dinner. If the woman at your right was your assigned dinner partner, then you are obligated to dance with her.

When you are the guest of a woman at a party, or are the guest of a subscription party member, you will dance several times with her, and you should invite her to have supper with you.

At a Service dance, you will dance—or sit and talk for a few minutes—with the wife of the senior officer present, whether she is the hostess or not.

COLLEGE DANCE

A Midshipman or Cadet, or other young officer, may wear his blue service uniform with black bow tie at a college dance—which is the equivalent of "black tie." A summer dance would mean white service. A college man will wear "black tie"—which means his tuxedo, or a white dinner jacket in the summer.

When a dinner precedes a dance at a woman's college, the girl usually pays for the dinner—in advance, so no one will be embarrassed. But if you invite her out for dinner, then you will pay for the meal. You will pay for all taxi fares during the weekend—and also any flowers, movies, etc.

After your return to the Academy, or station, you should write a "thank you" note to the girl, and also to the hostess in the house where you stayed, if she was a family friend or relative of the girl. In turn, you should try to repay the hospitality of the girl by inviting her to the Academy, or station, for a hop or dance.

A HOP WEEKEND

When you invite a girl to your Service Academy for the first time, write the letter in a simple but sincere manner. If she has never been to the Academy before, you should include a brief but general idea of any plans for the weekend. You should write her three or four weeks in advance of the hop.

After the girl accepts your invitation, then write a more specific letter in return. She will not want to arrive either unprepared or overloaded with luggage. If she has not been in the Academy town before, she will want to know the best way to come—by bus, train, plane, or car.

When she is to arrive by bus, the bus schedule must be checked beforehand. You will want to tell her the time that you can—or cannot—meet her, owing to drills, classes, etc. If you know that others girls from her area or college will be arriving that weekend, you might mention their names so that she may have company on the trip.

REGULATIONS CONCERNING CARS

When a "drag"—or any person—is to arrive in your Academy town by car, that person should know who can, and who cannot, ride in cars. The regulations governing the riding in cars by Midshipmen at the Naval Aacdemy are authorized by the Superintendent, and may be modified or changed whenever necessary. *The main regulations are:* Midshipmen cannot own a car within a seven-mile radius of the Naval Academy Chapel; First Classmen may ride in cars within this radius, but cannot drive the car anywhere.

DRESS FOR "DRAGS"

Your "drag" will be anxious to know what clothes to bring on her hop weekend, so tell her of the events that you plan to attend. A formal hop means her prettiest formal dress, either long or ballerina length, but *not* short and not a cocktail style dress.

The informal or afternoon hop means an afternoon-style dress, but the extreme cocktail-type dress is not desirable. White gloves are usually worn. Semi-formal hops are occasionally held on Saturday evenings in place of formal hops, when Midshipmen wear the uniform of the day and drags wear cocktail style dresses.

Sunday morning Chapel services may be attended by the girl wearing a suit, hat, gloves, or a plain afternoon dress with a coat or jacket in season, hat, and gloves. High heels are fine for dress occasions, but not for walking —and considerable walking is accomplished over a hop weekend. Therefore, walking shoes are a "must" for the weekend.

A football game, or any sports event, means sports clothes. The suit worn on the trip may be worn at such a contest, or a skirt and sweater. Although shorts may be worn for sailing, tennis, or other sports, brief shorts are frowned upon, and bathing suits are never paraded away from the beach. Your young lady should be advised that soft-soled shoes should always be worn for sailing or tennis.

"DRAGGING" EXPENSES

When a girl comes to the Service Academies for a hop weekend, or during June Week, she can expect to pay for her transportation to and from the Academy. She will pay for her meals en route and for any during the visit which have not been arranged for by you, her host, or by friends. She will also pay for her room during the visit, unless she has been invited by friends to be a guest in their quarters or home.

As a Midshipman or Cadet, you can expect to pay for anything to which you invite your guest, or guests, such as meals, movies, etc. You pay for flowers for your "drag," which you order in advance, and for taxis—when you are permitted to ride in them.

As almost everyone knows, a Midshipman or Cadet receives about ten dollars—and less—a month for spending money. For those who have little or no financial assistance from home, this amount does not go far.

CHAPTER 4

Receptions and Cocktail Parties

RECEPTIONS

According to Webster's dictionary, a reception is a "Ceremony of receiving guests." There are many kinds of receptions—afternoon or evening, formal or informal. They are of a limited duration of time, and a few or many people may be invited.

Receptions are usually held in honor of someone—a dignitary, a bride and groom, a debutante, or a newcomer. They are also held to mark a special occasion, such as the commissioning or christening of a ship, a golden wedding anniversary, or the christening of an infant. But no matter what the occasion may be, the routine of holding a reception is basically the same.

The purpose of a reception given in honor of someone is to have as many friends and acquaintances of the hosts meet the guest (or guests) of honor, as possible. In the Services, one type of reception is called an "at-home"—as, for example, when the senior officer of a large command designates a certain day for "calls made and returned."

When this type of reception is held, it means that the senior officer of a very large command cannot possibly receive and return individual calls made by all the officers and station personnel and their families. Thus the at-homes are held as often as necessary, ranging from one or two a year, to one every month or so.

Guests usually leave cards—and their call is considered repaid. When a tray is provided in the entrance hall—or any convenient place—you leave the necessary number of cards; when there is no tray, you are to assume that the senior officer does not care for cards to be left. (See Chapter 5, *Calls and Calling Cards*.)

Time

The hours of the reception are indicated on the invitation, and usually span a two-hour interval. The invitation does not have an R.s.v.p.* unless it is necessary for the hosts to know how many guests they can expect to attend—information particularly needed when the place of reception is held in limited quarters.

Receptions are held at various hours, according to their nature. An in-

* *R.s.v.p.* may be written R.S.V.P. and means "Please reply."

formal reception may be held in mid-afternoon or early evening; a formal debutante reception may be at five o'clock in the early evening, or at half past ten or eleven o'clock at night.

An official or formal reception usually starts at nine o'clock in the evening, and a very formal reception and dance may be held at ten or half past ten o'clock at night.

When a ship is christened or commissioned during the afternoon, a reception customarily follows the ceremony. When the christening or commissioning ceremony takes place in the morning, a luncheon usually follows. The ship's sponsor, officers, and dignitaries of Service and State will be among the guests invited to the ceremonies.

Dress

At *informal receptions,* formal clothes are not worn if the reception is held in the late afternoon. When guests are going on to a formal dinner where evening dress is required, they should not appear at the reception before six o'clock.

Dark business suits or the uniform of the day may properly be worn at informal daytime receptions, or lighter colored suits and white uniforms during summer months. Women wear afternoon dress with rather elaborate hats, and gloves.

At *formal receptions,* the formality of the occasion is indicated by the words "black tie" written or engraved in the lower right-hand corner of the invitation. "White tie" indicates a very formal occasion, and "decorations" or "tails" always means full evening dress. (See Chapter 2, *Service and Civilian Dress.*)

An eight o'clock reception is usually "black tie" unless specified otherwise. Women wear evening dress and long gloves, and men wear dinner jackets—or blue uniform with black bow tie, or summer whites.

When men wear "white tie" to State receptions, women should wear long white gloves. A woman usually does not remove her right glove, but may tuck its fingers in at the wrist before going down the receiving line.

At *formal daytime receptions,* you will wear the prescribed uniform of the day, or you can wear the cutaway, the prescribed civilian dress for very formal occasions, such as an inauguration reception, or when a speaker appears at a very formal public function. Such dress is worn at a very formal wedding and reception, when you are a member of the bridal party. Women wear an afternoon dress, a more elaborate hat, and white gloves.

At large official receptions, or at a large reception somewhat of a public nature, "Dress Optional" is frequently engraved or written at the lower right-hand corner of the invitation. Such a card may carry an "R.s.v.p."

White House Receptions

Dress for an afternoon reception at the White House is the same as at any afternoon reception.

As a guest, you *must* be on time at a White House reception. You should arrive at the White House gate no less than ten minutes before the hour of invitation, which will give you time to be checked at the gate and to leave your hat and coat in the designated room.

You will be directed to the place of reception, where a military aide will announce guests' names. All men precede the women they are escorting down the receiving line. You will say, "Good evening, Mr. President," and, "Good evening, Mrs.—," and pass on—unless the host or hostess stops you briefly to say a few words. Otherwise, you do not open a conversation with either the President or the First Lady while going down a White House reception line. You do not leave cards, and you do not leave the reception until after the President and his wife leave the room.

Arrival and Departure

There is no particular time limit on how long you will stay at a reception. You may arrive at any time between the hours indicated on the invitation. *It is imperative that you first pay your respects to your host and hostess.* Usually you stay a little longer at small receptions than at large ones.

Usually, you stay about forty-five minutes at a reception, but you may stay until the closing hours at a formal reception and dance. You should not arrive uncomfortably near the closing hour of the reception—unless you have been asked to stay on for supper by the hosts. A guest who arrives late at an afternoon reception and lingers on through the dinner hour can be a problem to the hosts, who may have other social obligations.

Receiving Line

There are differences in the way receiving lines are formed at various official, formal, and informal receptions. Customarily, the host stands first in line at *official* receptions, with his wife at his side. The hostess stands first in line at social, *non-official* functions, with her husband at her side.

At *official* receptions held in honor of a dignitary, an aide will announce the names of guests to the host. The protocol established by the State Department, not counting the aide, is:

1. The official host
2. The guest of honor
3. The guest of honor's wife
4. The official host's wife.
5. Extra man, if possible, to avoid leaving a woman at the end of the line.

When the guest of honor is the President of *any* country, a reigning King and/or Queen, or a dignitary of the Church (Pope or Bishop), the host and hostess will relinquish their positions in favor of their guest. The line would be:

1. President, King (or reigning Queen)
2. The honored guest's wife (or husband of Queen)
3. The official host
4. The official host's wife.

At many Washington receptions, when the honor guests are of high rank or position, the receiving line is frequently arranged in the following manner (for example, when the Secretary of Defense gave a reception in honor of the Secretary of the Navy):

1. The host
2. The hostess
3. The guest of honor
4. The guest of honor's wife.

Some hosts invite a man appropriately connected to the occasion to stand at the end of the line, in order that a woman need not be in this position. Other hosts feel that this is incorrect, since a reception is to honor certain individuals only.

When the guest of honor is a very high ranking dignitary or official, it is customary to offer him the option of a date for the occasion, and to consult his staff concerning the guest list and general arrangements. A host will remember not to invite anyone of higher rank than the guest of honor. But if this is unavoidable, the ranking guest should be asked to waive his right for the occasion in favor of the guest of honor. (See pages 187-188.)

At some formal—and at most less formal receptions—guests are received in the same way as at a formal dinner. The hostess greets each guest and presents him or her to the guests of honor standing nearby; then the guest is greeted by the host, who is near the hostess but is mixing among the guests and introducing newcomers into groups.

The receiving line at receptions should be kept as small as possible. Usually, those in the line are the host, hostess, and guest or guests of honor. No one likes to go down a long line—which generally means that a guest's name is mixed up midway in the line. Names are not announced at small and informal receptions.

The receiving lines at wedding receptions, at-homes, and formal dances, are discussed in chapters pertaining to those subjects.

When a President, King, Queen, or dignitary of the Church, or a person of very high rank, attends a reception, all other guests must arrive before they do. In the case of a King, President or Pope, women are presented to them, rather than the customary rule of presenting men to women.

Garden Party

The procedure for guests going through the receiving line at a large reception may be illustrated by the Superintendent's Garden Party, which is held each spring during June Week at the Naval Academy. The party is given for the parents and "drags" of the Midshipmen of the First Class.

The Superintendent and his wife receive as many as three thousand guests during the hours of 9 to 12 P.M., inside the Superintendent's Quarters. The guests greet their hosts, then go into the garden, where non-alcoholic punch and small cakes are served.

From there guests go to Dahlgren Hall, where dancing continues until midnight. In case of rain, the receiving line forms inside the Hall. Staff officers and their wives will assist in hospitalities throughout the evening, but usually they are not in the receiving line.

The Superintendent, his aides, and the Midshipmen will be in evening dress uniform. The officers' wives and the Midshipmen's guests will also be in evening dress. Although the majority of parents and other relatives of the Midshipmen will wear evening dress—the men in dinner jackets and the women in evening attire—many persons coming from a distance may not be able to bring formal attire.

In this case, women are properly attired when they wear their prettiest afternoon dress, with white or pastel colored gloves—but no hat. Men wear a dark or conservative business suit, with white shirt. It is not mandatory, but it is in good taste, that women guests take off their right glove and hold it in their left hand when shaking hands with those in the receiving line.

Customarily, the Superintendent is first in the line—due to his official position—with his wife at his side. If he prefers, however, he may have his wife stand first in line to receive the guests.

The aide will announce the names of guests as they arrive, and he will stand nearer the entrance to the reception room, either at the head of the line or facing the host—whichever way names are more clearly heard. As the guests approach the line, the aide will turn and face the couple. He will wait for the male guest to state the name of the woman he is escorting. If the male guest does not do so, the aide may say, "Your name, please?"

Guests do not shake hands with the aide, and *last* names only are given. As the man states the woman's name, she steps ahead of her escort and is presented to her hosts. The form of presenting names depends upon the number of guests. At a very large occasion—such as the Garden Party—the presentation is brief:

Midshipman guest, to aide: "Miss Smith."

The aide turns to the Superintendent and says, "Miss Smith" (or, if time permits, "This is Miss Smith").

The aide then looks back toward the guest and says, "Admiral Blank" or, "Miss Smith, this is Admiral Blank."

Miss Smith may say, "Good evening, Admiral Blank," and the Superintendent may say, "Good evening, Miss Smith." Then the Superintendent will turn to his wife and say, "Mrs. Blank, Miss Smith."

As soon as the young lady is presented to her hosts, the aide will turn to the Midshipman, who will then give his name: "Mr. Jones." The aide then turns to the Superintendent and says, "Admiral Blank, Mr. Jones," or simply, "Mr. Jones." The Superintendent and his wife will shake hands with each guest as they greet her or him.

The Midshipman may say, "Good evening, Sir." or, "Good evening, Admiral Blank." or, "How do you do, Sir."

As stated previously, Midshipmen and Naval officers up to and including the rank of lieutenant commander give their titles as "Mister" at official and social occasions at the base or station, unless it is desirable that identification of the officer be made. Officers of the rank of commander and above state their rank, with admirals of all grades stating their rank as "Admiral." Officers of the rank of lieutenant and above in the Marine Corps, Army, and Air Force, use their titles.

You will remember to shake hands lightly—but with a degree of firmness. Your hosts have many hands to shake during the evening, and a pressure grip is to be avoided. Guests may arrive at any time between the hours stated in the invitation, but it is customary at this reception that the Midshipmen attend by battalions at certain designated hours. When the line is very long, guests may dance first, then later go through the line—but all guests *must* go through the line.

Upon leaving, you do not look up your hosts and say "Goodbye." This is a very large reception, and it is not expected or desired that guests again shake hands.

Departure

At receptions other than the Superintendent's Garden Party, the receiving line may form again at the end of the evening, and once again you will go down the line. You will thank your hosts as you shake hands, express pleasure for the evening, and say goodbye.

At a reception to meet a newcomer, the line is usually broken up after the first hour, but the hosts and guests of honor usually stay near the door, mingling with other guests. At a large affair, you do not look them up; at a small reception, you do. In the latter case, you thank them—and leave.

COCKTAIL PARTIES

Cocktail parties vary in size from a handful to many people. They are, perhaps, the easiest means of entertaining a large number of guests—who may arrive at any time within the customary two hours stated in the invitation.

The main difference between cocktail parties and receptions is that cocktail parties are informal, there is no receiving line, cards are not left, and alcoholic drinks are always served. They are also held during or near the close of daylight hours. Receptions may have fruit punch or alcoholic punch served, they may be held in the evening as well as in the daytime, and usually they are of a formal nature.

A host and hostess will be near the door when guests arrive, and guests are always greeted in an informal manner. If you are a stranger, your host or hostess will probably introduce you to someone nearby—but after this, you are on your own. You may talk with stranger or friend, and you may stay as long as the invitation specifies.

Customarily, a choice of two drinks (three at most) is offered at cocktail parties, as well as whiskey and soda, ginger ale, and perhaps sherry. Fruit juice or tomato juice or soft drinks should be available for non-drinkers. A host will never insist that a guest take a drink when he does not want one.

Some cocktail parties may be small affairs, for perhaps a dozen friends, with the host mixing and serving drinks from a tray placed at a convenient spot in the room. Cocktail food may consist of a bowl of nuts or potato chips with a dip, with guests serving themselves or assisting in passing the food around the room.

Drinks at parties are frequently served from a bar which has been set up in a designated room, with a waiter in attendance. Guests are expected to order their choice. When you arrive, the host may say, "Won't you go over to the bar and have a drink?" You will ask your date—or anyone whom you have brought—what she would like to drink, then you get both drinks.

Some hosts prefer that drinks be served on a tray by a waiter. If your host, or the waiter, should ask if you prefer a drink not offered, you may state your preference; otherwise you do not request a drink not offered, other than non-alcoholic beverages. If you must request anything at a party —such as a glass of ginger ale or water, etc.—you make your request of the servant, not of your busy host or hostess.

At small cocktail parties, the host usually acts as bartender. If he does not limit or state what he has to drink, you may ask, "What are you serving?" However, a wise host will first state what is on hand, and then ask each guest which he prefers. Most hosts mix drinks beforehand; frequently drinks are stored in the refrigerator, "deep freeze" fashion, with ice added when needed.

Canapes (Cocktail Food)

Canapes (or cocktail food) is growing progressively more substantial, but a guest is invited to a cocktail party, not a buffet supper, and should eventually move away from the table or tray of food. Roast ham, turkey, or beef, with hot and cold breads, sea food, elaborate dips, broiled olives wrapped in bacon, bite-size biscuits filled with hot mixtures, miniature hamburgers on toothpicks—any or all of these, and more, may be served at a large party, and several are often served at even small affairs.

Frequently, the hosts invite several guests to stay on for supper (which is already prepared), but without such an invitation in advance, no guest should linger so long after the hours of the party that he forces himself to be invited.

Most cocktail food is eaten with the fingers, except that some food, such as shrimp, is served on or with toothpicks. Food, however, is not offered until after a guest has been served a drink. Napkins are always handed to a guest, or are available on a buffet table nearby.

At large parties, a staff of waiters is necessary to serve drinks. Not counting servants in the kitchen who mix drinks, prepare food, wash glasses, etc., two waiters are needed to serve each fifty guests. In this case, guests will serve themselves at the buffet table. When food is not served buffet style but is to be passed around by the waiters, then extra help is necessary.

Cocktails are customarily offered to guests in the late afternoon, an hour before dinner, and less frequently before luncheons. Cadets and Midshipmen at any of the Service Academies are *never* offered alcoholic drinks, and such alcoholic drinks are prohibited aboard any ship of the U. S. Navy.

Rules to Remember

- If you can't hold your liquor, don't drink it.
- If you do not drink, say so; *you don't have to drink*. When a drink is offered to you, simply say, "No, thank you." without any explanation of *why* you don't want it. Remember the old service admonition: *"Never take a drink just because another man is thirsty."* In case of a toast, however, you go through the motions of drinking.
- If you want a non-alcoholic drink, it is proper to ask for it. You may say, "I'd like a ginger ale or a Coke, if you have some" etc.
- Do not boast about how much you can drink, or insist upon drinking drink for drink along with others—when you know you can't handle it. This is a juvenile trait, or, at best, immature.

- You should never help yourself to a drink in someone else's home —unless you are very close friends and know that you are welcome to do so.
- You should not ask for a different drink from the one offered to you, unless you want a non-alcoholic drink. If your host says, "Would you care for something else?" then you are free to ask for a different drink.
- Do not set a damp or cold glass on a table without something underneath it—a coaster, napkin, magazine, or anything convenient when coasters are not provided.
- You need not offer a drink to every casual visitor in your home; also, it is not polite to force drinks on a visitor, and you should always have something non-alcoholic to offer non-drinking guests.

CHAPTER 5

Calls and Calling Cards

In times of war or national emergency the social life in the Services is relatively informal. Many social customs were held in abeyance during World War II and the Korean conflict; some have been slow to come back, and others may never return, due to the changing times.

One of the customs which has changed since the advent of the more recent wars is that of making formal calls. Formerly, there was a rigid system of etiquette observed in making official and formal calls. The system of official calls is unchanged, but that of making and returning formal calls is now more simplified.

In some parts of the country, formal calls are being reestablished. Many old hands in the Services desire the return of formal calls as a gracious way of living. The more formal system of calling in the pre-war Services had its merits—mainly in the promotion of friendships between senior officers, and their wives, with junior families.

However, there are problems involved in today's living that did not affect the old Services particularly. With few servants in the modern household, there is far less time to make calls; junior officers and their wives frequently have no one with whom to leave their children when making calls. There are many more officers serving at larger bases than ever before—thus more officers' families on whom to call.

The commanding officer of a large station could not possibly take the time today to receive and return all the calls that were required to be made in the pre-war days. A formal call is of about twenty minutes duration, its purpose being to pay your respects to the person on whom you are calling, and to become acquainted.

REQUIRED CALLS

The number of required calls is relatively small. They consist of a call on the Commanding Officer, the Executive Officer, the Head of your Department, and your Department Executive Officer (or senior assistant, should he be so designated). A new officer reporting for duty is expected to call on his senior officers on the first day after his arrival (always within 48 hours). This requirement holds whether you are serving ashore or afloat.

CALLING TIME

In the Naval Service, the customary time for making *social* or *"first"* calls is between 4 and 6 P.M. In the Marine Corps, the favorite hours are from 5 to 6:30 P.M. In the Air Force, the customary hours are from 4 to 6 P.M. on weekends, and in the Army the hours are between 7:30 and 9:30 P.M. A formal call ashore is about twenty minutes duration—never less than fifteen or more than thirty minutes. An informal visit among friends is considerably longer, but you should always avoid staying too long and wearing out your welcome.

An *official call* in an office or aboard ship is not less than ten minutes duration and no more than fifteen, unless the caller is requested to stay longer.

In tropical climates, the social calling hours might be made later because of the heat which is prevalent in the afternoon; the hours may be earlier in the North where daylight hours are short. Working hours and the distances from the station may necessitate changes in the usual calling hours at some stations.

Many commanding officers have designated certain days and hours to receive calls, and these days are considerad to be "at home." As with required calls, no notification of the prospective call is necessary, since you will ask the aide or Executive Officer concerning the days for calling when you first report to the station.

At certain stations where there are no regular calling days, it is becoming customary for a junior family to telephone the senior family first and ask when it will be convenient for them to call.

DRESS

You will wear your uniform when making an official call, and sometimes when making a social call. It is customary to wear civilian dress—usually a business suit—when making social or "first" calls ashore. At less formal calls, sports jackets may be worn, but this depends upon the hour of the call, the day, or the occasion. But a sports shirt with no tie or jacket is *not* correct dress for any type of call.

A woman will wear an afternoon dress, or suit, but not a cocktail-style dress. She will usually wear a hat and gloves.

"FIRST" CALLS

You always leave cards when making "first" calls. A card tray is usually placed on a table in the entrance hall, or in a conspicuous place in the living room. Cards should be left on the tray at a convenient moment either upon your arrival or departure, but you *never* hand them to the host or hostess.

The number of cards that you leave depends on the number of adults in the family you are calling on, and the type of card which you use. You will call upon each adult member of the family, man or woman, therefore you leave a card for each. If you are married, your wife leaves a card for each adult woman only; she never calls on a man, not even the President.

When a steward or maid opens the door of the house where you are calling, you may hand the cards to him or her. When you wish to be received, but the family is not at home, you leave the cards and the call is considered made. Otherwise, do not leave your cards but return at another time. If you want to leave cards without being received, you will say to the steward or maid, "Will you please give these to Mrs. Smith?"

When a member of the household opens the door, you may introduce yourself—but do not give him or her your card. If admitted, you leave your card on the table; when your host is not in, you may ask if you may leave your card, then you step inside and lay the card on the table yourself.

Wives of senior officers at many stations have regular days to receive callers. When a senior officer insists that you stay longer than the customary length of a first call—twenty minutes—you may do so, but it is better not to stay much more than the prescribed length of time, or more than thirty minutes. If you have known the family previously, or have served with the officer at another station, your call will probably be a little longer than the usual time.

It is customary in the Services (particularly the Navy) for the host to offer drinks to callers—either tea, coffee, soft drinks, or alcoholic beverages. Some hosts feel, however, that offering a drink to "first" callers is an invitation to extend the call and therefore, it is optional for a host to offer drinks. When drinks are offered, a guest should never accept more than one.

Since the purpose of a call is to become acquainted, a host can be defeated in this purpose by having to act as bartender instead of talking with the guests. Also, many younger Service families are finding that the prevailing custom of serving drinks during calls is becoming a financial burden. When guests do not accept drinks, there is no problem involved.

RETURN CALLS

All calls should be promptly returned. The usual interval for returning a call is within two weeks, but there are variations depending on the size of the station and the number of calls to be made. The procedure for returning calls is the same as when making them.

Should the family not be at home when you return a call, you may leave cards and the call is considered as having been returned. If you want to visit with the family, do not leave your card but return at a later date.

When cards are left, all calls must be returned, whether the callers were received or not—with the exception of certain bachelor calls.

A woman may make or return a call and leave cards for her husband when he cannot accompany her. A man *can not* leave cards for his wife when she does not accompany him.

SEPARATE ARRIVALS

Upon occasions when an officer's wife precedes him to a new station, she is not expected to make formal calls until after he arrives and can accompany her. In like manner, until the wife's husband arrives there is no obligation on the part of the other members of the naval community to call on her. However, other wives usually call informally to assist her in any way that they can. Such informal calls are not to be considered substitutes for a formal call.

Should you precede your wife to the station, formal calls should be delayed until she arrives, but this must be explained to the Executive Officer in order that you do not seem remiss in your social obligations.

If your wife will not arrive for several months, you should make your required and formal calls as usual; then later it would be courteous for you both to call together informally. It is not courteous for anyone to call at a time when the family you are calling on obviously will not be at home.

When you are reporting to a new duty station and learn that a senior officer or his wife will be absent for some time, you may discuss the problem of calling on one, or waiting to call on both, with the Executive Officer.

LEAVE-TAKING CALLS

Leave-taking calls are those you make, prior to your detachment, on the officers constituting the required call list. However, most calls made at detachment time seem to be made *on* the officer and his wife being detached rather than *by* them. This change from former custom arises from the fact that packing and making preparations for the move are exhausting, and that detachment may come earlier than expected. Since the departing couple is usually entertained at parties before detachment, it does not seem necessary for them to call on the families whom they saw only a night or so before.

At some stations, leave-taking calls are made in the same way as first calls. When you leave cards, you write "p.p.c." in the lower left-hand corner of the card to indicate that the call was *pour prendre congé*—"to take leave." Most Americans prefer simply to write the word "goodbye." If the family is not at home, be sure to leave cards.

Leave-taking calls are not generally made at large stations where the Commanding Officer and his wife are contacted infrequently. Instead, telephone calls are usually made to friends before you leave, and notes of appreciation are written at your new station and then sent back to those who entertained you.

Such leave-taking calls are not to be confused with the official calls that are made by officers on the Commanding Officer and Executive Officer in their offices prior to detachment.

NOT AT HOME

Upon occasions when you call at a home or quarters and are told by a maid or steward that your would-be hosts are not at home (and you know they are), do *not* take offense. The maid or steward means no more than that the officer and his wife are not receiving guests for reasons of their own. This is correct procedure, and is completely within the privileges granted a senior officer who has many obligations—or any host and hostess, for that matter.

Junior officers and officers of intermediate rank are always received whenever practicable, so do not consider failure to receive you a rebuff. You should just leave your card, and you will receive credit for the call anyway.

CALLING CARDS

At no time does any individual leave more than *three cards*. (For example, a husband and wife may leave a total of six cards at one call.) You will remember that a man calls on adults, man or woman, but that a woman only calls on another woman. The following rules apply to the individual cards a husband and wife leave:

- When calling on a senior officer and his wife—2 officer cards and 1 "Mrs." card.
- When calling on a senior officer and his wife, and his mother— 3 officer cards and 2 "Mrs." cards.
- When calling on a senior officer, his wife, his mother, and his father—3 officer cards and 2 "Mrs." cards.
- When calling on a senior officer, his wife, his mother, his mother-in-law, and adult daughter—3 officer cards and 3 "Mrs." cards.
- When a husband and wife use *"joint"* calling cards (Lieutenant and Mrs. John Smith Jones), this rule applies:
- When calling on a senior officer and his wife, leave—1 officer card and 1 joint card.

Cards in addition to joint cards are left in accordance with the general rules given for individual cards.

CHAIN OF COMMAND

Flag officers pay official calls upon seniors in the chain of command. Commanding officers and unit commanders call only on seniors in the type of ship to which they are assigned. Officers junior to commanding officers call upon their commanding officer in his cabin on board ship within 48 hours after reporting for duty.

When these officers have established a residence at the port of call, the order of making required calls follows a general pattern. It is customary that reporting officers call on the families of the commanding officer first, then on the executive officer, the head of their department, etc. These calls are made within a week or ten days after your arrival. Calls should be returned within another two weeks.

It is customary in Washington, D.C., for flag officers to leave cards on the Chief of Naval Operations and his wife, and for other officers to inquire whether their immediate chiefs wish to receive callers. It is courteous for officers returning from foreign duty to call at the embassies of countries in which they have served.

Naval officers of the grade of captain and above should leave cards at the White House once a year. Callers are not received, but the names of those who have left cards are frequently added to invitation lists for teas and receptions.

CALLS ON FOREIGN STATIONS

Officers are expected to pay calls within their own embassy group, on officials of the host government, and on diplomatic representatives of other governments.

Upon the arrival of a naval attaché at a foreign capital, he will make introductory calls upon the civilian heads of the foreign Naval and Air Establishments corresponding to the Secretary of the Navy and the Secretary of the Air Force, and/or the Secretary of National Defense, in addition to the military chiefs of these activities. These introductory calls are made in uniform at the office of the officials concerned and cards are usually left. Other calls are made in accordance with local customs.

"DESIRABLE" CALLS

Newcomers should, of course, make calls on seniors in command with whom they will be working; other officers make calls on contemporaries in their department or on the station, as well as on senior newcomers in their department; all officers make calls on newly married couples and on families with new babies.

A call on a newly married couple means a welcome of the couple into the Service community—and the bride into the Service. Calls made on the arrival of a new baby shows a sincere interest in the family of a fellow officer.

BACHELOR CALLS

Bachelor officers have as much responsibility in making official and formal calls as married officers do. The return of the bachelor officer's call is not required, however, mainly because of the inadequacy of his quarters for receiving visitors.

The bachelor's formal call is usually repaid by his later being invited to dinner or some other occasion by the family on whom he called. The old custom of returning the bachelor's call by leaving cards in his mailbox at the Bachelor Officers Quarters (BOQ) has been abandoned.

When a senior bachelor officer has a home of his own, his formal call will be returned. Although both a husband and wife will make or return the call, only the husband will leave a card, since a woman never calls on a man.

MIDSHIPMEN AND CADET CALLS

It is expected and desirable that Midshipmen and Cadets at the Service schools make formal calls at prescribed hours on senior officers and professors. Calls should also be made on officers who are family friends.

You may ask the senior officer beforehand if it is convenient for you to call on a certain day and hour, although a Sunday afternoon between three and five o'clock is a customary time for calling. If the officer asks you to come for Sunday dinner, or to stay on for badminton, TV, etc., you should feel free to do so.

Otherwise, you should *not stay over thirty minutes*—unless your hosts specifically ask you to do so. A senior officer may be very busy, and he may have other callers and obligations.

A new Sponsor Program for the Plebes at the Naval Academy stimulates the practice of calling. The program calls for officers and professors to invite the Plebes to their homes for luncheons, dinners, and other informal social occasions. Plebes are invited to call on officers and professors whenever they can.

CALLS MADE AND RETURNED

At any large activity, such as the Service Academies or a War College, the complement of officers is so large that the senior officer is unable to receive many individual calls, or to return them. The senior officer usually receives guests at a reception, tea, at-home, etc., at which time all officers and their wives in the activity are invited to attend. It is announced in advance that the attendance at the party serves as "All calls made and returned."

Upon arrival, guests will leave cards in a card tray or receptacle placed on a table, usually in the entrance hall. However, some senior officers at various stations discourage the leaving of cards at such parties, and when no tray is provided, you are not expected to leave cards.

At the Naval Academy, the Superintendent and his wife receive guests at a series of at-homes held during the early part of the academic year. The officers and professors of the Severn River Naval Command, and their wives, as well as friends in the Annapolis area, are invited to attend the at-homes between the hours of five to seven. Cards are usually left.

An aide will be standing near the entrance to the reception room, and will announce the name of each guest to the Superintendent, whose wife will be at his side. If the Superintendent prefers, his wife may stand first in line to greet the guests. They will greet and shake hands with each guest.

If you are a guest, you will give the name of the lady you accompany to the aide, and you give the last name only: "Mrs. Jones." The aide will announce her, then he will turn to you, and you will say, "Captain Jones." It is easier for the aide to remember names if they are stated singly.

Staff officers and their wives do not stand in line, but they will assist in greeting guests and directing them to the punch bowls placed in the various rooms. You will stay about forty-five minutes.

The line does not form again at the end of the reception, but if your host and hostess are nearby and not busy with other guests, you may thank them and say goodbye.

OFFICERS' CARDS

An officer's personal card is about 3⅛ inches long by 1⅝ inches wide, or slightly wider. The length of your name and title will determine its exact size.

When your name is the same as that of your living father, you will add "junior" written in full. If your name is very long, "junior" may be written "Jr." The Roman numeral II is used to identify a younger man who has the same name as an older living relative, such as a grandfather, uncle, or great-uncle. Other numerals, III, IV, etc., would be used accordingly.

An officer's rank of commander or above in the Navy, or major or above in the Marine Corps, or captain or above in the Army and Air Force, should precede his name in the center of the card.

Since your name and title should not be abbreviated, and initials are not used, officers with long names and titles should choose a style of lettering that is not too wide, or use a slightly larger card, 3⅜ by 1⅝ inches in size.

Cards of Navy Department officials may carry only their titles on the card. This form is also correct for an Under Secretary and for Service Secretaries, although the latter are no longer of Cabinet rank.

A very senior officer is entitled to use only his rank and surname on his card, but many officers prefer to give complete identification and to have their names fully engraved. Official cards of high ranking officers afloat usually have their command engraved in the lower right-hand corner.

The card of an attaché is larger than the regular card since it will carry some five or six lines of engraving. The customary size is about 3½ inches long and 2 inches wide, corresponding in size to official cards of State Department representatives.

SELECTION OF CARDS

Your choice of calling cards will reflect your good taste. Only engraved cards are correct. According to American usage, the name should be engraved in full, without abbreviations or initials. Titles, branch of service, and staff corps designations should not be abbreviated.

Clear lettering should be chosen rather than a heavy or unusual type. Many men prefer the more masculine block lettering, or the shaded block. Script has always been correct, but Roman, shaded antique Roman, or London script are popular letterings. Go to the very best engraver you know of, and take his advice in the matter.

Cards should be of excellent quality paper; this is customarily white, but may be a very light cream color. The lettering is always black. The engraver will give you the engraving plate, and you can have additional cards made up at any time thereafter. When you advance in rank, the plate may be easily altered at less cost than for a new plate.

Although the cost of cards varies in different sections of the country, a hundred cards with plate will cost about ten dollars. It is practical for a married junior officer to have one plate made in such form that it can be used for three types of cards by merely blocking out unwanted words; if you are not married, the "and Mrs." can be added at any future time. Samples of plates for such cards are shown below:

LIEUTENANT AND MRS. JOHN SMITH JONES

LIEUTENANT
UNITED STATES NAVY

or: LIEUTENANT AND MRS. JOHN SMITH JONES
or: MRS. JOHN SMITH JONES
or: JOHN SMITH JONES

LIEUTENANT
UNITED STATES NAVY

On the cards of all officers attached to a diplomatic office, two sizes of lettering are used, with the larger for the name and the smaller for the title. Such officers sometimes have two sets of calling cards; one engraved in the language of their own country, the other engraved in the language of the country to which they are assigned. It is customary for such an officer serving in the Orient to have his name and title in the characters of the Oriental language put on the back of his cards.

The various types of cards are:

Official Cards

Ashore

Admiral John Paul Smith
United States Navy

Chief of Naval Operations

General Randolph Henderson

Commandant
United States Marine Corps

Afloat

Admiral George Washington Jones
United States Navy

Commander in Chief Pacific

Flag Officers' Personal Cards

Vice Admiral Jones

United States Navy

Rear Admiral Robert Edward Decatur
United States Navy

Flag Officer's Joint Card

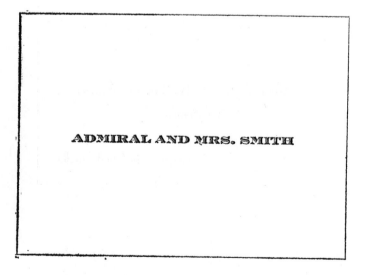

ADMIRAL AND MRS. SMITH

(Including and below the rank of rear admiral, full names are used.)

Rear Admiral and Mrs. Robert Edward Decatur

Personal Cards, Senior Officers

Captain Stephen Sidney Preble

United States Navy

COLONEL PAUL JOHN O'BANNON

UNITED STATES ARMY

Colonel Richard Walter O'Bannon

United States Marine Corps

Commander James Richmond Briggs
United States Coast Guard

Commander James Richard Briggs

United States Maritime Service

Naval Attaché

Captain Albert Truxton
United States Navy
Naval Attaché
Naval Attaché for Air
Embassy of the United States of America

Rio de Janeiro

Marine Attaché

Richard Brinton Butler

First Lieutenant, United States Marine Corps
Assistant Naval Attaché
Assistant Naval Attaché for Air
Embassy of the United States of America

Tehran

Staff Corps Attaché

Commander Dan Murray Hill

Supply Corps, United States Navy
Assistant Naval Attaché
Embassy of the United States of America

Paris

Marine Officer's Personal Card

Carl Langley Hall

Lieutenant
United States Marine Corps

Personal Cards, Retired Officers

Albert Edward Dewey

Captain
United States Army
Retired

or

Rear Admiral Willard Arthur Saunders

United States Navy
Retired

Joint Card

Lieutenant Commander and Mrs. Peter Winston

Personal Card

William Orrmond Paul

Midshipman
United States Navy

Staff Officer's Personal Card

WILLIAM EUGENE HOWARD

LIEUTENANT, JUNIOR GRADE
MEDICAL CORPS
UNITED STATES NAVY

WOMEN'S CARDS

A woman's calling card is about the same length as a man's card, but is wider. The customary size is about 3⅛ inches long by 2¼ inches wide, but the size varies slightly according to the length of the name. It is desirable that a wife's card match her husband's in color, style, and type of engraving.

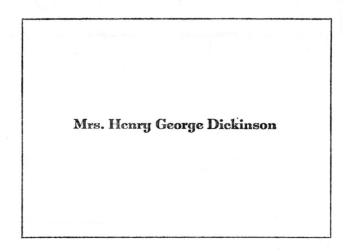

A woman officer in the Services uses a similar card with the same type information engraved in the same way as an officer's personal card.

JOINT CARDS

The *joint card* that married couples frequently use is about 2½ by 3½ inches in size. When used in making formal calls, one such card may be used along with any additional individual cards as needed, or two joint cards are used in accordance with the number of adults in the family. The officer's branch of Service is never indicated on the card, but his individual card will provide this information. (See page 56.)

A flag officer's joint card may have only the rank and surname engraved in the center of the card; a Rear Admiral and officers of less rank will use their full names. It is customary for officers of the rank of lieutenant and up to use their rank to precede their names on joint cards.

The joint card is also useful for extending and replying to invitations, and is frequently enclosed with gifts. Notes of thanks, condolence, etc., are written across them; an address is sometimes engraved in the lower right-hand corner of the card. Matching envelopes are usually ordered with the cards.

INFORMALS

The fold-over card, known as *"informals,"* are widely used for informal invitations and brief notes, but they are *not* used for calling cards. The name is engraved on the outside, and the message or invitation is written on the inside of the card.

Another style of informal is the *"message card,"* a single flat card about 3½ by 4½ inches in size. The address is engraved above and to the right of the name, with the name engraved in the center or near the top center of the card. Message cards are not used for calling cards.

ABBREVIATIONS ON CARDS

There are a number of conventional abbreviations on calling cards. Although some of these abbreviations are not often used in this country, you should be aware of their meaning. Such abbreviations are customarily written by hand:

p.p.c. (*Pour prendre congé*)—"To take leave." This indicates that one is leaving town. The initials are written in the lower left-hand corner of the card.

p.c. (*Pour condolénce*)—"To condole"; to extend sympathy.

p.f. (*Pour féliciter*)—"To congratulate;" to extend congratulations; to felicitate.

p.r. (*Pour remercier*)—"To thank"; to reply to a "p.f." card (above) or instead of a dinner call.

n.b. (*Nota bene*)—"Note well"; this calls attention to any words or messages written on the card.

R.s.v.p. or R.S.V.P. (*Répondez s'il vous plaît*)—"Please reply." These initials are customarily written on invitations, when an answer is requested.

The custom of bending the upper right-hand corner of the card toward the name is rarely observed today. But it is still occasionally done to denote that a call was made in person, or upon all members of the household.

SECTION III

YOUR TABLE MANNERS

CHAPTER 6

Manners at the Table

Good table manners in the Services are good table manners anywhere. Customs may vary abroad and in various parts of the United States, but good fundamentals in eating are generally the same. The proper use of table silver should be as easy and as familiar to you as the proper use of any mechanical device you consider important to your career.

Mealtime is the time for enjoyment, not only of foods but also the company of others. Pleasant conversation, coupled with the relaxation that comes with knowing what to do, will mean pleasure in dining any place— in a luxurious hotel, in a home, or at an embassy.

Good manners are not turned on or off, in accordance with the importance of the occasion or the individual, yet neither do they mean rigid formality. The desirable attitude at even the most formal occasion is *relaxed politeness,* plus the ability to make interesting "small talk."

But it takes everyday practice before manners at the table become easy and automatic. Poor manners at home will invariably mean poor manners in the wardroom or the Commandant's quarters.

TABLE TRADITIONS

The modern day use of table silver goes back to A.D. 1100, when the wife of an Italian nobleman introduced the two-tined fork into table usage in Venice, because she did not like to pick up meat with her fingers.

The use of forks was not entirely satisfactory, and their use spread but slowly, even in Italy where they had the blessing of the nobility. Complete acceptance of the fork came only with the Renaissance, which also ushered in the use of the table knife to displace the common hunting knife which every freeman carried at all times on his belt and used at the table for cutting.

France and England were slower in accepting these customs, and it was not until the mid-1600's that English craftsmen commenced the manufacture of table knives and forks, and then spoons. These utensils were made of silver, and were considered a rarity.

As a result of the scarcity of table silver, it fell to the lot of the English gentry to formulate the table manners of the land. It is from them that Americans inherit their table manners, modified somewhat by native American thought and customs.

73

The first table napkins made their appearance in Reims, France, in the court of Charles VII. They were used exclusively in the palaces of kings and princes, and from the early part of the fifteenth century, they were lace trimmed and intricately embroidered.

Later, in the seventeenth century, napkins were an important decorative part in table setting. They were folded and pleated to represent flowers, birds, fans, etc. Ornate foldings are still used occasionally in Europe, and it is claimed that there are 400 ways of folding napkins. In this country, however, a few simple foldings are preferred.

MEALS

Dinner is the main meal of the day in the United States, when it is the evening meal except for Sundays and holidays. Luncheon is everyday noon meal, and a light or informal evening meal is usually called supper. (In certain sections of this country, dinner is the noon meal and supper the evening meal.)

Suppers are also held after formal occasions, such as weddings, dances, receptions, etc., and may be served very late. Buffet meals served in the evening are referred to as suppers, never dinners—even when guests are in evening attire. Luncheons and dinners are the only completely served meals.

EATING CUSTOMS

You may use the American or Continental way of eating, but the favored American custom is to hold the dinner fork in your left hand to pin down the food for cutting, and then to transfer the fork, tines up, to the right hand for the purpose of eating. The Continental, or European, custom of eating is to transfer the food to the mouth from the fork while it is still held in the left hand, tines down. Either fashion is correct.

CUSTOMS AT THE TABLE

The simplest silver service at any meal is the knife, fork, and spoon. The fork is placed at the left of the plate, and the knife and spoon at the right, with the knife closest to the plate.

In the United States, the *knife* is always held in the right hand, with the handle in your palm and your index finger along the back of the blade. After using the knife, never lay it down afterwards on the table. You place the knife across the upper half of the plate, or on the right side of the plate, with the blade facing in.

The *fork* is held in the left hand while being used with the knife to cut food. The handle of the fork will rest in your palm, with your index finger extending along the back.

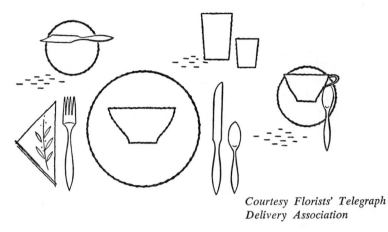

*Courtesy Florists' Telegraph
Delivery Association*

At all other times, the fork is preferably held in the right hand, tines up, with the handle controlled by your thumb and first two fingers in a manner similar to holding a pencil. The end of the handle should extend out between your thumb and index finger.

After the fork is used, lay it on the plate below the knife, or at the left, and parallel to the knife, with the handle at the right, and the tines up.

The *spoon* is held in the right hand in the same manner as the fork. Correctly, the only spoon to appear on the table at the beginning of a meal is a soup spoon—except at breakfast. However, a modern hostess frequently places the dessert spoon at the right of the knife, or above the plate and parallel to the table edge, at an informal meal.

The most commonly used spoon is the teaspoon. It is used at informal meals for soup served in cups, desserts, cereal, tea, coffee, cereals, grapefruit, etc.

ADDITIONAL SILVER

In settings other than the simplest, you will also find other table silver, such as a butter knife, salad and/or dessert fork, a sea food fork, dessert spoon, iced beverage spoon, soup spoon, coffee or demitasse spoon, etc.

The individual *butter knife* (sometimes called a *butter spreader*) is

*Courtesy Florists' Telegraph
Delivery Association*

usually laid across the top of the butter plate, with the handle at the right, the blade facing the edge of the table. The individual butter knife is used only to spread butter on a piece of bread. It is not used to take butter from the butter plate. A knife to be used for the purpose of taking butter from a butter plate will be placed on the butter plate—when such a plate is used. The individual butter knife is much smaller than a dinner knife.

The *salad fork* is shorter than the luncheon or dinner fork, and may be used for either a salad or dessert course. The placing of the fork depends upon the time the salad course will be served. When the salad is served after the main course—as is customary—the fork will be placed next to the plate on the left-hand side, and inside the luncheon or dinner fork. When served as a first course at family or informal meals, the salad fork will be placed outside the luncheon or dinner fork. When there is no separate salad course and the fork is to be used for dessert, the fork is usually placed on the dessert plate.

A *seafood fork* is much shorter and slimmer than the salad fork, and may be placed at the outside of the forks on the left, but customarily is placed at the right or outside of the spoon. Sometimes the tines of the seafood fork rest in the bowl of the spoon, with the handle of the fork placed even with the handle of the spoon.

The *dessert spoon* is longer than a teaspoon and usually is placed on the dessert plate at formal meals. But the dessert spoon, and/or fork, may be placed on the table at the beginning of an informal meal.

The *iced beverage spoon* is a long-handled spoon, and is laid on the small plate or coaster placed under the iced beverage glass. When no plate or coaster is provided, you will leave the spoon in the glass, holding it against the far side of the glass with your first and second fingers while drinking. When finished, do not lay the spoon on the tablecloth but leave it in the glass.

Soup spoons are longer than the dessert spoon or teaspoon, and are oval-bowled. In using a soup spoon, dip the spoon *away* from you and avoid scraping the bottom of the soup bowl. After the spoon is used, it is placed on the soup plate on the right-hand side.

Coffee or demitasse spoons are used with small cups of after-dinner, or after-luncheon, coffee. They are usually about four inches long, and are customarily placed on the saucer when coffee is served.

The *serving fork and spoon* are placed on the platter or in the vegetable dish. These pieces are larger than the regular fork and spoon. In serving yourself, you hold these like other forks and spoons, with the fork in your left hand, the spoon in your right hand. You will slip the spoon under a portion of food, and, while holding the food in place with the fork, you transfer the food to your plate. Meats are usually portioned before serving, but if not, you will cut the food with the spoon and transfer it to your plate with the fork.

Table silver, or *flatware,* as it is called, is always placed on the table in the order of use, beginning from the outside and working in toward the plate. There will never be more than three knives and three forks placed on

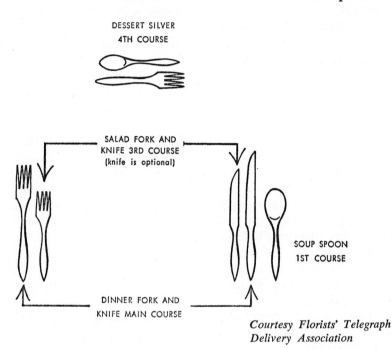

DESSERT SILVER
4TH COURSE

SALAD FORK AND
KNIFE 3RD COURSE
(knife is optional)

SOUP SPOON
1ST COURSE

DINNER FORK AND
KNIFE MAIN COURSE

Courtesy Florists' Telegraph
Delivery Association

the most formal table at any time. If more silver is needed, it will be brought in with the courses they accompany.

TABLE CHINA AND GLASSWARE

There are three main types of *plates* used daily: breakfast, luncheon, and dinner. In setting the table, the plate is placed an inch from the edge of the table, and the silver and napkin are also placed an inch from the table's edge.

At a formal luncheon or dinner, there will be a *place plate* (sometimes called a *service plate*) on the table when you sit down. The first course, in its own plate, will be set in the place plate.

The butter plate, which is much smaller than the regular plate, is placed above the forks at informal and semi-formal dinners and formal or informal luncheons. It is never used at a formal dinner. The individual butter knife is laid across the top of the butter plate. When butter is passed in a butter plate, you place your butter directly on the butter plate—not on the luncheon or dinner plate. You also place bread, jams, etc., on the butter plate.

The *salad plate* is larger than the butter plate, and usually is flat and round. There are also crescent-shaped salad plates to be used when meat and salad are served in the same course at less formal meals. However, salad is usually served as a separate course, but at informal or family meals it may accompany the main course.

The *dessert plate* is about eight or nine inches in diameter, and is interchangeable with place plates.

Soup plates are used at formal dinners, and although they are called "plates" they really are a broad bowl about an inch deep and usually have a broad flat rim—but also may be rimless. The soup plate sets in an underplate, with the rim of the underplate showing about half an inch.

Soup cups are used at luncheons, with the standard soup cup looking like a two-handled teacup—only larger. There is always a matching saucer.

A *cup and saucer* are set at the right of the knife and/or spoon. No cup or bowl is set on the table without a saucer or plate under it. Soup, cereal, or dessert bowls are always placed in a plate or served with their own plates under them. A coffee cup is always in its saucer. When you hold a coffee cup, avoid curling your little finger.

Demitasse cups and saucers are much smaller than coffee cups and saucers. Demitasse coffee is served after informal as well as formal dinners.

The *water goblet* is placed above the knives, and is usually filled before guests sit down.

Wine glasses are placed in the order of their use at the right of the water goblet, but nearer the table's edge. Wines are poured with the courses they accompany. It is correct to hold long-stemmed water goblets or wine glasses with the thumb and first two fingers at the base of the bowl, but not around the bowl itself. Small-stemmed glasses are held by the stems, and tumblers are held near the base.

NAPKINS

Napkins are placed at the left of the forks at luncheons and informal meals, and in the place plate at formal meals. You will place your napkin, unfolded in half, in your lap immediately after you sit down at the table—or after grace is said. To lay the napkin smoothly, pick it up by the right top corners and unspread in one motion across your lap.

At the end of the meal, replace the napkin *unfolded* at the left of your plate. At formal dinners, the napkin may be laid at the right of the plate. When paper napkins are used at informal meals, these are laid at the left of the plate, and when you are through with them, you never crush them or roll them into a ball.

HOW TO EAT:

Artichokes are eaten by pulling off each leaf, with the base of the leaf dipped in a sauce and eaten. When down to the heart, you scrape or cut off the fuzz with a knife, then cut and eat the heart. Leaves are piled on the plate or butter plate.

Avocados, when halved, are eaten with a spoon. When peeled and served in a salad, they are eaten with a fork.

Bacon is eaten with a fork unless very crisp, then it is eaten with the fingers.

Cake is eaten by hand unless sticky, then with a fork. When cake is served alone as dessert, use a fork.

Caviar is served on small pieces of toast with cocktails, or in a bowl before dinner or at buffet suppers.

Cheese is frequently served at the table with the salad course. Cheese, fruit, and coffee are frequently served together as the final course, instead of dessert.

Chicken, broiled or fried, is held with the fork in the plate, while you strip the meat off the bones with your knife. Or, if not greasy, you may hold the chicken in your left hand against the plate, while you strip the meat off with the fork. At informal occasions, such as picnics, family meals, etc., fried chicken is eaten held in the hand.

Corn on the Cob is usually served only at informal meals, and may be held with the hands or by small spears inserted in each end. Salt, pepper, and butter are sometimes mixed in small pats or balls before the meal, or you can mix them yourself on the dinner plate before eating. Butter only a few rows of kernels at a time. Kernels may also be cut off the ear with the dinner knife.

Cream Puffs or Eclairs are eaten with a fork when served at the table.

Fish, unless served in pieces, is held in the plate with the fork while you slit it with the tip of the knife from head to tail. Insert the tip of the knife under the end of the backbone and lift out the skeleton. Lay the skeleton and bones on the side of the plate out of the way, or on plates provided by the host.

Frog Legs are eaten in the same manner as chicken.

Fresh Fruits (except citrus fruit) served at the table may be eaten either the American or Continental way. Continental fashion is to skin the fruit, halve and stone it, then cut it into small pieces and eat these with the fork. The American way is to halve, quarter, and stone the fruit with the knife and fork, but not skin it (except peaches); then you eat the quarters with your fingers. Fresh grapes and cherries are eaten whole. The pits are removed with the fingers.

Grapefruit, or Oranges, are usually served in halves, and eaten with a teaspoon. Do not squeeze the fruit after eating.

Honey is taken by the spoonful. With a twisting motion of the serving spoon, catch any drops, then transfer the spoonful to the butter plate.

Ice Cream is served with a fork and/or spoon; the fork is for the solid part, the spoon for the softer. Ice cream is always eaten with a spoon when it is served in a sherbet glass.

Olives are held in the fingers while the flesh is eaten, and the stones are then placed on a butter plate.

Oranges and Tangerines, served other than at the table, are peeled and held in the fingers, and segments eaten by hand; served at the table, they are of course eaten with a spoon.

Pâté de Foie Gras, an imported paste made of goose livers, is frequently served on toast at cocktail parties, or with cocktails before dinner. Or you may find it placed in its own earthenware crock on a tray with a knife, and served at a buffet supper.

Pickles are held with the fingers and eaten when served with a sandwich, but are eaten with a fork when served with meat at a table.

Potato Chips are eaten with the fingers.

Potatoes, French fried, are eaten with the fork after being cut in shorter lengths, if necessary. Do not spear the potatoes with the fork, and then bite off pieces of them.

Radishes are taken with the fingers and placed on the side of the plate, or on the butter plate until you eat them.

Roast Beef may be carved at the table by the host, but is sometimes partially carved in the kitchen before bringing into the dining room. The carving of a three-rib roast is illustrated:

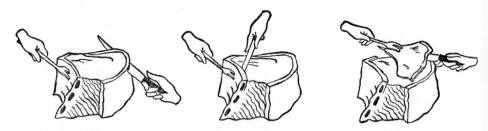

Salad is eaten with a fork. When iceberg lettuce is served, it may be cut with a knife and fork, then eaten with the fork.

Sandwiches are eaten by hand. The large or double-decker sandwiches may first be cut in half, then in quarter pieces, with a knife. They are then eaten by hand.

Seafoods are often eaten both with the fingers and with table silver.

Clams are usually served steamed, until the shell has opened. If not fully open, bend the shell back with the fingers, then hold it in the left hand just over the dish and lift out the clam by its neck with your right hand. Pull the body of the clam out and discard the neck sheath. Hold the clam in your right hand, dip it whole in melted butter or broth, or both, and eat in one bite. You place the empty shells on the butter plate or on a dish especially provided for that purpose. Fried clams are eaten with a fork, since they are too greasy to hold. Clam broth is drunk in a separate bouillon cup or small bowl.

Lobster and Hard-Shelled Crabs, boiled or broiled, demand dexterity. The major part of the meat is in the stomach cavity and the tail or claws. The claws of both the lobster and crabs demand careful— but similar—handling:

For crabs, etc., the general objective is the same as that for lobsters. The best meat is in the large claws and the main body of the crab.

Oysters and Clams on the half shell are eaten raw, with an oyster fork. They are lifted whole from the shell, sprinkled with lemon juice or

1. Twist off the claws.

2. Crack each claw with a nutcracker, pliers, knife, hammer, rock or what have you.

3. Separate the tail-piece from the body by arching the back until it cracks.

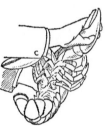

4. Bend back and break the flippers off the tail-piece.

5. Insert a fork where the flippers broke off and push. PUSH

6. Unhinge the back from the body. Don't forget that this contains the "tomalley", or liver of the lobster which turns green when it is cooked and which many persons consider the best eating of all.

7. Open the remaining part of the body by cracking apart sideways. There is some good meat in this section.

8. The small claws are excellent eating and may be placed in the mouth and the meat sucked out like sipping cider with a straw.

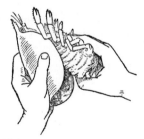

Courtesy State of Maine Department of Economic Development.

dipped in cocktail sauce, and eaten in a single mouthful. When served as a first course, the half shells come to the table imbedded in cracked ice. Regardless of size, do not cut oysters or clams with your fork before eating them.

Shrimp, Oysters, Scallops, when fried, are eaten with a fork. When shrimp are French fried, they may be held in the fingers by the tail, dipped in sauce, and eaten to the tail. Unshelled shrimp, which are never served with heads on, are held in the fingers, shelled, and eaten whole except for the very tail.

Spaghetti is twisted around the fork, cocoon fashion, and eaten from the fork tip. It is sometimes cut with the side of the fork before winding, but it is never bitten off.

Tortillas (thin Mexican corncakes) are laid flat on the left hand, or plate, and are filled with frijoles (kidney beans) or special sauce, as provided, then rolled and eaten from the end with the fingers.

Turkey (or poultry) is usually carved at the table by the host, and is eaten like chicken. There is an art in carving:

Midshipmen, Cadets, and other junior officers should make every effort to become adept at carving. It is quite customary at the Service Academies when a Midshipman or Cadet is invited to the home of an officer for Thanksgiving or Christmas dinner, to have the host request one of the invited Midshipmen or Cadet to carve. This is considered part of his training.

CHAPTER 7

Eating Habits

There are many simple rules in eating that may seem elementary, but they are the rules by which you are judged. The difference between good or crude manners is the way you observe the following rules:

Do *not* talk with food in your mouth, make noises while eating or swallowing, chew food with your mouth open, or blow on hot liquids to cool them.

You will avoid such unattractive eating habits as smacking your lips or taking too-large mouthfuls from food piled high on your fork. Use your napkin before drinking from a glass of water in order not to leave traces of food on the glass. Never lick your fingers after they have been in contact with food—use your napkin.

If something is out of reach at the table, do not rise out of your seat to obtain it, but ask for it to be passed. However, you may reach for anything you conveniently can without bothering your dinner partner.

You will avoid curling your little finger on a cup handle—and be sure to remove the spoon from the cup after stirring and before drinking. Remember to place the spoon in the saucer, at the right of the cup handle, and not on the tablecloth. If the liquid seems hot, test it by sipping a spoonful—but do not continue drinking by spoonfuls.

You may tilt a soup bowl away from you when almost empty, and you must remember to dip the spoon in the bowl *away* from you. Clear soup served in a cup or bowl with handles may be drunk. You must not place the bowl of the spoon in your mouth, but should sip somewhat from the side.

Bread and rolls are broken in half, and then into smaller pieces with the fingers. Do not cut breads with a knife. If butter is served, you butter each piece of bread before eating.

Jams and condiments go directly onto the butter plate, not onto the bread.

You must never place your elbows on the table while eating, but you may do so momentarily between courses if you do not turn your back on your dinner partner or lean too heavily on the table.

You should keep your elbows at your sides when cutting food; they move as easily up and down as sideways, and if held in, cannot hit your partner.

Do not slump at the table, but do not sit too rigidly or "at attention," either. Avoid twisting your feet around the chair legs or extending your legs under the table.

Loud talk and laughter at the table are disturbing to others. The monopolized or too-intimate conversation between partners, to the exclusion of others, is equally ill-bred.

Be careful of controversial or unpleasant subjects, such as politics, religion, or death. Be careful of talking "shop." Carry your share of the conversation; do not make it a burden for others. But always remember not to discuss personal affairs or women at the table, or before groups anywhere. Also, never criticize a senior in wardroom talk or in a group.

It is annoying to others if you drum on the table with your fingers, crack your knuckles, or fiddle with the silverware. Do not crunch ice from the water goblet—it makes an unusually loud sound. It is crude to pick your teeth in public, to run your tongue around your cheek to dislodge foods, or to rinse out your mouth with water.

Olives, celery, etc., may be placed on the butter plate or dinner plate, and cranberry sauce may be placed alongside the turkey, or mint jelly alongside the leg of lamb. Gravies and liquid sauces go directly over the foods they accompany.

Usually, what goes into the mouth may be taken out in the same way— when necessary, and only then. A cherry stone in a pie would be removed on the fork, and olive pits are removed with the fingers. But fish bones or a sliver of glass should be removed with the first finger and the thumb rather than a fork, and placed at the side of the plate or on the butter plate. You will remember not to call attention to these little embarrassments at the table.

Common sense will dictate what to do in unexpected situations, such as uncontrolled coughing, choking, sneezing, blowing your nose, or when a foreign object is taken into your mouth.

When a sip of water does not help a fit of coughing, or when you are choking, you will necessarily leave the table. If it is your dinner partner who is choking, you may assist her or him on leaving the table and going to another room. If you have to sneeze, use your handkerchief, or your napkin, if you have time.

Although it is better not to attend a dinner when you have a cold, sometimes it is necessary that you attend unless quite ill, particularly at an official or state occasion. If you must use a handkerchief at the table, do so as unobtrusively as possible. If your cold is a serious one, it may be better to be excused from the table than to disgust the other guests.

Upon returning to the table, you should not apologize profusely, if at all. A murmured "sorry" may be said to the hostess, or in the general direction of the hostess at a long table. By apologizing or acting embarrassed over an embarrassing situation, you only draw attention to an incident that is best forgotten.

When you drop a piece of silver at the table, do not pick it up. When you have used the wrong piece of silver and obviously need another piece, ask the waiter for it. Do not apologize for the mistake. The less the incident is noticed, the better. You will make fewer mistakes at the table if you will remember always to start from the *outside* of the array of silver, and work in toward your plate.

WHEN WOMEN ARE GUESTS

When women are guests before and at a meal, there are certain rules customarily observed: you rise to your feet when women enter the room and remain standing until they are seated. An exception is when women prefer to remain standing in conversational groups other than your own. In that case, you may return to your own seated group and sit down.

Women are seated at the table as soon as they enter the dining room. You will not take your seat at the table until after all women have been seated. You do not rise from the table until your hostess rises. At a formal occasion, you may remain standing at your place until the women have left the room and entered the living room, and then you may remain at the table with the host and other male guests for coffee and cigarettes. You normally rejoin the women in the living room after half an hour or so.

The following rules are customarily observed with women guests:

- You will assist the lady at your right with her chair by stepping behind the chair and drawing it back. She will usually sit down from the right. You will move the chair forward as she starts to sit down. You will assist with her chair when the meal is over, remembering that she will usually arise from the right side of the chair.
- At a small luncheon or dinner you start eating only after all guests have been served and after the hostess starts eating.
- At a large luncheon or dinner you may start eating after a few near you have been served.
- At formal dinners your host and the ranking woman guest will enter the dining room first, with the ranking woman seated at the right of the host. Other guests will enter in pairs, with no order of precedence. The hostess and ranking male guest will enter the dining room last. He will be seated at her right.
- When a very high ranking officer, or a dignitary of state, is a guest, the hostess and the high ranking officer or dignitary will enter the dining room first, and the host and ranking woman guest will be next to enter.
- At luncheons, there are *no partners* when entering the dining room.

You will enter the room with whomever you were most recently talking.

- At informal or less formal meals, such as buffet suppers, the hostess and women guests usually enter the dining room first, with the men following.
- You may assist your partner with her plate at buffet meals, or she may prefer to fill her own plate. She does not fill your plate, but the hostess may ask a guest to assist in serving at the table.
- The ranking woman guest, or the woman at the right of the host, should be the first person to leave the host's house or quarters at the end of the dinner or other occasion. So wait until the high ranking guest, or guests, leave before taking your own departure.
- It is the woman who suggests that it is time to leave the dinner or other occasion.
- Upon your departure, you should tell your dinner partner at your right, the woman at your left, and as many guests at a small party as you can, that you enjoyed the pleasure of their company at dinner, or for the evening. You will express pleasure for the evening, and thank your host and hostess for their hospitality. After saying "goodbye"—*leave*.

CHAPTER 8

Dining in Public Places

Restaurants in the United States vary in as many ways as American ingenuity can express itself. They range from the milkshake-and-hamburger spots to expensive supper clubs. Hotel dining rooms and coffee shops cater to the most particular gourmet as well as the man who eats and runs.

There is an adage to the effect that experience is the best teacher. For the average man, it is good that experience has a few foundation stones on which to build. Mainly, you should remember that the more elaborate or formal the restaurant, the higher the bill and the slower the service.

SELECTING A RESTAURANT

Three basic principles should be followed in choosing a restaurant: (a) the quality of food you desire; (b) the amount of money you can spend; (c) the length of time you can stay.

You should learn something about the restaurant before entering its doors. In a strange city or in a foreign country, guide books will give such information. You can always ask a bell captain in a reputable hotel—regardless of whether you are staying there—about a good place to eat, and the approximate cost. You can mention the type of place you have in mind, inquire if there is music and dancing, and state that you like seafood or Italian food, etc. When money is an important consideration, you had better find out in advance whether or not a supper club has a cover charge.

When making a cross-country trip, quick information concerning good eating places can be found in excellent and inexpensive books or pamphlets, which may be purchased in almost any drug store, any place, or in travel guides put out by chain hotels or motels.

ENTERING THE RESTAURANT

You may check your coat and hat at a restaurant, hotel, or supper-club, and your lady guest may check her coat or any bundle she may be carrying. Usually, women prefer to wear their coats into the dining room and lay them back across their chairs. You wait at the entrance of the dining room until the headwaiter comes up, and then you may say, "Have you a table for two?"—or any desired number. You may tell the headwaiter where you would like to be seated, but when there is a crowd you may not get what you want.

Women will precede the men and follow the headwaiter to the table. When there is no headwaiter or hostess, you go first to find a table. In a mixed group of several couples, the women are given the desirable seats, which usually are those facing the room at large or any view that is offered. Usually, the preferable seats are away from the aisle. At tables in an open space, women sit opposite each other; at banquettes or wall tables, they will have the wall or inboard seats. At a small table for two, the man sits across from the woman, or by her at a banquette.

You should help a woman with her coat by laying it over the chair back, or stand by while the waiter does this.

ORDERING

In most restaurants there are two methods of ordering a dinner: *table d'hôte* (pronounced "tahble doat") and *à la carte*. The first method means paying a single price for the complete meal as outlined on the menu. The second method involves paying a specific price for *each* item order. If a complete dinner is desired, it is more economical to order *table d'hôte*. Ordering *à la carte* is always more expensive, but also more selective; you get what you want.

The host will perhaps make suggestions to his guest or guests concerning the ordering of the dinner, such as "I understand that the chicken tetrazzini is excellent here. Do you care to try it?" or "Seafood is their specialty. Do you care for lobster?" Regardless of suggestions, the host always asks his guests, "What would you like?"

When you take a lady out to lunch or dinner, she will tell you what she wants even though the waiter asks her directly, and then you will place both orders. When you are host to a group, your guests will tell you what they want, and sometimes how they wish certain dishes prepared—steaks well done, rare, etc. The waiter takes the individual orders from you after the guests tell you what they want. Dessert is usually ordered following the main course, when the waiter again brings menus for everyone to study.

Depending upon the part of the country you are in, the size of the city, and the type of restaurant involved, many different menus are encountered which may list local dishes, or menus entirely in French, or foods which are completely disguised. When you do not know what the dish may be, ask the waiter.

Most menus for a complete dinner include an entré, such as tomato or fruit juice, shrimp or fruit cocktail, or soup; a main course of meat and two vegetables, plus salad, dessert, and coffee. When young ladies accompany junior officers, it is to be hoped that they are aware of his financial status, but a young man should not ask someone to have dinner with him in an unknown restaurant *unless he is solvent*.

When you are host to a large group at dinner or luncheon, it is best to order the menu in advance. You may always telephone, but when you have time it is wise to talk with the headwaiter personally and make all plans in advance. The guests will accept what is placed before them at such a dinner or luncheon, and there will be little effort for a host and/or hostess.

WAITERS

A good waiter or waitress will give a couple or a group time to study the menu and determine what they care to order. But you should always remember that every waiter or waitress is a human being, and a little consideration toward them may prove the difference between good or indifferent service.

You address a waiter as *"Waiter."* not *"Hey, you!"* or *"Boy."* and a waitress as *"Waitress."* not *"Miss."* In speaking to the waiter, you refer to your guest as "The lady." When a waiter or waitress is busy, you do not attract their attention by clapping your hands, drumming on the table with silverware, or hissing. When a waiter passes nearby, within hearing distance, but fails to notice you, you may call "Waiter!" in a clear tone—but don't bark an order for attention.

The host will make any complaints concerning improperly prepared or served food, or when a mistake of any consequence has been made in the order. A very small error is not worth mentioning, but when anything of importance needs correcting, you do so quietly, but with firmness. Mistakes do happen, but they may not be the fault of the waiter, who serves the food, but does not prepare it.

If the waiter assigned to your table disappears continuously, or takes too long to serve you, this may be mentioned to the headwaiter. But do not lose your temper and shout or create a scene.

PAYING THE BILL

When it is time to leave, you quietly say to the waiter, "The check, please." The waiter may bring the check on a small tray, with the check face down, and set the tray by the host or whoever did the ordering. In a small eating place, the check may be laid on the table, face down. The host will look at the bill long enough to see if it is correct, and then place the money on the tray. The waiter will take the tray to the cashier and return any change; you usually leave this for the tip, deducting or adding to the sum, if necessary. Or, in small eating places where the bill says, "Please pay the cashier," the host takes the check directly to the cashier and pays there. In this case, be sure you leave a suitable tip on the table for your waiter or waitress.

Tips customarily are between *ten and fifteen per cent* of the entire check.

Pennies should not be left unless they add to an even amount, but it is better not to leave them at all.

If you should find an error in the check, you call this to the attention of your waiter. If he should insist that the bill is correct—when you are certain that it is not—you may discuss this matter with the headwaiter, the cashier, or the manager. After all, it is your money that is involved. But unless the amount involved is considerable, it is better to pay the amount demanded rather than create a scene that will be unpleasant for your guests.

When a stag or mixed group goes "Dutch treat," one person may be designated beforehand to pay the check, with others in the party settling up later. This avoids the clutter of paying at the dinner table, but it is inexcusable for anyone to forget to settle accounts immediately afterward with the one who has paid.

If you are a guest at a dinner held in a hotel or restaurant, you should not offer to help your host pay the bill. You should repay his hospitality later with a dinner, or similar social occasion, of your own.

RESTAURANT MANNERS

Although a man should rise to his feet when a woman stops to chat at his table, this can be awkward to do, as well as inconsiderate of others, at a crowded table. You need not rise completely to your feet under such crowded conditions, even when introductions are underway. A half-rise, or a brief attempt to rise, is acceptable.

It is thoughtless of anyone to stop and talk at a table when hot or very cold food is before those eating. It is better just to nod or speak and then go on your way; later you can talk briefly with your friends during a lull in the service, or over coffee. When someone stops at your table, you need not ask him to sit down unless you and your guest so desire.

You do not rise when the restaurant hostess stops at your table to inquire about the service and the quality of your food. This is a courteous, business gesture—not social.

In any public eating place, you should never wipe the silver with your napkin; if it appears unclean, ask the waiter for fresh silver. When you drop a piece of silver or a napkin, leave it alone and ask for another. Do not write or chart a course on the tablecloth, and avoid cluttering up the floor space with your feet or bundles.

CHAPTER 9

Toasts

Toasts are given upon various occasions—after weddings, or at bachelor dinners, birthday parties, christenings, engagement parties, dinners, anniversaries, or at a "wetting down" party, etc. A "wetting down" party is one held in celebration of an advancement in rank in the Naval Service.

Champagne is the favorite wine for toasts, but dessert wines, sherry, port, marsala, or angelica wines are suitable. Liqueurs and soft drinks are not suitable. The person receiving the toast remains seated; all others stand.

When you are the one receiving the toast, you will remain seated and not even sip the drink—or you will be drinking to yourself. After everyone else sits down, you may rise and thank them or offer a toast in return.

At a *wedding reception,* the first toast is always offered by the best man and is always a toast to the bride. The bride usually accepts the toast by smiling and remaining seated. At a reception where all guests are seated at tables, the second toast at the bride's table may be proposed by the groom to the bride's mother, with other toasts to the bridesmaids.

At a reception where everyone stands, the bride cuts the cake with the bride and groom eating the first piece; then everybody else has a piece of cake, and the toasts begin.

At a bachelor dinner given by a groom for his ushers (See Chapter 31, *The Military Wedding),* the groom's toast to the bride traditionally is, "To the bride." He will rise to his feet when giving the toast, and all others at the table will also rise to their feet.

At a *small dinner* a toast may be proposed by anyone as soon as the first wine has been served, and guests stand only if the person giving the toast stands. More than one toast may be drunk with the same glass of wine, and you may informally say, "To your health." or "Your health." You might say, "Many happy returns." at a birthday party.

You will remember that it is an insult to refuse to participate in a toast; if you are averse to alcoholic drinks, you may simply lift your glass and go through the semblance of drinking.

It is customary for the *toastmaster or master of ceremonies* at a luncheon or dinner to give his toast after the dessert. The toast should always express the personal sentiment of the toastmaster or master of ceremonies (M.C.), and it should be brief and appropriate to the occasion.

A very high ranking officer or a dignitary does not always return a toast. At a service organization dinner, a dinner chairman would propose the first toast to the president of the organization. The organization president may bow in recognition of the honor and remain seated while others stand.

At a *child's christening,* the toast to the child's health would be given during the reception, luncheon, or tea which usually follows the christening ceremony. The toast would be proposed by the child's godfather.

CEREMONIAL TOASTS

All American officers should be familiar with the international customs observed when toasts are exchanged on board foreign ships or in foreign messes ashore, or at official dinners or luncheons given in honor of visiting dignitaries.

On these occasions, toward the end of the meal, the host—or the highest official of his country present—proposes a standing toast to the head of state (Sovereign or President) of the guest's country. This toast is customarily followed by the national anthem of the country concerned. The highest ranking guest then responds with a toast to the ruler of the host country, followed by its national anthem.

The preliminary ceremonial toasts may be succeeded by toasts to the countries or services represented. The order and subjects of all toast should be previously agreed upon so that the host and guests will know what is expected of them. All present drink to a ruler or country, but they do not drink toasts proposed to themselves or to their own Services.

When the guests represent more than one nation, the host proposes a collective toast to the heads of their several states, naming them in the order of the seniority of the representatives present.

To this collective toast the highest ranking foreign officer present will respond on behalf of all the guests by proposing the health of the head of state of the host.

Occasions and toasts typical of certain countries are given in the next few paragraphs.

British Customs

At an official dinner given by a British officer to an American officer, the British officer rises during or after dessert to toast the President of the United States, and then the orchestra plays "The Star-Spangled Banner."

After the guests are seated, the American officer rises to toast "Her Majesty, Queen Elizabeth II," and the orchestra plays "God Save the Queen." These toasts are sometimes followed by short speeches and toasts to the Services represented.

At regular mess dinners in the Royal Services, the senior member of the mess proposes the toast, "The Queen." and all members in a low voice repeat "The Queen." and sip the toast. If an American officer should be a personal dinner guest in a mess where a toast to the Queen is drunk every night, the mess president might propose a toast to the corresponding U. S. Service after the usual toast to the Queen.

The proper reply by the American officer then would be a toast to the corresponding Royal Service. At official dinners, the Britisher would toast "The President of the United States," and the senior American would reply with a toast "To Her Majesty, Queen Elizabeth II."

Officers of the Royal Navy have the unique and traditional privilege of remaining seated when toasting their sovereign at mess, although those serving in the Royal Yacht choose to rise.

French and Italian Customs

Officers of these Services are more likely to begin a toast with the phrase, "I have the honor, etc." At a dinner for a senior American officer, the French host would probably say, "I have the honor to propose a toast to the President of the United States," and the American officer might reply with the toast, "It is my great honor to propose a toast to the President of the Republic of France."

Scandinavian Customs

In the Scandinavian countries ceremonial toasts are not customary, but instead the host "skoals" (toasts) each individual guest. No one drinks any wine at the table until after the host has made a general skoal welcoming all the guests. Then skoaling proceeds all during the meal, and women in particular must be on the alert to respond to individual skoals from the men.

Each man is supposed to skoal the woman sitting at his right at least once. The procedure is for him to raise his glass slightly from the table, and looking straight into his partner's eye draw the glass down and toward his body, bow slightly, say "Skoal" and drink—not forgetting to salute again with his glass before putting it down. This skoal must be returned a few minutes later.

During the dinner the host and hostess are supposed to skoal everyone around the table, but it is incorrect for guests to toast them immediately. At the end of the meal, the guest of honor (seated at the left of the hostess in Scandinavian countries) makes a little speech of thanks, and skoals the host and hostess on behalf of all the guests, who join in this skoal.

CHAPTER 10

Tipping Charts

IN AMERICA

It's easy to trip over tips, particularly since tipping varies in certain sections of this country, as well as abroad. Like death, poverty, and taxes, tipping is always with us.

Originally, tips were given to individuals for services better or beyond those expected. Nowadays, tips are expected for almost any kind of service, but you should never tip a person for inefficient or discourteous service; neither should you allow yourself to be bullied into too large a tip by a scornful attendant.

Never over-tip; that is considered to be flashy. But neither should you be cheap and under-tip. Learn at the start what a fair tip is—and then stick to your system.

If a crafty waiter brings you only large coins or folding money, don't allow yourself to be intimidated; just ask him courteously to bring you some smaller change.

When you do tip, be pleasant about it. You should glance at the person you are tipping, and for good service you should say, "Thank you."

It is a wise man who always carries a quantity of small change for small tips.

When Not to Tip

While it is important to know when to tip, it is equally important to know when not to tip. If you make a mistake and offer a tip to someone who should not be tipped, you will discover your error when your tip is waved away. In such a case you simply re-pocket your money.

You do not tip professional people, including nurses, ship's officers, government employees, lawyers, doctors, stenographers, department store workers, golf professionals, or owners or managers of such places of business as restaurants or nightclubs, or barber shops.

You do not tip airline employees, including pilots, stewards and stewardesses, reservation clerks, porters in airline uniforms, limousine drivers, etc. About the only person around an airport who can be tipped is the porter or redcap, who is an employee of the airport—not of an individual airline.

A headwaiter, usually referred to in nicer restaurants as the *maître d'hotel* and who ranks as a manager, is not tipped—unless he has given special attention to arranging in detail a reservation for your supper party, etc. You do not tip ushers in theaters.

You generally do not tip delivery people—unless someone has given special service, such as a Western Union boy who delivers a telegram at a late hour or in bad weather. You may give presents at Christmas time to any delivery person, such as your postman, a newspaper boy, garage attendant, or garbage collector.

A newspaper boy or garbage collector may prefer a present of folding money—say a dollar or two—but gifts of a carton of cigarettes, cigars, a tie, may be given to others, and in the case of women, you can give candy.

You do not tip nurses or doctors, but you may tip maids and attendants at a hospital. In a private or semi-private room, you may give a dollar to each attendant; you do not tip in wards.

If you would like to give something to your nurse, a small present of fruit, candy, or cigarettes, etc., is acceptable.

Tipping Chart

Wine and Dine
> In a Restaurant:
>> WAITER—10% to 15% of the bill; when check is over $15, about 10%.
>> HEADWAITER—no tip unless he made advance arrangements, then 10% of the bill.
>> WINE STEWARD—when he serves, 10% of the wine bill; otherwise, the tip goes to the waiter. (Tip should not be under $1.)
>> CHECK ROOM—25¢.
>> DOORMAN—15¢ to 25¢ for getting a cab; a little more when he parks your car.
>> BUSBOY—no tip.
>> MEN'S ROOM—15¢ to 25¢ when attendant brings towel, uses whisk broom; etc., otherwise no tip.
>> AT A COUNTER—10% of your check, or follow "No Tipping" sign.
>> CAFETERIA—usually no tip.
> In a Nightclub: (Generally the same as in a restaurant; but—)
>> ENTERTAINERS—do not tip; you may buy the star a drink.
>> REQUESTS—special numbers by stars, either no tip, or $1—up.
>> CIGARETTE GIRL—10¢ to 25¢.
>> AT A BAR—bartender 15% of check (do not tip manager or owner).
> Private Club: (Generally no tipping of employees, such as at Officers' Club, country club, private club, etc. Members usually chip in and give employees gifts at Christmas time.)

Hotels and Motels
> At a Hotel:
>> BELLBOYS—25¢ a bag in average hotel.
>> 40¢ to 50¢ a bag in expensive hotel.
>> 10¢ for small objects brought to room (cigarettes, etc.).
>> 25¢ for large objects brought to room (pitcher of ice, etc.).

DOORMAN—15¢ to 25¢ for each service.

$1 a month during a long stay.

ROOM WAITERS—10% to 15% of each check, or 25¢ minimum for one person (40¢ minimum in an expensive hotel).

CHAMBERMAIDS—no tip for brief stay; for longer stay, about 10% of bill, depending on good service.

VALETS—usually no tip, since they are generally concessionaires and not employees.

ROOM CLERKS,

MANAGERS,

STAFF—no tips.

At a Motel: No tips.

At a Resort: (Generally the same as for hotels, plus)

HEADWAITER—usually tipped at the end of your stay, or every two weeks.

BOATMEN,

GUIDES—$1 to $5, according to amount of service, for a one- or two-week stay at a resort. (This is in addition to their regular wages.)

CADDIE—25¢ for a fee of $2 or less, at average resort.

50¢ for a fee of $2 or over.

Transportation

In a Taxi:

DRIVER—15¢ to 25¢ for fares up to $1.50. 20% to 25% for fares from $1.50 to $10. 10% for fares $10 and over. (You usually give no less than 50¢ for a short trip and tip combined.

On a Train:

PULLMAN PORTER (day trip)—25¢ to 50¢, depending on service.

Berth—50¢ to $1 a night, according to service received.

Roomette—$1 to $1.50 a night.

CONDUCTOR—no tips except for special services, $1 and up.

DINING CAR WAITERS—same as for waiters and headwaiters in restaurants.

ROOM SERVICE—15% of each check.

STATION REDCAPS—15¢ a bag, plus 25¢ for extra pieces.

On a Plane: (No tipping of stewards, stewardesses, pilots, reservation clerks, limousine drivers, or anyone in airline uniform.)

AIRPORT REDCAP (not employed by the airlines)—25¢ a bag.

On a Ship:

(Non-Service)

SHIP'S OFFICERS (including doctor) not tipped. 10% of the cost of your ticket is divided among those who give service; when traveling with your wife, 8% is divided up, usually:

CABIN STEWARD—30% of tipping kitty.

DINING ROOM STEWARD—30% of kitty.

STEWARDESS—10% of kitty.

DECK STEWARD—10% of kitty.

(Remaining amount is for others who give good services.)

Hired Car: 15% to 20% of bill for short trip. 10% to 15% of bill for long trip.

Grooming

Barbershop:

BARBER—15¢ to 25¢ for one service. 25¢ to 35¢ for two or more services. (Do not tip owner.)

SHOESHINE BOY—25¢ for shine and tip.

MANICURIST—15¢ to 25¢, depending on cost of manicure.

At a Hospital

NURSES are never tipped, but you may give a nurse an inexpensive gift of a book, fruit, flowers, candy, etc.

ATTENDANTS—$1 each after a week to 10-day stay. $3 to $4 after a stay of a month or longer.

Private Clubs (No tips to any employee at a private or country club, but Christmas presents are given by members to each employee.)

CADDIE—25¢ for a fee under $2. 50¢ for a fee over $2. (In tournaments, the fee is higher.)

GOLF MASTER—no tip.

GOLF PRO—no tip.

LOCKER ROOM ATTENDANT—$1, by a guest; $1 to $2 a month by a member.

GROOM—50¢ for hired horse. $1 to stable boy of host's stable, or $2 to head groom to divide among boys.

PINBOY—5¢ for each frame bowled.

WAITERS—15% of drink bill.

Special Sports

SKIING PRO—no tip. (Tips are usually included in the cost of the lodge; otherwise, tip as you would in a hotel.)

SHOOTING—$2 for general helper. $4 to $5 for guide for the day. (This is in addition to the guide's wages.) (Take your own ammunition when you are a guest at a lodge.)

FISHING—you replace any tackle (except lines) as soon as possible after any accident. The host always divides the catch, regardless of who caught the fish. Prices vary in all sorts of fishing, including charter boat fishing. Dutch treat is a customary way of group fishing, and the tips above fees may be:

CAPTAIN—$10.

MATES—$5 each.

GUIDES—$2 a day (in addition to their wages).

House Guest (You usually do not tip servants unless you have spent more than one night in a home; you usually do not tip anyone you have not seen—unless they did a special service for you. You tip just before your departure, preferably not in front of your hosts. You may give presents instead of tips—cigars, or a carton of cigarettes to menservants; candy to maids, etc.)

MAID (in small household)—$2 after a weekend stay.

BUTLER (in large household)—$5 after a weekend, or longer stay.

COOK—$2 or same as for butler, with good service.

MAID—$2 or same as for butler, with very good service.

VALET—$5 for very good service.

CHAUFFEUR—$1 to $2 or more if you received extra service, such as having your car washed, etc.

Tipping in Europe

Courtesy *Good Housekeeping Magazine*

This chart represents a basic guide to tipping in Europe for the American abroad. The amounts given* constitute modest tips, for routine service, for the average traveler who is neither voyaging on a shoestring nor staying at the most expensive resorts. In some cases the amounts may seem small, and you may increase them as you wish. But remember that although the voyager from the United States is likely to overtip by European standards, Americans *are* expected to tip a little more than Europeans. Even if there is a service charge, you sometimes tip extra.

Besides the 13 categories that are given in this chart, the traveler should remember that guides are always tipped in Europe. If there is no fixed fee for the guide, tip the European equivalent of 10 cents to 25 cents, depending on the length of the tour. If there is a fixed fee, tip 10 per cent of that amount. One other person who should always receive a small tip, equivalent to about 15 cents a night, is the porter who shines the shoes left outside the hotel-room door.

	France	England	Italy	Spain	Portugal	Switzerland	W. Germany
Station Porter	100 francs (28¢) a bag or 300 francs (85¢) a load of luggage	1 shilling (14¢) a bag, but not less than 2 shillings for a complete service	100 lire (16¢) a bag or 200 lire (32¢) a trunk	3 to 5 pesetas (7¢ to 11¢) a bag	4 escudos (14¢) a bag	1 franc a bag (23¢)	10% above the regular fee
Concierge	100 francs (28¢) a service; 500 to 600 francs ($1.43 to $1.71) a week even if no services are performed	3 to 7 shillings (42¢ to 98¢) for special service	150 lire a day (24¢); 500 lire (80¢) for special service	15 pesetas (33¢) a day, or more, depending on service performed	10 to 20 escudos (35¢ to 70¢) a service	2 to 4 francs (47¢ to 93¢) a special service	1 to 2 marks (24¢ to 48¢) a special service

Bellhop and Baggage Porter	200 to 300 francs (57¢ to 85¢) for a load of luggage; 100 francs (28¢) a service	1 shilling (14¢) a bag, but not less than 2 shillings	50 to 100 lire (8¢ to 16¢) a bag or a service	3 to 5 pesetas (7¢ to 11¢) a bag; 2 pesetas (4¢) a service	4 escudos (14¢) a bag; 3 escudos (10¢) a service	Included in the hotel service charge	20 pfennige (4¢) a bag or a service
Chambermaid	100 francs (28¢) a day; 400 to 600 francs ($1.14 to $1.71) a week	Whether your hotel has a service charge or not, add a tip, but not over a shilling a day or 7 to 10 shillings (98¢ to $1.40) a week	100 lire (16¢) a day; 500 lire (80¢) a week	3 to 5 pesetas (7¢ to 11¢) a day; 15 to 25 pesetas (33¢ to 55¢) a week	5 to 10 escudos (18¢ to 35¢) a week	Included in the hotel service charge. Tip 1 franc (23¢) for a special service	Nothing for a short stay; 2 marks (48¢) a week
Doorman	50 to 75 francs (14¢ to 21¢), depending on effort, for calling a cab. If you stay a week, tip 200 francs (57¢) even if no service performed	1 shilling (14¢) for calling a cab. Otherwise nothing unless you stay a week; then tip 3 to 5 shillings (42¢ to 70¢)	50 to 100 lire (8¢ to 16¢) for calling a cab, otherwise nothing	2 pesetas (4¢) for calling a cab, otherwise nothing	1 to 2 escudos (3½¢ to 7¢) for calling a cab	Included in the hotel service charge	20 to 50 pfennige (4¢ to 10¢) for calling a cab, otherwise nothing

* The sums given in U.S. currency are the nearest practical equivalents of European currency as of March 20, 1957.

Tipping in Europe—continued

	France	England	Italy	Spain	Portugal	Switzerland	W. Germany
Taxicab Driver	20% of the meter	Three pence for every 2 shillings on the meter. Sixpence is the minimum tip (7¢)	15% of the meter, but not less than 100 lire (16¢)	2 to 5 pesetas (4¢ to 11¢); 3 pesetas is average tip	10% to 15% of meter	10% to 15% of meter	15% of meter
Restaurant Waiters	Tip 5% of bill over service charge. If none, tip 12% to 15% of check. Tip wine steward 10% of cost of wine	15% of check. Tip wine steward 10% of cost of wine	100 to 200 lire (16¢ to 32¢) over service charge, usually no more than 100 lire. Tip wine steward 10% of cost of wine	5% to 10% of check over service charge. Tip wine steward 10% of cost of wine	5% to 10% of check over service charge. Tip wine steward 10% of cost of wine	10% to 15% of check. If service charge, leave small tip extra. Tip wine steward 10% of cost of wine	5% of the check over usual service charge. Tip wine steward 10% of cost of wine
Night-Club Waiters	200 or 300 francs over service charge, depending on size of bill. If no service charge, tip 15% to 20% of bill. Tip headwaiter 300 francs if service performed	15% to 20% of check. Tip headwaiter 7 shillings if he performs service	100 lire per person (16¢) over service charge. Tip headwaiter 500 to 1,000 lire (80¢ to $1.60) if you have large party	5% to 10% of check over service charge. Tip headwaiter 20 pesetas (or 44¢) if he performs service	5% to 10% of check over service charge. Tip headwaiter 10 escudos (or 35¢) if he performs service	10% to 15% of check. If service charge, leave small change in addition. Tip headwaiter 2 francs (47¢) if he performs service	15% of the check over service charge. Give headwaiter 2 to 3 marks (48¢ to 71¢) if he performs a service
Checkroom Attendant	50 francs (14¢)	Sixpence to one shilling (7¢ to 14¢)	30 to 100 lire (5¢ to 16¢)	2 to 3 pesetas (4¢ to 7¢)	1 to 2 escudos (3½¢ to 7¢)	30 to 40 centimes (7¢ to 9¢)	20 to 50 pfennige (4¢ to 10¢)

Ladies'-Room Attendant	50 francs (14¢)	Sixpence (7¢)	30 to 100 lire (5¢ to 16¢)	1 peseta (2¢)	1 to 2 escudos (3½¢ to 7¢)	30 to 40 centimes (7¢ to 9¢)	10 to 20 pfennige (2¢ to 4¢)
Barbers	15% to 20% of the bill	15% to 20% of the bill	100 to 200 lire (16¢ to 32¢)	2 to 4 pesetas (4¢ to 9¢)	2 to 3 escudos (7¢ to 10¢)	10% to 15% of the bill	20 pfennige (4¢)
Hairdressers	15% to 20% of the bill	15% to 20% of the bill	100 to 300 lire (16¢ to 48¢)	5 to 10 pesetas (11¢ to 22¢)	5 to 10 escudos (18¢ to 35¢)	10% to 15% of the bill	50 pfennige to 3 marks (10¢ to 71¢)
Theatre Ushers	50 francs (14¢)	Nothing	50 lire (8¢)	1 peseta (2¢)	1 to 2 escudos (3½¢ to 7¢)	Nothing	Nothing

SECTION IV

ENTERTAINING AT HOME

CHAPTER 11

Entertaining at Dinner

Today's Service family is the forerunner in the new American custom of adapting the best of old European traditions to present day needs on a modest income. With the modern Service family living briefly in many states and various countries all over the world, it is only natural that the best of American as well as Continental or Far Eastern customs are modified into everyday living.

The goal of any host and hostess is to serve the best food in the most pleasant surroundings to congenial guests. The Service family combines the French tradition of good food with a Yankee minimum of time and expense. With the general lack of servants in the average household today, it is essential that modern entertaining fits today's needs—not yesterday's.

A young officer's household will probably have little, if any, help. A higher ranking officer's family may have a part-time maid—but household help is almost a vanished profession. Stewards are assigned to the quarters of high ranking officers, such as the Chief of Naval Operations, Army Chief of Staff, the Commandants of Districts, and the Superintendents and Presidents of the various Academies and Colleges.

When the occasion demands, waiters are available from a catering service or from an officers' club. Maids frequently serve at today's formal luncheon or dinner—a procedure which once was considered incorrect.

In keeping with the times, less formal dinners are the order of the day, with the semi-formal dinner or sit-down buffet the most favored. Buffet meals, with guests helping themselves, are favored from coast to coast.

The modern Service family entertains more often, more casually, and has more fun by entertaining all over the house, than ever before. The dining table may be in the dining room, in a corner of the all-purpose living room, or on the patio. It is characteristic of this family that men and women often exchange household duties that once were considered the duty of only one or the other. A man often enjoys selecting furnishings or decorations for his home, and the opportunity to find interesting and useful objects while serving in distant parts of this country or abroad is limitless.

It is gratifying to any host to know that friends come to his quarters because they want to—not have to. But it is not by chance that a luncheon or dinner, large or small, is successful. The party that seems so easy and smooth is that way because it was planned to the last detail, long in advance of the date.

However, officers and members of their families will attend many formal occasions through the years. As an officer, you will attend official, public, and state occasions, starting as a Midshipman or Cadet, and will continue to do so throughout your Service career—and on into retired life.

But formal or informal, you will want to know exactly what to do as the guest—or the host—at any type dinner or luncheon.

CLASSIFICATIONS OF ENTERTAINING

There are three general classifications of entertaining:

Informal: There may be no servants, therefore no service at the table. The host and hostess will serve two or three courses, probably buffet style.

Semiformal: There will be service at the table, with the host and hostess helping somewhat (mostly before the meal); from three to five courses may be served, but three or four are customary.

Formal: There will be full service at the table, with no assistance from the host and hostess; stewards or waiters will serve four or five courses.

INFORMAL DINNERS

The Family Dinner

The family dinner is one that you will attend the most often as a guest, or will most often give as the host. Since a dinner with a family is an intimate occasion, guests should consider it an honor to be invited into a home.

As a guest, you will be invited by telephone or in person, or perhaps by a brief note. As the host, you may extend the invitation in the name of the hostess: "Mary would like you to have supper with us on Saturday, at seven." If you are the only guest, and if there are children in the family, the dinner hour may be as early as six o'clock.

If you are a guest, the hostess will precede you into the dining room and will tell you where to sit. And if you are the ranking or oldest male guest, you will be seated at the right of the hostess.

When a blessing, or grace, is said at the table, it is said before anything is touched—including the napkin. You may be asked to say the blessing. A blessing that is acceptable to all faiths is:

> For what we are about to receive,
> Lord, make us truly thankful.   Amen

The food may already be on the table when you sit down, with the meat placed in front of the host to serve and the vegetables in front of the hostess. When soup is the first course, the soup cup or bowl will be in the place plate, and the main course of meat and vegetables will not be brought in until after the soup plates have been removed. When there is no servant, the hostess (sometimes the host) will remove the soup plates.

The table may be simply set, with mats or a cloth, and a small bowl of flowers will be the centerpiece. Two or three courses are customarily served:

Two courses:

Main course (meat and vegetables), and dessert,
or   Casserole with, or without, salad; dessert (cool weather menu),
or   Seafood, chicken or turkey salad, etc., and dessert (summer menu),
or   Main course, salad and cheese (no dessert).

Three courses:

Soup, main course, and dessert,
or   Main course, salad, and dessert,
or   Entrée (seafood, melon, etc.), main course, and dessert,
or   Casserole, salad, and dessert.

When the host and hostess serve the meal without the help of a maid, the host usually serves the meat. The stack of plates is placed directly in front of the host, with the meat placed in front of the plates, along with carving knife and fork. A portion of meat is placed by the host on each plate, which is then passed to the hostess for vegetables. The hostess usually indicates who is to receive the plate, with the first plate going to the woman at the right of the host.

Should the hostess not say to whom the plate will go, a male guest should pass it to the woman nearest him. All persons at the table will be served in this manner, with the next to the last plate for the hostess, and the last plate for the host. If the hostess prefers, the platters and dishes of food may be passed in one direction around the table, with each guest serving himself. If you are a guest at such a meal, you may hold the dish for the woman at your right to serve herself before you take your portion, then the dish would be passed on around the table. The bread tray is also passed to each guest, and the water glasses would have been filled before the family sits down.

Dessert may be served directly from the kitchen, after all plates and dishes have been removed from the table. When the dessert is to be served from the kitchen, the dessert silver will be in place on the dessert plate.

When dessert is served at the table, the stack of plates, along with the dessert, serving fork, and/or spoon, are placed directly in front of the hostess. The dessert silver may be in place on the table, parallel above each plate. The spoon will be above the fork, with the handle of the spoon at the right, and the handle of the fork at the left. If the hostess prefers, she may place the dessert silver on the plate before it is passed down the table.

Coffee is frequently served throughout the family dinner, in medium size cups (teacups), or it may be served with or after dessert. The coffee service may be placed on the sideboard or nearby table, with cups and saucers, sugar and cream. The coffee may be poured from the sideboard or table and placed at the right of each person at the table, with cream and sugar passed down the table.

Or the coffee service may be placed on the table, with the hostess pouring. She will ask each person his preference for cream and sugar, then she will pass each cup with the spoon in place on the saucer.

At a family dinner, you may take second helpings when offered—or even a third, if your hostess insists and if you really want the food. It is flattering to your host and hostess that you enjoy the meal, and you should say so. But if you do not care for a second helping, you need not feel any obligation to take it. When passing your plate for a second helping, leave your knife and fork on your plate, the knife above and parallel across the top or at the right of the plate, the fork placed below with tines up.

You will wait for the hostess to begin eating before beginning yourself (unless she especially asks you not to wait for her). And you will wait until she rises from the table before doing so yourself. She will precede everyone from the room, probably walking with the guests. When something needs to be done during the meal, or afterwards, you may offer to assist—such as bringing in the coffee service, stack of plates, etc.—but most hostesses prefer that guests do not help at a small or family meal. If nothing has been planned after dinner, you may leave within an hour.

Dinner with No Maid

A small two or three-course dinner for several guests may be served at the table by the hostess, or by the host and hostess, with everything arranged for convenience in serving. The dining table should be set early in the day with cloth or mats, and as much food preparation as possible must be completed in advance of the dinner.

Soup, dessert, and various foods may be prepared the day before (a frozen food compartment will permit other dishes to be prepared and stored days in advance of the dinner).

A menu should be planned which requires little last-minute preparation. A hostess may plan as a main dish something that can be placed in the oven before the arrival of the first guests and that will finish cooking during the cocktail hour. Casseroles and roasts are favorite foods of the sort that can be prepared early.

The host and hostess will not attempt to carry out the same type of service as would be done by a maid. The host will place ingredients and glasses for cocktails on a tray which is placed in a convenient but out-of-the-way

Place arrangement when the hostess serves.

table in the living room. Cocktail food is set out as soon as the first guests arrive, and tomato or fruit juice will be brought on a separate tray.

The dinner may be served by the host and hostess in the same manner as the family dinner. However, many hostesses prefer not to crowd the table with dishes and platters of food, and will place them, instead, on the sideboard or on a sturdy card table, along with the stack of plates.

Frequently, the host will carve and portion the meat, and will place each portion on a plate which is handed to the hostess for vegetables. She will place the plate before each guest at the table, serving from the left.

After the plates are removed by the hostess, she will serve the dessert directly from the kitchen, or she may remove the dishes and platter from the sideboard or card table and serve the dessert and coffee from there.

The hostess may prefer to serve coffee to guests in the living room, with the coffee service placed on a low table. The hostess would ask each person his preference for cream and sugar, and the cup would be handed to each guest—who would come forward—or the host or another guest would

Guest's place arrangement when the hostess serves.

hand the cups to the guests. The cream and sugar may be passed on a small tray, with each guest helping himself.

Informal Dinner, with Maid

When a maid serves 8 or 10 guests at a three-course dinner, where all the guests are seated, the hostess will assist in serving at the table. The first course of soup or an entree may be in place on the table when guests sit down. Upon the removal of the soup course, the main course will be brought in by the maid and placed in front of the hostess for serving.

The warmed plates will be set directly in front of the hostess, and the hostess will fill each plate. The maid will set the plate in front of each guest, serving from the left. The woman at the right of the host will be served first, the host would be second, then the woman at the left of the host and on around the table.

The hostess may prefer to pass each plate directly down the table, designating the plate for the woman at the right of the host, etc. This would leave the maid free to pour the water, pass the rolls, or work in the kitchen.

The maid may serve the main course on a platter, with the vegetables placed by the meat. The maid would offer the platter at the left of each guest.

After the main course is eaten, the maid will remove the plates, the bread and butter plates, the relish dishes, salt and pepper shakers, bread tray, and

Dessert silver placed above the place plate at informal dinner or luncheon.

serving platters, and then she will brush the table. The dessert may be served from the kitchen, or the maid may place the dessert in front of the hostess for serving.

Coffee may be served at the table with the dessert, but it is usually served in the living room for all guests. It is served in the same manner as at the "no-maid" dinner with the maid removing the used cups.

Ashtrays are usually on the informal table, either individual or one large tray for each two guests, which is placed between the guests' plates. Smoking usually starts just before the serving of dessert.

The rule for leaving informal dinners is for the ranking woman guest to leave first, at about ten-thirty o'clock—after which any of the remaining guests may leave as they please.

Buffet Suppers

The buffet (pronounced "boo-fay") supper or luncheon is the favorite form of serving a large number of guests in a small space with, or without, a maid. A buffet supper, luncheon, or late supper is the best type of get-acquainted party.

At such a meal the table is placed in a space convenient for guests to move around it and serve themselves. The table is usually covered with a cloth, placed over a silence pad. There will be a centerpiece, not too large, and several sets of salt and pepper.

The stacks of plates, napkins, rows of silver, platters, and bowls of food will be placed in sequence around the table. Serving forks and spoons will be near the dishes they accompany. Dinner forks may be the only silver on the table, since hostesses do not serve difficult foods to cut, but knives will be placed on the table if needed.

When there is no maid, everything will be placed in the dining room, for convenience in serving. A water pitcher and glasses, coffee service, and wine decanter and glasses may be on a sideboard or convenient table, if not on the dining table. Dessert and dessert plates and silver may also be on the sideboard, or they may be placed on the table or sideboard after the dishes for the main course have been taken away.

As a guest, you will fill your plate and carry it into the living room, or any other room designated by the hostess. Small tables or folding tables, are frequently provided by the hostess, but if not, you will sit any place and balance your plate on your knees. At very large buffet meals, you will probably eat while standing up.

When you are through eating, you may place your plate on the sideboard or dining table, leaving the host or hostess, or the maid to carry them into the kitchen. Or the maid may take the plates personally from before each guest, removing two at a time. Guests may serve themselves dessert from the table or sideboard, and the maid will serve coffee from a tray.

At buffet suppers, two or three courses are usually served, as well as hot buttered rolls or biscuits. The buffet luncheon food will be lighter, but with similar service. Although soup may be a first course, this is inconvenient to serve and is usually avoided by a busy hostess.

Buffet menus are varied, but may include:

> Roast beef, turkey, or ham; salad, and dessert. All three roasts may be served at very large occasions.
>
> or   Main course of meat and vegetables with, or without, salad and

dessert. The meat dish, such as chicken à la King, etc., is usually prepared in advance.

or Any of the curries that are favored in the Service set, with innumerable side dishes, plus salad, and dessert.

or A casserole with, or without, salad and dessert.

Sit-Down Buffet

The sit-down buffet is a more comfortable form of entertaining than is the stand-up buffet. The table is set as it would be for dinner—with the exceptions of the plates and the main course, which are placed on the sideboard for guests to serve themselves. The napkins, silver, glasses, salt and pepper, and butter plates are all in place on the table.

Place mats are frequently used on the table, and there will be a centerpiece. Small tables—usually card tables—are often arranged in the same

I.-SALT & PEPPER   2.-LARGE GOBLET

3.-SMALL GOBLET

The sit-down buffet.

manner as the larger table, except that the centerpiece on such tables is usually very small, to save space.

The dessert silver may be in place above the space for the plate, and butter plates are used as a matter of convenience. When dessert is served from the kitchen, the dessert silver will be brought on the dessert plate.

When there is a maid, soup is frequently the first course, and this may be in place on the place plate when the guests sit down. The maid will remove used plates while guests serve themselves at the sideboard. Coffee is usually served at the table.

At very large buffet parties, the coffee service, water, wine, and glasses may be placed on trays, with guests helping themselves.

SEMIFORMAL DINNERS

The main difference between the semiformal and the formal dinner is in the service. Fewer waiters will serve fewer courses to the same number of people. The semiformal dinner (particularly the sit-down buffet) is a favorite form of entertaining, because the very nicest appointments may be used. Table decorations may be as elaborate as any at the most formal table.

A table cloth of linen or damask or lace may be used, or mats of the same materials. The silver will probably be sterling, the glassware may be jewel toned, and butter plates and ashtrays are used. The first course of soup or seafood may be in place on the table when guests sit down, but it is

Place arrangement for a semiformal dinner or formal luncheon.

preferable that soup be served after guests are seated in order that it does not get cold.

A five-course menu may be easily changed for fewer courses, with three or four courses customarily served. A good sample for such a meal is:

First course: entrée, such as oysters or clams on the half shell, melon etc.
Second course: soup, usually clear
Third course: main course of meat and vegetables
Fourth course: salad
Fifth course: dessert.
A *four-course* dinner could omit either the first or second course. A *three-course* dinner could omit the first or second course, and the fourth course (salad) could be served along with the main course; or both the first and second courses could be omitted.

All courses are served at the table. You may smoke just before dessert, unless ashtrays are not provided—from which you may assume that your hostess does not wish you to smoke at the table.

After-dinner coffee is usually served to the women in the living room and to the men at the dining table, though coffee may be served to both men and women in the living room. The ranking woman guest will make the first gesture toward going home, not later than ten-thirty o'clock.

FORMAL DINNERS

A formal dinner is always a dignified occasion, but it should not be a cold and formidable affair. Although most very formal entertaining has disappeared in the Services, there are still many official and state functions which high ranking officers must give and attend.

At such dinners the most delicious food is served, with the utmost efficiency, at a table set with the most beautiful and correct appointments. Full service, preferably by men servants, is required at the truly formal table.

Tradition rules that all guests sit at one table. You will wear "black tie," unless "white tie" is indicated on the invitation. Place cards are used, and the hostess will plan the seating arrangement, with due regard for the Service rank of those present, for congeniality of guests, and the number to be invited. When an equal number of men and women are at the table, care must be taken that men do not sit by other men or women by other women.

The formal table is customarily set with sterling silver, a damask cloth, fine china, and crystal glassware. There will be a centerpiece of flowers flanked by silver candlesticks or candelabra. Customs have changed in recent years concerning the number of courses served, with four or five the usual number, but as many as seven or as few as three are occasionally served.

Although guests are seated according to protocol at an official or state

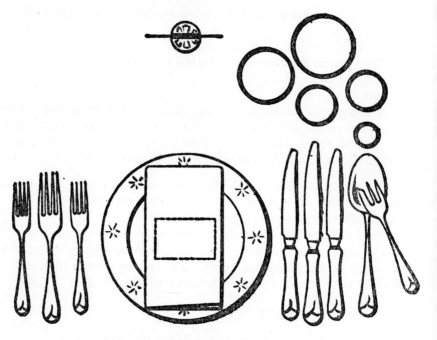

The service for a formal dinner.

In the center, upright in a holder, is the menu card. From left to right, at the edge of the table are: fish fork, meat fork, salad fork, plate with napkin and place card, salad knife, meat knife, fish knife, soup spoon, and oyster fork. In the upper right are the glasses. Starting at the top and going clockwise they are: champagne, white wine, sherry, red wine, and water glasses.

dinner, they are seated according to congeniality in most homes, as well as with due regard for the rank of Service officers attending.

The high ranking man is customarily seated at the right of the hostess, and the high ranking woman will be at the right of the host. The host and hostess may be seated at opposite ends of the table, or they may sit opposite each other at the center of a very long or round table.

If you are a guest, you should arrive at the designated time—usually eight or half-past eight of an evening. You should be on time. In quarters, a steward will open the door for you, say "Good evening, Sir," and direct you to the coatroom. In homes of civilians with considerable means, a butler usually is at the door.

You will find a small envelope in a tray on a hall table, with the name of your dinner partner enclosed. At large dinners, a small folded card with the man's name on the outside and his partner's name on the inside on a small diagram, will show the seating positions at the table. Such cards are frequently used instead of the usual card and envelope.

Your hostess will be standing just inside the living room door to greet guests, and the host will be nearby. A guest, or guests, of honor will be with them. It is customary that when the guest of honor is a dignitary, an aide to the host will meet the guest at the gate of the station or base and will escort the guest to the host's quarters. The host will be waiting in the hall to greet the honored guest, and to present other guests to him.

It is the duty of the host to see that each guest meets his dinner partner before going into the dining room. At large official dinners, aides will introduce dinner partners when necessary; at other dinners, the host may ask a friend to make necessary introductions.

Your host, or an aide, will introduce you into a group, then it is up to you to meet and talk with many other guests. A choice of one or two cocktails, as well as sherry and fruit or vegetable juice, will be offered before dinner. You usually take one, but no more than two cocktails before dinner.

When dinner is announced, the hostess will turn to the ranking male guest and say, "Shall we go in to dinner?" *But it is the host and the high ranking woman guest who lead the way into the dining room.* When a guest is late—not counting the honor guest or guests—the general rule is to wait some fifteen minutes for a man and twenty minutes for a woman, before going in to dinner.

When the guest of honor is a man of very high position, or a dignitary of note, the hostess and guest of honor will enter the dining room first, with the host and ranking woman following. All other guests follow in pairs, in no order of precedence.

Place cards are usually laid flat on the napkin in the place plate, or they will be standing at the head of each plate. Names are handwritten, with titles and last names only: "Mrs. Smith." "Captain Jones." "The Ambassador of Thailand." or "The Secretary of the Navy." The latter are addressed as "Mr. Ambassador" and "Mr. Secretary."

Women are usually seated as soon as they enter the dining room, not always waiting for the hostess to enter and be seated. Stewards may assist with some of the ranking women's chairs, but you will probably seat your dinner partner at your right. You will step behind her chair, draw it back carefully, then as she starts to sit down from the right, you will push the chair forward.

The number one steward will be standing behind the hostess's chair, directing the service. As soon as all guests are seated, the first course is placed in the place plate, which is on the table when guests sit down. There will always be a plate before you until dessert is served.

The service customarily begins with the woman at the right of the host (See Chapter 14, *Table Service*). The number one steward will pour wine as soon as the first course is served, and will serve other wines with the courses they accompany. If you do not care for wine, simply say, "No, thank you."

At dinners held in homes, and at small formal dinners anywhere, you start eating as soon as the hostess begins (or the host, at a stag luncheon or dinner). At large formal dinners or banquets, you start eating as soon as those near you have been served. Menus for formal dinners are varied.

A very formal seven-course menu, with the wines that accompany each course, may be changed to four- or five-course menus by omitting certain courses.

Seven-Course Menu

COURSE		ACCOMPANYING WINE
First course:	entrée (shrimp cocktail, oysters on the half shell, etc.)	white Burgundy
Second course:	soup (usually clear)	sherry
Third course:	fish, hot or cold	white Rhine
Fourth course:	main course of meat and vegetables	claret
	main course of game and vegetables	Burgundy
Fifth course:	salad	no new wine
Sixth course:	dessert (ice cream, sherbet, etc.)	champagne
Seventh course:	fruit (pears, grapes, etc.)	champagne

A *five-course dinner* could omit the fish and fruit courses. A *four-course* dinner could be:

> Entrée, soup, main course, dessert,
> or   Soup, main course, salad, dessert,
> or   Soup, main course, salad or asparagus, dessert,
> or   Entrée, soup, main course with salad, dessert.

A *three-course* dinner could be soup, main course with salad attractively served, and dessert. Rolls, condiments, and after-dinner coffee are always served. Candy is frequently served after the final course, but is not necessarily offered.

Demitasse and liqueurs are customarily served in the living room to the women, and at the table or in the library to the men. It is a French custom to serve coffee in the living room to both men and women.

Cigarettes are offered at most formal dinners, but some hostesses prefer that there be no smoking at the table. Individual ashtrays may be placed above the plate, or between each two guests at the table. Urns or other containers of cigarettes may be placed on the table, and individual ashtrays offered each guest. Cigars and cigarettes may be served to the men after the women leave the table.

When the hostess rises, you will stand and again assist your partner with her chair. You will remain standing until the women leave the room, then you may move toward the host's end of the table—or the host may move toward the dignitary—or you will go with your host and other men into the library. You rejoin the women in about half an hour.

If dancing or games have not been planned for the evening, and if you are not going on to the theater or some function, the guests will form in conversational groups. The high ranking woman guest will make the first move to leave when the time for departure comes—which usually is about ten o'clock—or within an hour after the dinner is over.

Upon departure, you will shake hands with your host and hostess and thank them for their hospitality. The hostess will rise when guests rise to leave, but she will not leave the living room. The host, however, accompanies all guests to the door of the living room, and may even walk to the front door or into the hall with high ranking guests.

Although it is impossible to tell each guest goodbye at a large dinner, you should speak to your own dinner partner before leaving, as well as with others with whom you were just talking. The steward or butler will open the door for you and will say, "Goodnight, Sir." You will answer, "Goodnight and thank you."

RÉSUMÉ

Informal Dinner Rules to Remember:

- Invitations may be extended by telephone, in person, by note or by calling card. You may answer in the same manner.
- The time is anywhere from 6 to 8 P.M., with 7 P.M. customary.
- You will wear informal dress—usually a dark or light business suit, in season, or sports attire if indicated. Women will wear afternoon, cocktail, or sports attire, as indicated. The hostess may designate what to wear when the invitation is given, or a guest should feel free to ask.
- There will be two or three courses served, with the host and hostess serving, or assisting in serving.
- The table will be set simply but attractively, with a tablecloth or mats, and a centerpiece.
- One or two wines may be served, if desired. The bottle or decanter may be placed on the table, with guests serving themselves.
- Write a "Thank you" note to your hostess after being entertained, or telephone her. Regardless of the informality of the luncheon or dinner, it's the hospitality of your hosts that you are thanking them for—not the expense.

Semiformal Dinner Rules:

- Invitations may be extended by telephone, by letter, or by the semi-engraved card. You will answer promptly and in the same manner,

except that the semi-engraved invitation is answered by handwritten note, third person.
- The time is usually 8 P.M., and you wear "black tie." Women will be in evening dress.
- Three or four courses are customarily served.
- The dinner may be buffet style, or sit-down buffet.
- Butter plates and ashtrays are usually on the table.
- Small tables seating four, six, or eight, are frequently used for seated dinners; tables for eight are popular, since they offer wider conversational range for guests.
- Elaborate appointments, place mats or tablecloth, are customary.
- Guests may leave at about 10:30 or 11 P.M., when nothing is planned after dinner.
- Remember to write a "Thank you" note, or telephone your hostess.

Formal Dinner Rules:

- Invitations will be handwritten or engraved in the third person, and you must reply in the third person on white or cream colored note paper. You will answer promptly.
- The time is usually 8 or 8:30 P.M., and you must be on time.
- You will wear "black tie" or "white tie" as indicated on the invitation; by telephone, the hostess will indicate which to wear. Women wear evening dress.
- There will be full service at the table, with from three to seven courses served—customarily, four or five.
- Butter plates are not used on the formal table, and butter therefore is never passed. Nothing is passed at a formal table; everything is served.
- "Turning the table" means cooperating with your hostess mid-way of the meal by talking with the person at your left.
- You will not leave until after the high ranking guests leave, which may be thirty minutes after the dinner is over, or usually within an hour. When there is no guest of honor, the woman who sat at the right of the host is the first to leave.
- Courtesy requires that you write your hostess a note of thanks within two or three days after being entertained. Or you may telephone.

CHAPTER 12

Entertaining at Luncheons, Breakfasts

LUNCHEONS

Most luncheons that you will attend will be official occasions, frequently held in honor of a high ranking officer or dignitary who may be a visitor to your base or station. These luncheons are often "stag," with no women attending, but when the guest of honor's wife is in attendance, other women will be invited.

The service for a formal luncheon is like that for a semiformal dinner. Three courses are customary, or four at the most. An informal luncheon may have two courses, since the food served at noon time is lighter than that served at evening meals.

The high ranking guest will be seated at the right of the host at a stag luncheon, or at the right of the hostess when women are present. Place cards are used for eight or more guests, and the table may be covered with a lace or linen cloth, but not damask. Mats are frequently used, and there will be a centerpiece but no candles.

Butter plates are used at formal as well as informal luncheons, and ash-trays are usually in place on the table. The first course will be in place on the table when guests sit down, and each course is served at the formal table by waiters or maids. The hostess serves or assists in serving at the less formal table.

Tomato juice and sherry are usually offered about thirty minutes before luncheon, and cocktails may also be served. Coffee is served to both men and women in the living room after formal meals, and at the informal table with, or following, dessert.

Time

The lunch usually starts at 12:00 or 1 P.M., depending upon duty hours. You should stay about half an hour, or forty-five minutes after luncheon, unless you must return to your ship or station. You will wear the uniform of the day, or plain business suit. Women will wear afternoon dress or suits, hats and gloves. Luncheons may be longer when women attend. The high ranking woman will properly start to leave no later than three o'clock.

Luncheon invitations may be given in person, by telephone, letter, "informals," calling cards, or the partially engraved cards. You may answer in the same manner—except you always reply by handwritten note in answer to the engraved card.

When speaking of the noon meal, you will say "lunch." The steward announces, "Luncheon is served." But you will say, "Shall we go in to lunch?" or "Yesterday I lunched with your classmate."

Menus

The menu for any luncheon is varied. A two-course summer luncheon could be: fruit or seafood salad, and dessert. A two-course winter luncheon could be: casserole with, or without, salad and dessert.

The three-course luncheon could be:

        Soup, main course, dessert,
    or Main course, salad, dessert,
    or Fruit (melon or grapefruit), main course, dessert,
    or Casserole, salad, dessert,
    or Soufflé, salad, dessert.

Soup is usually in place on the table when guests sit down. A two-handled cup or bowl, with matching saucer, is customarily used. These cups are sometimes called "bouillon" cups, and a wide bowl would be called a "cream-soup" cup or bowl. When soup is served at the informal table, the hostess may serve from a tureen placed in front of her.

Sherry is often served with the soup course, and may be the only wine served at luncheons. A white or red wine may be served, or both may be served at formal meals. Iced tea is frequently in place on the summer table when guests sit down, and hot tea may be served at the table, with the service the same as for coffee—except that the hostess always pours.

BREAKFAST

Breakfast is usually a simple meal, served informally except for such occasions as wedding breakfasts, hunt breakfasts, etc. A small bowl of flowers or fruit may be on the table, and the table is frequently bare. Mats of almost any gay material, may be used. As a rule the early morning hours are an undesirable time to entertain.

The silver at each place is usually a fork, knife, and cereal spoon. A butter knife will be in place on the butter plate at a more formally set table. The coffee cup will be at the right of the knife, and the coffee spoon will be in place on the saucer at the right of the cup handle.

Jam is served in a dish set on a small plate, with the spoon in the plate. Fruit or fruit juice is usually in place on the breakfast plate, or the juice glass may be set at the right of the water glass—when water is on the table.

Plates may be arranged in the kitchen and brought in individually, or the food may be placed in dishes set on the table and passed around the table. Food is frequently kept hot on the sideboard, along with the coffee and toast, with everyone serving himself.

At a family breakfast, the food is placed on the table for convenience in serving. When guests are present and time is not important, a leisurely breakfast may be served by the hostess or a maid. Then, fruit or fruit juice will be in place on the breakfast plate, with dry cereal placed above the plate on the table. The butter plate and knife will be set above the fork, and hot cereal and food will be served from the kitchen or from the sideboard.

RÉSUMÉ

Luncheon Rules to Remember

- Invitations are extended by telephone, in person, by informal notes or calling cards, or by the partially engraved cards for formal occasions. You will answer in the same manner, but always by a hand-written note in answer to the partially engraved card.
- The time is usually 12:00 or 1 P.M. You are expected to be on time.
- There are *no* luncheon partners when entering the dining room. You will walk in the room with whomever you were talking when luncheon was announced. You do *not* offer your arm to a woman when entering the dining room.
- Butter plates and ashtrays are placed on the formal as well as the informal table.
- Men and women usually have coffee together in the living room after the more formal luncheon. Coffee or hot tea may be served at the less formal table.
- One wine is customarily served at the luncheon table, but two may be offered. Lighter wines are served at luncheons.

CHAPTER 13

Setting the Table
and Seating Plans

The basic rule in setting any table, formal or informal, is that crowding must be avoided—there should be at least twenty-four inches of table space for each person—and everything on the table must balance. The centerpiece is in the middle of the table and is balanced by any other decorations placed around it—unless the table is placed against a wall, such as at a large buffet when space is needed; in that case, the centerpiece would be placed closer to the wall.

Guests may be seated with regard to congeniality as well as with regard to Service rank or official position at dinners and luncheons held in homes and private clubs. However, when guests are all Service personnel, it may be safer to seat them according to rank in order to avoid hurt feelings. Only at official and state occasions are guests seated according to strict protocol.

The traditional table arrangements for six, eight, or eighteen guests shown here may be adapted for various numbers of guests:

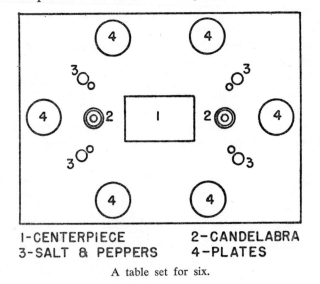

1-CENTERPIECE   2-CANDELABRA
3-SALT & PEPPERS   4-PLATES

A table set for six.

SEATING ARRANGEMENTS

It is customary at mixed dinners and luncheons that the high ranking man sits at the right of the hostess, and his wife is seated at the right of

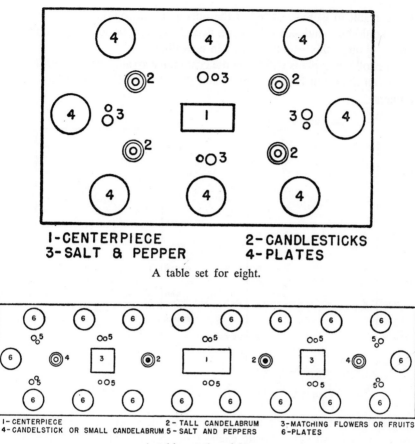

1-CENTERPIECE   2-CANDLESTICKS
3-SALT & PEPPER   4-PLATES

A table set for eight.

1- CENTERPIECE   2 - TALL CANDELABRUM   3-MATCHING FLOWERS OR FRUITS
4- CANDELSTICK OR SMALL CANDELABRUM 5 - SALT AND PEPPERS   6 -PLATES

A table set for eighteen.

the host. But at occasions governed by protocol, the high ranking man is seated at the right of the hostess and the *high ranking woman* is seated at the right of the host.

The high ranking woman may be a Congresswoman or Senator and not the wife of the high ranking man. The second ranking man is then seated at the left of the hostess and the second ranking woman is at the host's left. The third ranking woman sits at the right of the man of highest rank, the fourth woman is at the left of the man of second rank. Under this arrangement a hostess may find that a man would be seated alongside his wife, and since this is not done, it is the wife who is moved.

It is also customary for the host and hostess to sit opposite each other at the ends of the table, or they may sit across from each other at the center of a long or round table. However, an equal number of men and women could result in women sitting at the outside places on one of the sides, and this should be avoided. In this case, two places may be set at each end of the table—though this usually results in crowding.

The following plans will show the customary arrangements, with *Plan 1A* the usual dinner or luncheon plan, and *Plan 1B* usually used at large official dinners:

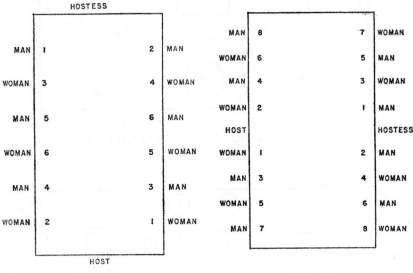

Plan 1A.   Plan 1B.

Small dinners for six or ten, fourteen or eighteen, etc., are easily arranged, with the hosts sitting opposite each other and with married couples sitting by other guests. Women will not be sitting at the outside places, when such numbers of guests are at the table.

However, any *multiple of four*—such as tables of eight, twelve, sixteen, etc.—mean that the host and hostess cannot sit opposite each other without having to place two men or two women together when there is an equal number of each sex present. When this happens, the hostess may relinquish her position at the end of the oblong table and move one seat to the left, which places the male guest of honor opposite the host. When one couple is not married they will sit side by side as in *Plan 2A*. When all couples are married, follow *Plan 2B*.

Seating In-Laws

When your or your wife's parents are guests in your home, your mother or mother-in-law is seated at your right at the table, and your father or father-in-law is at the right of your wife.

When both sets of in-laws are on hand, your wife's mother is seated at your right, and your mother is seated at your left. Your father is seated at

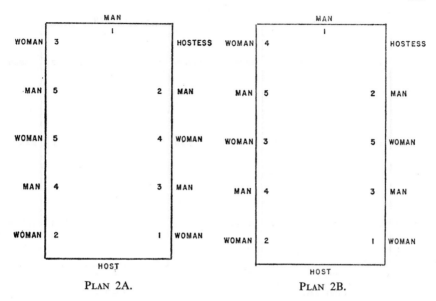

PLAN 2A.   PLAN 2B.

your wife's right and her father is at her left. If many in-laws should be gathered in your home, such as at a holiday dinner, then the rule of seniority may be followed. When children are present, alternate them and the grand-parents. Teen-agers may prefer to have a separate table.

If special guests have been invited to a dinner when both sets of parents are present, then the guests of honor take precedence—unless the parents are considered the guests of honor with the other guests invited to meet them.

Bachelor Host

A *bachelor host,* or a host who is entertaining in the absence of his wife, may choose from several seating arrangements, depending upon the number of guests, their rank, etc. The high ranking guest will be seated at the right of the host.

At a mixed luncheon or dinner, the host may ask a woman guest to act as hostess to balance the table when the number is not divided by four. In this case, *Plan 1A* may be followed, with the ranking male guest seated at the right of the guest-hostess.

The host may prefer to ask the ranking male guest to sit opposite him, when *Plan 3A* may be used. *Plan 3B* may be used when the ranking man and woman are not married to each other and the bachelor host does not want a hostess or co-host at a dinner divisible by four.

Unmarried Women Guests

When a bachelor asks a young unmarried woman to be hostess or to as-

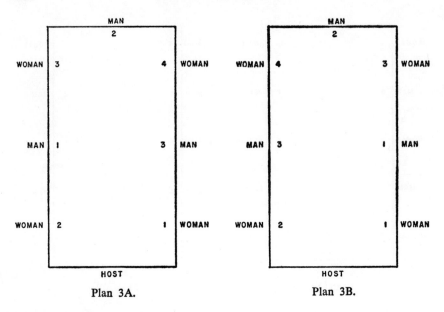

Plan 3A.   Plan 3B.

sist at a luncheon or dinner party at his home or club, he should remember that this might be interpreted as a sign of intimacy of relationship when none is intended. When one particular young lady is asked to act as hostess at this special occasion, other guests may hear the sound of wedding bells—when none are planned. In such a case, the bachelor should make certain that the young woman leaves the party at the same time the other guests leave.

A bachelor officer will want to know that the buffet style of entertaining is not only the easiest to plan and serve, but it also eliminates the necessity for seating a hostess at the table.

For the sake of propriety, a bachelor host at a house party should have a married couple or an older lady—preferably a relative—in his home when unmarried women are guests.

Stag Dinners and Luncheons

A co-host is frequently appointed to assist the official host at a large stag dinner or luncheon. This is usually done in order to balance the rank at the official table.

Usually, the host and co-host sit opposite each other at the center of a long table. When there is no co-host, or when the dinner or luncheon is small, the host will sit at the head of the table and the juniors at the foot.

Speakers' Table

Tact and diplomacy are required in seating toastmaster and speakers at a banquet. The host or chairman will be seated at the center of the long or main table, with the guest of honor at his right and the second ranking guest at his left. The toastmaster is customarily at the left of the second ranking guest.

When official or dignitaries of state or very important unofficial guests

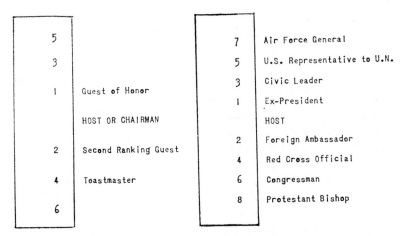

The customary banquet table.   The seating of distinguished guests.

are present, these distinguished persons may be seated in between the guests of official rank after the guest of honor and second official guest are seated.

Forfeiture of Positions

The only time that a host and hostess, excepting the President of the United States and the First Lady, relinquish their positions at the head and the end of their luncheon or dinner table is when their guest is a President or head of any country, a King or a Queen.

Then, the reigning King or Queen will sit at the head of the table, and the wife or husband, respectively, will sit at the other end of the table.

In order that they do not "give honor to themselves," the host and hostess will sit at the *left* of the President or Royalty, and their wives, respectively, with the high ranking man and woman guests sitting at the *right* of the honored guests. This will place the high ranking guests in the traditional guests of honor position.

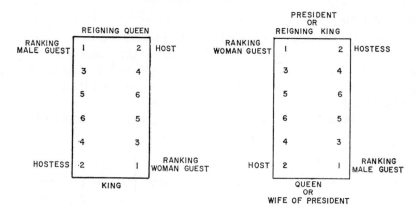

PLACE CARDS

Place cards are used at the luncheon or dinner table, formal or informal, mainly as a matter of convenience in seating guests without confusion or according to protocol. Cards are of heavy plain white or cream colored paper, with plain, or gold or silver beveled edges.

The cards are about 1½ by 2 inches, or 2 by 3 inches in size. The flag of an admiral or general, seal of a ship, or a crest may be embossed or stamped in the top center or the upper left corner of the card.

The cards are customarily placed on top of the napkin in the place plate, or laid flat on the table above the plate.

Folded place cards are about 3 by 3¼ inches in size, and are folded in half, with the name written across the lower half of the card. They usually stand directly above the place plate.

Names are written by hand on place cards, in black or dark blue ink. At formal occasions, names are usually written in script, such as "Mrs. Jones," "Captain Smith," "The Ambassador of Norway," "The Secretary of the Navy." At informal occasions, names may be written in the same manner,

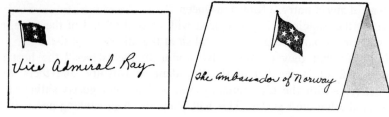

Flat place card.   Standing or folded place card.

but at more intimate occasions first names are often used: "Marion," "Allan," etc.

MENU CARDS

Menu cards may be used at official dinners, at state and public occasions, and occasionally in a home—such as for an anniversary dinner. A crest or coat of arms may be embossed at the top center of the card, which is of heavy white or cream colored paper. An admiral's or general's flag, or the seal of a ship are customarily used.

The card is about 4 by 5½ or 6 inches, with a gilded or silvered beveled edge. It is usually placed in a stand, or laid on the table. In homes, the cards may be placed in front of the host and hostess, and one for each three guests down each side of the formal table. They are placed about 6 inches above the plate.

The word "Menu" is written by hand in black ink beneath the crest, and one dish is written on each line centered directly underneath. The first letter on each line is capitalized and each course is separated by a space or asterisks.

Appetizers, bread, relishes, jellies, candy and coffee are not written on the menu as they are on hotel menus. Menus for formal dinners are usually engraved in French, but on naval ships—for instance at formal dinners in flag messes—they are printed, embossed, or handwritten in English.

Menus are frequently considered as souveniers, such as the menus at the Inaugural Luncheon or the menu at the Christmas Dinner given annually for the Brigade of Midshipmen at the Naval Academy.

THE MODERN TABLE

Although such things as table decorations—china, linens, and sterling silver patterns—are usually confined to a "woman's world," it is a sharp young man who will take time to learn something about the furnishings of a household, since sooner or later most men get married. For young officers, informal tables are now set with imported steel because it is attractive and easy to polish. However, sterling silver flatware is essential for more formal entertaining.

In the present day world of the Midshipman, Cadet, or bachelor officer (who may have no immediate thoughts of marriage), it is well to know what is correct in furnishings for the home since you will have the opportunity to buy excellent articles at prices usually much lower than at home, when you are on the Midshipman Practice Cruise or have duty abroad. Furthermore, such articles make excellent Christmas, wedding, birthday (or any anniversary) gifts, as well as gifts for a hostess when you have been an overnight guest in a home.

Today's modern table is one of utility as well as beauty. Mats have replaced the tablecloth on most tables—even the more formal table. Harmony in color and design, and balance of table appointments and decorations, are the main rules in setting any table, formal or informal.

The type of entertaining to be enjoyed usually determines the formality of the silver and china service. Table linens may be in every color of the artist's palette and in a wide range of fabrics.

Fine bone china, or any of the serviceable potteries or earthenwares, may be the choice of the hostess; glassware may be crystal clear, or colored, plain, or etched. Silver flatware will usually be sterling, possibly of imported steel, with another set of silverplate or stainless steel for breakfast and informal use. But sterling or silver plate, porcelain or pottery, fine table service is never mixed with coarse accessories any more than fine evening accessories would be mixed with sports attire.

There are a number of rules that are followed in setting the table:

TABLE LINEN

- The formal dinner table is traditionally covered with a white or ivory colored damask tablecloth. The more modern pastel colored damask cloth is frequently used.
- The tablecloth never overhangs the table by more than 18 inches, and no less than 12 inches. A silence pad should fit the top of the table, with the tablecloth placed over the pad.
- Matching damask napkins should be between 18 and 22 inches square—or 24 inches square for the very formal table.
- A lace or linen tablecloth for the formal luncheon or semiformal dinner table must not overhang the table. Elaborate mats are used at the most formal luncheon—and occasionally dinner-table.
- Luncheon napkins are from 14 to 16 inches square. They may be of linen, plain or with matching lace, or damask.

HOW TO FOLD NAPKINS

Large formal napkins are used at formal dinners or banquets when the service is quite formal. There are three customary ways of folding napkins: (1.) Fold the napkin once in each direction, then fold the square into thirds. Place on the place plate. (2.) Fold the napkin into a square, then fold opposite corners together to form a three-sided shape. Place on place plate. (3.) A standing napkin—which is frequently used on European tables but rarely on American tables—has a roll placed inside the fold. Make a square, then

Formal napkin folds.

a triangle, tuck one point of the triangle inside the other and fold the points down so that one lies a little above the other, and until the top one is left pointing straight up. Place on place plate. (When formal napkins are monogrammed with three initials of equal size, their order is the order of the hostess's name: Mary Senn Fisher would read: "MSF" or "mFs." A single initial is: "F.")

Informal napkins are from 14 to 16 inches square, and are used for breakfast, luncheon, tea, or informal dinners, or buffet suppers. They are usually placed at the left of the forks, with the open edges toward the plate and the table edge.

Napkins are customarily placed one inch from the edge of the table, on a line with the place plate and table silver. There are several ways to fold napkins at the informal table: (1.) Fold the napkin into a square, then fold

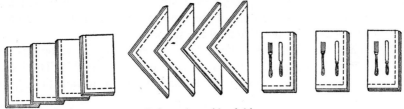

Informal napkin folds.

it in half again. (2.) Fold a smaller napkin from corner to opposite corner to form a triangle, and place beside the plate with the triangle pointing *out* from the plate. (3.) Napkins for buffet suppers are folded in triangles or rectangles, and are placed near the stack of plates. Napkins may be placed in folded rectangles on the buffet table, with silver for each guest laid on each napkin. (4.) Napkins may be placed on the place plate when a first course is not on the plate.

FLATWARE

Silver flatware is always placed on the table in the order of its use, starting from the outside and working in toward the plate. There are several rules that are followed in placing table silver. Below is a résumé of those rules:

- The silver, napkins and plate are lined up *one inch* from the edge of the table.
- Forks are placed at the left of the plate—with the exception of the seafood fork, which may be placed at the right of the spoon, or at the left of all other forks.
- There are never more than three forks in place on the table at any one time. If more forks are needed, they will be brought in with the course they accompany.
- Knives and spoons are at the right of the plate, with the blade of the knife facing in toward the plate.
- Teaspoons are not placed on the luncheon or dinner table, unless used for soup or fruit. Teaspoons are placed on the breakfast table.
- Spoons for tea and coffee are placed on the saucers, at the right of the handles, before service.
- Dessert spoons and/or forks are usually brought in on the dessert plate, with the fork at the left, the spoon at the right of the plate.
- At informal meals, dessert spoons and/or forks may be placed on the table above the plate. The spoon will be above, with the handle at the right, and the fork will be directly below the spoon, with its handle at the left.
- The iced beverage spoon, used mainly at luncheons, may be placed on the table at the right of the soup spoon, or it may be laid above the plate, with the handle of the spoon at the right.
- The individual butter knife is customarily placed across the top of the butter plate, parallel with the edge of the table. The handle of the knife is at the right, the blade facing in toward the edge of the table.

CHINA

A china service is composed of plates for breakfast, luncheon, and dinner; coffee and tea cups, serving dishes, as well as various size plates for various uses.

There are large flat plates (usually called "dinner plates") for the main course; a slightly smaller plate for luncheon, and a plate that may be used for dessert or salad. Various size plates are needed for the soup cup or bowl, butter, oysters, fruit, fish, etc.

Place plates are the plates that are on the formal or semi-formal table when guests sit down.

Although all china used throughout the meal need not match, it is a rule that all plates used together at the same time *must match;* that is, all dinner plates used in the main course must be alike, all dessert plates alike, etc.

There are three sizes of cups most customarily used: the demitasse or small coffee cup used after formal and semiformal meals; the teacup or medium size coffee cup at luncheons and less formal meals; and the large coffee cup for breakfasts and informal meals.

The sizes of the main types of plates are:

- The plate for the main course (the dinner plate): about 10 inches in diameter.
- The luncheon plate: 9 inches.
- The flat dessert or salad plate: about 8 inches.
- The butter plate—a small flat plate for bread and butter—between 4 and 6 inches.
- The soup plate, between 9 and 10 inches, with broad flat rim, used only at formal dinners; the handled soup or "bouillon cups" and bowls are used at luncheons. The broad bowl—generally called a "cream soup bowl"—is used at less formal dinners and luncheons.

SERVING DISHES

A complete set of serving dishes is required to serve each six or eight guests. At a meal for 12 to 16 guests, a second set of serving dishes would be required. Serving dishes may match the china service, or they may be silver. They should blend with the china service if they do not match exactly. There are many shapes and sizes, with oblong or oval dishes having broad flat bottoms and deep sides the most useful.

Two pairs of vegetable dishes are necessary, if you entertain often, with a smaller pair for everyday use and a larger pair for the serving of many persons. The customary sizes are:

- Vegetable dishes, 12 to 14 inches, one or two pairs.
- A bowl 5 or 6 inches deep, for soft foods, etc.
- A shallow bowl, about 10 inches in diameter and 2 or 3 inches deep, for serving fruits, desserts, etc., or used as a centerpiece.
- Bread tray or basket, of various sizes and materials. A silver tray may be used for serving asparagus, celery, carrot sticks, radishes, etc.
- Sauceboat or gravy boat.

Platters:

- A small oval platter, 15 inches long, for meat or fish for a few persons.
- A large oval platter, 18 inches long, for large roasts and cold meats; it is particularly useful at buffet meals.

• A round platter, 12 inches in diameter, for serving pies, cakes, canapes, cookies, etc.

WATER AND WINE GLASSES

The stemmed water goblet is used on the luncheon or dinner table, and is customarily placed above the knives. The goblets are usually filled with water before the guests sit down. Stemless water glasses are used at the less formal table, and after or between meals. Goblets and glasses come in a variety of sizes, shapes, and quality of crystal or glass.

Wine glasses are placed on the table in several ways—customarily at the right and forward of the water goblet. Wine glasses are placed in the order of their use, and are filled immediately after the course they accompany has been served. Glasses are filled about two-thirds.

The basic triangle at a *formal luncheon* or *semiformal dinner,* with two wines served, is:

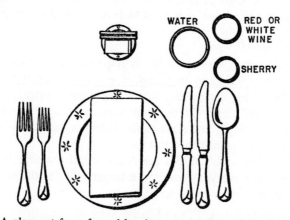

A place set for a formal luncheon or semiformal dinner.

Wine glasses are held by the thumb and first two fingers at the base of the bowl. Small stemmed glasses are held by the stems, and the tumblers are held near the base. Brandy snifters are held in the palms of both hands to warm the brandy.

When you hold a glass of chilled wine, hold it by the stem so that your fingers do not warm the glass, and thus the wine.

TABLE DECORATIONS

The center of interest on the luncheon or dinner table is the centerpiece. The size of the centerpiece depends upon the size and shape of the table, but it should not be so tall or large that guests cannot see over it. When candles are used, the flame must either be above or below eye level.

The basic formal table decoration is a centerpiece of matching china or porcelain bowl or tureen, filled with white flowers, flanked by silver candelabra or four candlesticks. A long table will have matching replicas of the centerpiece placed midway down each side of the table—and both sides of the table must be alike.

In addition to the candelabra on the long table, four or more candlesticks with white or cream colored candles, may be placed in rectangular fashion around the centerpiece. When two candlesticks are shorter than the others, they are placed at the ends of the table.

A single candelabrum, or a small bowl of flowers artistically arranged, may be used on the small formal or semiformal table. Flowers are customarily used, but modern table settings include the use of almost any material or container in good taste—fruit, vegetables, figurines, or driftwood. Modern or antique containers may be of silver, china, porcelain, or crystal for the most formal table, and wood, pewter, glass, or pottery for the less formal table.

ASHTRAYS

Ashtrays are customarily placed on the most formal table today, but until recent years smoking was not permitted at the table. Individual ashtrays of sterling, china, or porcelain may be placed above the place plate, with two cigarettes laid across the top of the tray, and a small book or box of matches laid in the lower part of the ashtray.

Larger urns or containers of china or porcelain, or of sterling, may be placed on the table, with individual ashtrays. At formal dinners, the guests may be offered cigarettes in silver boxes placed on a tray and served by a waiter just before dessert.

Ashtrays, either individual or for every two guests, are usually in place on the semiformal and informal table when the guests sit down.

SALTS AND PEPPERS

One salt and pepper set may be placed on the informal table and passed around the table when needed. Antique condiment sets are frequently used on the informal table, and unusual or antique sets can add interest to a table.

On the formal table, individual sets may be placed directly above the place plate, or one set may be placed to the right of the line of glasses of a guest and used by the guest next to him as well as by himself. Sets are customarily placed in a rectangle around the centerpiece, with the pepper above and the salt below.

Open salts and peppers require a very small sterling or glass spoon.

CANDY DISHES

Candy is served at the table less frequently now than in former years. Candy dishes are considered a part of the table decorations, however, and may be placed between the candelabra and the place plates at each end of the formal table.

At a long table, the candy dishes would be spaced, equal distance, midway down the sides. The candy may be passed by the hostess or served on a tray by a waiter.

FINGER BOWLS

Finger bowls may match the glass at the table, but not usually so. The finger bowl is brought to the table in one of two ways:

- On the dessert plate, with the dessert spoon at the right and the dessert fork at the left of the plate. The bowl is taken off the plate by the guest, who sets it on the table above and to the left of the plate. The guest places the dessert silver on the table, with the fork at the left and the spoon at the right of the plate. When a lace doily is under the finger bowl, this is also removed from the plate and is placed on the table under the finger bowl.

- Or the finger bowl may be brought on the fruit plate, when fruit is the final course served. The finger bowl and fruit knife and fork are removed from the plate by the guest, and are placed on the table in the same manner as described above. When the finger bowl is brought in with no silver, the guest will know that no other course will be served.

Finger bowls may be brought in at any meal, but are most frequently offered at formal meals, or after the serving of lobsters or clams or any food that is greasy or that must be handled. The finger bowl is three-quarters filled with cool water—or with warm water, when foods have been greasy to handle.

TABLE LISTS

A young couple just starting out may begin the table service with a "starter set" for two. "Open-stock" china or silver or glassware means that extra pieces or sets may be purchased at most stores at most any time. Established patterns are advisable, since replacements may be purchased whenever needed.

Sets of 4 or 8 are preferable for a young couple, with service for 12 the average in most households. When purchasing a service for 6, it is well to know that when the number of *dinner plates* and *coffee cups* is doubled, the same list will take care of 12 guests at a two-course luncheon or dinner.

The average sizes in plates most frequently used are: dinner, 10 inches; luncheon, 9 inches; dessert or salad, 8 inches. The place plates used at formal meals are approximately 9 or 10 inches in diameter.

In the average household, the medium size cup, or teacup, is used more often than any other sized cup, and the new *place spoon* may be used for dessert, cereal, or soup—but not for cream soup. The soup bowl used for clear soups is used more than the cream soup bowl by the average family.

A place setting includes the dinner plate, salad plate, butter plate, teacup, and saucer. A service for 6 persons would include:

China

    6 Dinner plates
    6 Butter plates
    6 Salad or dessert plates (12 preferable)
    6 Teacups and saucers
    2 Large coffee cups, family use
    1 Sugar bowl
    1 Cream pitcher
    6 Soup bowls
    6 Soup plates
Extra pieces:
    6 Demitasse (after dinner) cups and saucers
    6 Luncheon plates
Serving dishes:
    Platters, small, medium, or large
    Platter, round buffet
    Vegetable, open or closed

Sauce boat
Useful pieces:
  Casserole
  Water pitcher of silver, glass, or pottery
  Salad bowl, wooden (preferable)
  Individual salad bowls
  Cereal bowls
  Butter dish, of china or silver
Tea, coffee service:
  Silver or china

Most table service sets can be purchased or ordered at your nearest PX or Navy Exchange at considerable savings.

Glassware

Thin crystal, plain or etched, is used for formal and semiformal occasions. Modern glassware comes in all qualities, colors, and designs, and is used instead of crystal at less formal occasions. Water goblets and wine glasses may match, but not necessarily so. Glasses should harmonize in color, quality, and design for various occasions. A desirable list is:

- 6 Water goblets, stemmed, holding about 10 ounces (formal)
- 6 Water glasses for informal occasions
- 6 Wine glasses, stemmed, holding from 3 to 5 ounces
- 6 Sherry glasses, stemmed, 2 ounces
- 12 Cocktail glasses, 3 to 4 ounces (the cocktail and wine glasses may be interchanged if the wine glass is not too large; a large sherry glass may be used for cocktails)
- 12 Highball glasses, also used for iced fruit juices, soft drinks, etc., 12 to 14 ounces, no stems
- 6 Fruit or vegetable juice glasses, no stems, 4 to 5 ounces
- 6 Liqueur glasses, stemmed
- 6 Finger bowls (usually for formal entertaining)

Silver

The sterling silver pattern selected should be for a lifetime. Service families frequently use Swedish steel. A minimum place setting includes the knife, fork, teaspoon, salad fork, soup spoon (or the new place spoon) and butter spreader.

The place spoon doubles for soup, cereal, and dessert. The salad fork serves for dessert. There are also new place knives and forks that can be used for breakfast, lunch, or dinner.

For a complete place setting, it will be necessary to eventually add coffee spoons, oyster forks, iced beverage spoons, and individual steak knives. Serving spoons and forks are essential in table service. Service lists for 4, 8, and 12 persons are:

Starter Set (Service for 4)

- 8 Teaspoons
- 4 Knives
- 4 Forks
- 4 Salad or pastry forks
- 4 Soup or place spoons
- 4 Butter spreaders

- 2 Table or serving spoons
- 1 Sugar spoon
- 1 Butter serving knife
- 1 Gravy ladle
- 1 Cold meat or buffet fork

Medium Set (Service for 8)

- 16 Teaspoons
- 8 Knives
- 8 Forks
- 8 Salad or pastry forks
- 8 Soup or place spoons
- 8 Butter spreaders
- 8 Cocktail or oyster forks
- 8 Iced beverage spoons
- 3 Table or serving spoons
- 1 Cold meat fork

- 1 Butter serving knife
- 1 Gravy ladle
- 1 Sugar spoon
- 1 Cheese serving knife
- 1 2-pc. salad set
- 1 Pie server
- 1 Lemon fork
- 1 Jelly server
- 1 Tomato or flat server
- 1 2-pc. steak set

Regular Set (Service for 12)

- 24 Teaspoons
- 12 Knives
- 12 Forks
- 12 Salad or pastry forks
- 12 Soup or place spoons
- 12 Butter spreaders
- 12 Coffee or cocktail spoons
- 12 Cocktail or oyster forks
- 12 Iced beverage spoons
- 12 Steak knives, individual
- 4 Table or serving spoons
- 2 Sugar spoons
- 2 Table or serving forks
- 2 Cold meat forks
- 1 Butter serving knife

- 1 Gravy ladle
- 1 Jelly server
- 1 Tomato or flat server
- 1 Cheese serving knife
- 1 2-pc. Steak set
- 1 3-pc. Roast set
- 1 2-pc. Salad set
- 1 Cream or sauce ladle
- 1 Olive or pickle fork
- 1 Pie server
- 1 Cake slicer
- 1 Bonbon or nut spoon
- 1 Lemon fork
- 1 Sugar tongs
- 1 Punch ladle

TEA AND COFFEE SERVICE

A tea set includes a teakettle (usually with an alcohol burner and stand), a cream pitcher, a sugar bowl, and a tea caddy, which is a bowl into which dregs of the teacups may be emptied. Sugar tongs or a spoon, a fork for serving lemon, and a strainer are needed, and all these should be placed on a tray.

A coffee set includes a coffeepot, a cream pitcher, and a sugar bowl, with sugar spoon, and all these should be placed on a tray. The tray should be large enough so that there is no crowding.

A tea and coffee set are usually combined, with the same sugar bowl and cream pitcher, sugar tongs, spoon, and tray useful for either service. Trays are of silver plate, rarely of solid silver. There are three sizes of trays most useful in a household:

1. Eight-inch tray, used for serving one or two glasses of water or drinks; may be placed in the hall for calling cards, etc.

2. Medium size 13-inch tray, for serving iced beverages, cocktails at small dinners and luncheons, or liqueurs at larger dinners, etc.

3. Large tray approximately 16 by 24 inches, for tea and coffee service. Useful for serving sandwiches, cakes, or at informal parties to place in a room with decanter and glasses or food for guests to serve themselves, etc.

CHAPTER 14

Table Service

Due to the general lack of servants in the modern household, the semi-formal dinner is usual and the formal seated dinner of former years is less customary. According to national statistics, less than *one per cent* of the families in America have a full-time servant and only about *four per cent* have servants of any kind—most of whom are part-time. The percentage of families with servants of any kind has dropped from six to four per cent in fifteen years.

Today, four or five courses are served at the most formal dinner. Occasionally, when guests are going on to an official or social occasion such as a reception, lecture, or a Service Ball, only three courses are served.

For a formal dinner of five courses, two or three waiters or stewards are needed to serve ten or twelve guests, not counting the cook in the kitchen. Two complete services (sets of serving dishes) are necessary. At a very formal dinner, one waiter will serve each four guests.

In the Services, most entertaining is done at home—and done often. Fewer courses, thus fewer waiters, are needed for the semiformal dinner of three or four courses. Two waiters and a cook may serve fourteen guests at a seated three-course dinner, and, if very efficient, may serve sixteen guests.

Almost twice this number of guests may be served with the same amount of help at a semiformal buffet supper or sit-down buffet, when the very nicest table appointments are used and guests will serve themselves.

A waiter or steward, or maid, can serve eight guests at a seated dinner of three courses in a home. But a hostess will assist in serving at the table for a luncheon or dinner for ten or twelve, when there is help in the kitchen.

Many a versatile hostess serves a buffet supper for twelve guests with no maid or cook, but this takes advance planning and food preparation. No guest wants to see his hosts in a frenzied, exhausted condition—and no host wants to appear in such a condition. The hosts, too, should enjoy the party.

ESSENTIALS OF SERVICE

The service at the table must be efficient, quiet, and unobtrusive. Guests should not be rushed in eating, and there should be no long waits between courses.

The hostess is never served first except at family meals or very informal meals. When the hostess serves at the table, she may designate to whom the first plate will go—usually the woman at the right of the host.

Second helpings may be offered at informal and semiformal meals, but not at formal meals. Small side dishes of vegetables or fruit are not placed on the formal or semiformal table.

Fruit and vegetable juice are not offered as a first course or placed on the more formal table, but they may be offered in the living room before the meal to non-alcoholic drinkers.

When there is service at the table:

- Nothing is ever taken directly from the waiter's (or steward's) hand, or vice versa. Whatever it is, must be brought on a tray—a glass of water, etc.—with the tray held in the waiter's left hand, his right hand at his side.
- Stewards, waiters, or a maid will address the host and male guests as "Sir" and the hostess and women guests as "Madam."
- The steward or waiter will be in white coat, the maid will be in dark or conservative colored uniform with apron.
- The woman at the right of the host is always served first and is always offered an untouched dish.
- Everything is served at the formal luncheon or dinner. Nothing is ever passed by the guest at the formal table.

RULES OF SERVICE

The rule of *informal* service is: Serve left, remove from the right. (An exception is the removal of the butter plate—from the left.)

The rule of *formal* service is: Serve left, remove from the left.

There are a number of rules of service which should be observed:

- A waiter (or steward) will place one plate at a time at a formal luncheon or dinner. He will place the plate in front of the guest, serving from the left, and he will never reach in front of a guest.
- A waiter (or steward) will place two plates at a time at an informal dinner. He will place one plate with his left hand to the left of the guest, then will place the other plate with the right hand to the left of the next guest.
- The serving dish is offered at the left of each guest at a comfortable level for serving. Dishes are offered with the servant's left hand, with the right hand held close at his side or slightly behind his back. If the dish is very heavy it may be held with both hands.
- The dish or platter will rest on a folded napkin placed on the flat of the servant's hand. At no time will he grasp the dish or platter by its rim.
- A large serving spoon and fork are placed in each serving dish, face down, with the handles toward the guest.
- At semiformal or informal meals, a waiter (steward or maid)

may carry a serving dish in each hand, offering first the vegetable dish in his left hand, then the other vegetable dish in his right hand. The matching vegetable dishes may be placed on a tray and served to each guest, with the tray held on the left hand of the servant. A vegetable (usually potatoes) may be placed on the meat platter.

- Plates are removed after each course at luncheons or dinners when *all* guests have finished eating. Plates are removed at very large dinners or banquets after each guest has finished eating.
- At a formal luncheon or dinner, the waiter will hold the fresh filled plate in his *right* hand while removing the used plate from the left of the guest with his left hand. The fresh plate is set down at the left of the guest.
- At informal meals, to speed service, the waiter will remove two plates at a time. After removing a used plate and a butter plate (or two used plates if butter plates are not used), he will then bring back two fresh plates placing one with the right hand to the left of a guest and the other plate placed with the left hand to the left of the next guest.
- Two waiters (or stewards) may work as a team in removing used plates, with the first waiter removing the used plate from the left, and placing it on the large tray carried by the second waiter. The first waiter will take up a fresh plate from the tray, and place it before the guest, from the left side.
- The table is cleared of crumbs before dessert, with the waiter (or steward) holding a tray below the edge of the table, at the left of the guest. Crumbs, place cards, etc., are brushed into the tray with a folded napkin or table brush.
- The order of removal at an informal luncheon or dinner is: plates, butter plates, serving dishes and platter, pepper, salt, bread tray, and crumbs.

ORDER OF SERVICE

At a dinner with *one service* (complete set of serving dishes) for six or eight guests, the woman at the right of the host is served first, then the host, then the woman at his left, and on clockwise around the table.

According to the placing of the table, the location of the kitchen, etc., the service may be counter-clockwise, always starting with the woman at the right of the host, then around the table, with the host served last.

At a dinner with *two services,* and from 12 to 16 guests, the *first* service will start with the woman at the right of the host and the *second* service will start with the woman seated to the right of the man at the right of the hostess.

When a very important man is guest of honor at the dinner, the second service may be started with the guest of honor at the right of the hostess.

When there are *three services,* and 18 or more guests, the *first* service goes to the woman at the right of the host, then clockwise; the *second* will start where the first would leave off (or after six servings), then the *third* will take up where the second would leave off. However, all services must be synchronized so that food is offered at about the same time.

At times it may be better to start one of the services (never the *first*) with a man. When there are 14 people, the man at the right of the hostess may be the first to be served at that end of the table, and when there are 20 persons, a service may start with the man at the left of the hostess.

A custom that is not practiced very often in this country, but that is observed in many foreign countries, is the serving of all women before the men. This is customary at very formal dinners and in most Service messes. In this case, the woman on the right of the host is served first, then the woman on his left, and so on, ending with the hostess. Then the men are served in the same way, ending with the host. Men and women frequently leave the table together and go into the living room for demitasse.

COFFEE SERVICE

Informal Service

Coffee is served in several ways at informal luncheons and dinners. There are three main sizes of coffee cups: demitasse, or small cups used mainly after formal or semiformal meals (but also after informal dinners); medium or teacup size for less formal meals; and large cups for breakfast or family meals.

Coffee is frequently served at the informal table with, or following, dessert. At a family meal, with or without guests, coffee may be served throughout the meal. The coffee tray is usually prepared in advance, ready to be served by the hostess whenever needed. The tray may be placed on the sideboard, or the hostess may place the service on the table at her place, and serve each person. The cups may be passed down the table, after they are prepared with cream and sugar, or the cream and sugar may be passed around the table, with each person helping himself.

At informal luncheons or dinners, when there is a maid or steward, they may place the coffee service before the hostess, who will pour and prepare each cup with cream and sugar. The cup may be passed around the table, or the maid or steward may place it at each person's right.

The servant may place the coffeepot on a small tray, with an empty cup, sugar, and cream. He will stand at each guest's right and ask his preference concerning sugar and cream, then place the cup at the right of the plate. Or the servant may stand at the left of each guest, with the guest helping himself to sugar and cream and placing the cup on the table himself. Additional cups will be on the sideboard convenient for serving.

The hostess may pour coffee in the living room, from a tray placed on a low table in front of her. She will ask each guest his preference concerning cream and sugar, and will hand each cup to the guests. The host may assist in handing the cups to the guests, or another woman guest may assist.

Formal Service

Demitasse is usually served in the living room to both men and women after formal luncheons, and sometimes after formal, semiformal, or informal dinners.

Demitasse is customarily served in the living room to the women and at the dining table or in the library to the men, after formal and semiformal dinners. There are a number of ways of serving:

- Two waiters (or stewards) will work as a team, with the first waiter holding a small tray with a coffeepot, sugar and cream, and one cup. The second waiter (or steward) will follow with a large tray filled with cups and saucers. The first waiter will ask each guest his preference for cream and sugar, then will offer the cup on his small tray. Or the guest may help himself to cream and sugar.
- The waiter will have several cups on a tray, with cream and sugar, and, holding the tray on one hand, will stand before each guest and pour the coffee. Each guest helps himself to cream and sugar.
- At large occasions, the tray may be brought in with filled cups, cream, and sugar, with each guest helping himself.
- The favored form of pouring coffee is by the hostess. The coffee service will be placed in front of her on a low table, the hostess will ask each guest his preference concerning cream and sugar, and the cup will be handed to the guests, or the guests will come to the table for their cups. The spoon is placed on the saucer, at the right of the handle, before handing to the guest.
- The men will be served coffee at the dining table before the women are served in the living room. The service is the same, except that the host does not pour coffee at the table.

TEA SERVICE

The serving of hot tea at the luncheon or informal table is similar to the service of coffee—except that the hostess invariably will pour the tea. Although coffee is customarily served after luncheons and dinners, tea should be served to those who prefer it.

The maid (or steward) may place the tea service in front of the hostess, or the hostess will place the service on the table herself when there is no maid. The hostess will ask each guest his preference for lemon, cream, or sugar, then will pass the cup down the table. The first cup will go to the woman at the right of the host.

When only one or two guests care for tea, the teapot, lemon, cream, and sugar would be placed on a tray and offered by a maid at the left of the guest, with the cup placed on the table at the guest's right.

When there is no maid, the hostess may arrange a small tray and have the water hot before the meal, then quickly prepare the tea and serve it when needed.

COCKTAILS BEFORE MEALS

Cocktails may be offered before luncheons, and are customarily offered before dinner parties. Sherry, fruit juice or tomato juice are usually offered on separate trays, the juice being for those who do not care for alcoholic drinks. The juice glasses are filled before bringing into the living room.

There are several ways to serve cocktails before meals:

- At formal or semiformal occasions, the waiter (or steward) may bring a large tray into the living room, with filled shakers and unfilled glasses. He will stand in front of each guest and ask if he wants a cocktail, then pour it. The guest takes the glass from the tray.
- At more formal occasions, two waiters (or stewards) work as a team. The first waiter will hold a tray with one or two shakers, and a second waiter will follow with a tray with glasses for all drinks, and perhaps another shaker. The first waiter will ask each guest what he wants, etc., and offer the drink on the small tray.
- At large dinners, the tray of filled glasses is brought from the kitchen by the waiter, and offered to each guest.
- When there is no servant, the host may mix the cocktails in advance and place the tray with shakers and glasses in a convenient place in the living room before the guests arrive. The ice and the canapes (cocktail food) are brought in, upon the arrival of the first guests.
- The host may prefer to place all ingredients on a large tray, and mix each drink upon the arrival of the guests.

SERVICE FOR WINES AND LIQUEURS

Wines are served at meals with the courses they accompany, with the first wine (usually sherry) poured after all guests have been seated and after some have been served. One wine is customary at the less formal meal, but two may be offered. As many as four or five wines may be served at the formal dinner, but two or three wines are customary. After the serving of sherry, champagne may be the only wine served throughout the formal dinner.

The waiter (or steward) stands to the right of each person at the table, and pours the wine glass half or two-thirds full, according to the type of wine. An old custom is that a tablespoonful is poured first in the host's glass, in order that he determine the quality and clearness of the wine. Then the woman at the right of the host is served first, then the woman at the left of the host, and clockwise around the table. The glass of the host is filled last.

Wineglasses may remain on the table throughout the meal, except when three or four wines are to be served. In that case, the sherry glass is removed after the salad course. Wineglasses are refilled whenever empty.

Wines served at luncheons are lighter than those served at dinners. Sherry may be the only wine served at luncheons, or a white or red wine— sometimes both. Usually, red wines are decanted and the white wines are left in the bottle.

At informal meals, one bottle or decanter will serve each five or six guests, and a bottle or decanter may be placed at each end of the table for 10 or 12 guests. The host may fill the glass for the woman at his right, then the bottle is passed around the table at his left.

Champagne may be served in the living room after a very formal dinner, or at a home wedding reception or dance. The bottles and empty glasses will be placed on a tray, with a waiter pouring and serving each guest.

Liqueurs

Liqueurs are customarily served after dinners, *not* luncheons. They are offered after formal and semiformal meals, and frequently after informal suppers and dinners.

At a formal dinner, liqueurs are served to the men at the table following the service of coffee and cigars and cigarettes. The service for liqueurs is similar to that for cocktails. Two waiters (or stewards) will work as a team, with the first waiter holding a small tray and taking the liqueur and glass from a tray held by the second waiter, etc.

Liqueurs are served to the women in the living room after coffee has been offered, but before the cups have been removed.

At informal meals, the host or hostess will serve liqueurs from a tray arranged beforehand with bottles and glasses.

CHAPTER 15

Duties of the Host and Hostess

The "rule of thumb" at any party, formal or informal, is: good food, good conversation, and good company. The prime responsibility of the host and hostess is that guests enjoy the occasion. Not only must the food excel, but the guests must be congenial. An air of cold formality is to be avoided—even though the occasion is formal.

When incompatible personalities are brought together, a pleasant evening is frequently ruined. If it is unavoidable to have two such personalities at the same party, place them as far apart at the luncheon or dinner table as possible.

When a high ranking person or dignitary is your guest, he must not be lionized to the extent that other guests feel neglected. Special respect is due guests in high position, but each guest must feel equally welcome.

As the host, you must talk with all guests during the course of the evening. You will move from group to group and make a special effort to introduce newcomers or a shy individual into small groups. You will bring persons of less rank or position to meet the person of high rank, or the guest of honor.

A good host will "hear all and see all." You will notice when a guest is left out of a group, or when he seems bored. You will come to the assistance of a guest who cannot gracefully move away from a bore. You will be careful of interrupting a group that is obviously congenial and enjoying themselves—but you will interrupt a group when the conversation has turned to an unwise discussion, particularly if the discussion is to the discredit of another guest or person.

Although you will do everything within reason to make your guests comfortable, your hospitality should not be taken advantage of by a rude or unthinking guest. It is always difficult for the host to handle a situation where one guest makes himself undesirable by coarse conversation or by over-drinking, or by becoming insulting to another guest. However, you may tactfully introduce another subject of conversation, and you may suggest to the insulting guest that you show him something in another room, and thus draw him away from the group where he is not desired.

If necessary, you may have to assist the unwise drinker into another room, or you may ask a trusted friend to assist you in this task. But while guests often assist the host and hostess, they can not assume the duties of either. Since you are responsible for whatever happens within your home, no guest should be permitted to feel embarrassed about any-thing—whether he was awkward and broke something of value, or made an untimely remark. A thoughtful host will minimize the damage and will adroitly change the topic of conversation.

A good host will try to anticipate his guest's needs, but should never be either over-anxious, or over-casual. A host should not insist that a guest have another drink or more food when he refuses. You may offer again, but allow ten or fifteen minutes to elapse. Never urge a guest to have "just one more drink." And if a guest does not drink at all, never make a joke of it or point it out to other guests. Instead, offer any soft drinks that you have without comment.

When something goes wrong—when the food is burned, for instance, or when you run out of ginger ale—do not apologize profusely. Never apolo-gize for what you have—or do not have. If your quarters are small and the food not elaborate, do not discredit your hospitality by continually mentioning it. Guests should not feel forced to reassure their host that the evening *is* wonderful and the food *is* superb.

The host and hostess should be in the living room at least five minutes before the luncheon or dinner hour, relaxed and ready to greet the guests. Each guest should be greeted warmly, but not in a superfluous manner.

The hostess will speak to and offer her hand to each guest, and will make every effort to put the guest at his ease. The host greets each guest, shakes hands with him, then introduces him into a conversational group. When drinks are served, it is the duty of the host to ask each person what he cares for (after first stating what he is offering), and then make certain that he gets it.

The host and hostess must decide how long to wait for a late guest. When something is being served that may be spoiled by waiting, the hostess may not be able to wait. Also, sometimes the hosts may be plan-ning a theater party later, or to attend a lecture or dance, and thus it would be impossible to wait for the late guest.

Before the party, the host and hostess have planned what guests will do following the luncheon or dinner. Bridge or canasta, charades or dancing, are frequently enjoyed, but many hosts prefer that guests continue in con-versational groups.

At a buffet meal, when plates must be balanced in guests' laps, a wise hostess never serves food that must be cut. The hostess should not finish eating before the last guest, and she should always have a little food on her plate so that she can keep pace with the slowest eater.

As host, you may have to speed on his way a guest who overstays your hospitality. You can sometimes accomplish this by mentioning an early morning golf game, the next day's duty, or an important conference. And again you may also have to disentangle yourself from the guest who opens a new—and lengthy—conversation at the door after he has already said goodbye.

Concerning the friend who habitually "drops in" around mealtime, the host and hostess should feel no obligation to ask him to stay for the meal at times when this would be inconvenient. The hostess, or host, may say, "We have already made plans for the evening or I'd ask you to join us. . . . Perhaps some other time." Or you may say something as simple as, "I hope you will excuse us, but our dinner is ready now. . . ."

DUTIES OF THE GUEST

As a guest, you owe it to your host and hostess to be congenial and to mix and talk with other guests at the luncheon or dinner party. Upon arrival and departure, you will shake hands with your host and hostess.

At some time during the party, large or small, you will talk with your host and hostess for a short time, but you will not monopolize their time. A congenial guest will move from group to group, conversing with as many other guests as possible.

When your luncheon or dinner partner is a stranger to you, there are many agreeable subjects with which to start and maintain a conversation —current plays, a best seller, a TV program. If your partner is a Service wife, you can always discuss the merits of a recent duty station. However, each guest must carry his share of the conversation, and "small talk"— which does not include business or "shop."

If it is your misfortune to be seated at the table alongside someone whom you do not particularly care for, you must conceal your personal feelings. You are expected to talk with your partner at your right, but you must not forget the person at your left, either.

It is wise to refrain from mentioning the foods you do not care for— *that very dish may be on the menu!*

A thoughtful guest will offer assistance to the host or hostess when assistance seems needed in a servantless house, but he will never insist. If your offer in such a case is accepted, go about it quietly but efficiently. You must never "do the honors" in another man's house.

You must not point out an error in the service, or an oversight on the part of the host. If you can correct something unobtrusively, do so. If the dinner was not up to your expectations, do not discuss it with other guests —or with anyone else.

You should not take a lighted cigarette to the dining table, and should *never* use a saucer or plate as an ashtray. Although it is customary to have cigarettes and ashtrays on the most formal dinner table today, a hostess may prefer that there be no smoking at the table, and hence smoking is not appropriate until after dinner.

A guest should accept no more than one or two cocktails before dinner, and no more than one or two liqueurs after dinner. The guest who over-indulges in drink is a problem to a host—and a nuisance to everyone else.

Although no one wants to make an error in the use of silver at the table, do not worry about it if you do. And when you spill something, do *not* over-apologize and make everyone else uncomfortable.

But if you break something of value, you should replace it if possible. If you cannot exactly match a coffee cup, do not buy another pattern—it will be of little use to the hostess and just a waste of your money. You may, instead, send flowers and a note of apology to the hostess. The note should be brief but sincere, with an expression of regret concerning the mishap.

A thoughtless guest is one who asks his hostess at the last minute if he may bring a friend along—thus upsetting the seating plan at a more formal table. Also, it is very thoughtless to arrive late at a luncheon or dinner, and keep everyone else waiting. And a guest will soon wear out his welcome if he continually drops in at a friend's home at meal time, and then stays on to dinner.

A guest should not break an engagement for a formal luncheon or dinner, unless an emergency arises. This means at least a serious illness, a sudden transfer, an accident or death in the family, etc. But a sudden whim to not go because "you don't want to," or because a better invitation has been received, is no excuse at all after an invitation has been accepted.

An acceptance or refusal of an invitation should be made as soon as you can—usually within 24 hours after you receive the invitation. This gives you ample time to check your calendar and to make certain you have no other commitments on that date. When you refuse an invitation, you should give the reason for the refusal.

If you are a young bachelor officer, a Midshipman or Cadet, you are not expected to return the hospitality of your host and hostess. But you are expected to write a "thank you" note to your hostess, expressing your appreciation of the luncheon or dinner and the hospitality of the hosts.

The note should be written within a day or two after the party. It is not necessary to send flowers or candy to the hostess, but if the occasion was a very special one—such as Christmas dinner, or your birthday—the gift of candy or flowers would not be out of order. A small card would be enclosed with the gift—perhaps your calling card—with a few words of "thanks" written on it.

Other guests, however, will repay the hospitality of their host and hostess by later extending an invitation to them for a similar occasion. An invitation is not extended by saying, "You must come to dinner with us *some-time* . . ." but it *is* extended by setting the *date*.

SECTION V

GENERAL CORRESPONDENCE
AND INVITATIONS

CHAPTER 16

Correspondence

As an officer in the Service, you will probably be writing or dictating letters for the rest of your life, and whereas in conversation you are judged by what you say, in correspondence you are judged by how you write. Plain words and phrases are preferable in letter writing, just as they are in conversation. A letter difficult to compose is handled with more ease when written as though you were speaking to the person addressed.

When you choose your stationery, consider its use: whether for official* or business correspondence, or social or personal. White paper is customarily used for all types of correspondence, but personal stationery may also be cream color, gray, blue-gray, or a light tan.

Black and dark blue engraved or printed letterheads are used for business or personal stationery, but personal paper may also be engraved or printed in shades of dark green, gray, maroon, or brown. Initials, crests, and monograms are also used on some personal stationery. A man's stationery should look masculine, however, and feminine colors are to be avoided.

All engraving is more expensive than printing, and rag paper is more costly than wood-pulp. Wood paper is used for general correspondence, and rag paper for more personal or important correspondence. There are various textures of paper: *bond,* the one most customarily used, is firm but fairly transparent; *laid* means a paper with striations in the body; *granite* has shredded threads in the paper; and *lawn* has almost invisible lines drawn horizontally across the surface.

BUSINESS PAPER

Official or business stationery is white, with black or dark blue engraving or printing. The official letterhead is usually at the top center of the sheet but is also placed at the top left-hand side.

There are various sizes of business paper most frequently used:

- The traditional white bond paper, single sheet, 8 by 10 inches, with standard matching envelope of oblong shape and plain flap.
- A slightly larger sheet, with or without telephone number in the letterhead, 8½ by 11 inches.

* Since the official correspondence for the various Services is a part of the Regulations for each Service, it is not considered necessary to add such information in this chapter.

- A slightly narrower sheet for business-personal use, 7¼ by 10¼ inches, used for both longhand or typewriter.
- A smaller business-personal sheet, 7 by 8½ inches, used for business invitations.

BUSINESS LETTERS

Business letters are usually typed in the *block style,* with all lines flush with the left-hand margin and the date flush right, with double spacing to separate single-spaced paragraphs. The complimentary close and signature start at the center of the page.

A semiblocked form with indented paragraphs (about 10 indentions) is also used. The dates in business letters, civilian form, are written, "May 6, 1958," but the official Service form is usually "6 May 1958." No letter should be dated "5/6/58."

Customarily, there is a colon after the salutation, and a comma after the complimentary closing of a letter.

The *inside address* is written in the same way as on the envelope, with no punctuation at the end of the lines. In official naval correspondence, the order of address usually is: (a) administrative position; (b) station; (c) city, zone, and state. Sometimes, rank and name are "(a)."

In business, the order usually is: (a) title and name; (b) administrative position; (c) company name; (d) company address; (e) city, zone, and state.

The *salutation* is, "Dear Mr. Jones:" or, "Dear Captain Jones:" When names are unknown, "Dear Sir:" "Dear Sirs:" or "Gentlemen:" are used. A business woman is addressed, "Dear Miss Jones:" or, "Dear Mrs. Jones:" —but when it is not known whether she is married or not, use, "Miss." Two or more women are addressed as "Mesdames."

Paragraphs in business letters are not numbered as they are in official correspondence, but divisions of paragraphs may be lettered and numbered as in an official letter. The average one-page letter varies from one to six paragraphs, with the average between three and four. Paragraphs are complete thought units and should be arranged in proper sequence.

The body of the letter includes all necessary information, with well constructed sentences. There must be no errors in spelling, punctuation, or grammar. Avoid stilted or trite phrases; be courteous, and not annoying. Whenever possible, write a one-page letter. The second page is usually indicated by "—2—" at the center top.

The *complimentary close* is the polite phrase or word (adverb) with which you end your letter. Business letters are customarily closed by the "truly" phrase, with "Very truly yours" the most favored. "Sincerely" is next favored, and "Cordially" is used for a more personal-business letter. The complimentary close is typed *two-lines* below the preceding line of typing.

Your *signature* is typed or stamped *four lines* below the complimentary close, and hand-signed above the typed signature. For an officer, the order of signature is:

(1.) Name in capitals
(2.) Rank, if any, or
(3.) Functional title
(4.) Authority line, if any.

The signature for a business man usually is:

(1.) Name, not capitalized throughout
(2.) Functional title
(3.) The company name may be used if desired (frequently not used, since it is in the letterhead).

Signatures on the official Service letter vary from the business-form letter in the following respects: (1) the rank, if any, is included; (2) the functional title is added; and (3) the authority line, if any, is expanded to include the title of the command at whose direction the letter is prepared. Examples:

> J. B. JONES
> Administrative Officer
> Department of the Army

> J. B. JONES
> Rear Admiral, USN
> Acting Assistant Chief of Naval Personnel

> J. B. JONES
> Administrative Officer
> Navy Department

> J. B. JONES
> Rear Admiral, USN
> Head, Division of Administration
> By Direction of the Chief
> of Naval Operations

> J. B. JONES
> Rear Admiral, USN
> Chief, Bureau of the Budget

> JONATHAN B. JONES
> Colonel, USMC
> Administrative Officer

In signatures it is incorrect to use titles such as "Mr.," "Mrs.," "Capt.," "Dr.," "Prof." Men and women in business usually use the company's writing paper for all business correspondence, but important executives often have specially engraved or printed paper. Under the company's letterhead, at the left-hand margin, the full name is engraved with the title of office directly underneath. For example:

James Wilson Brown
Editor-in-Chief

An example of a business-form letter is:

HEADQUARTERS SEVERN RIVER NAVAL COMMAND
UNITED STATES NAVAL ACADEMY
Annapolis, Maryland

In reply refer to:
3397 110
27 June 1958

Superior Insurance Company
214 North Tenth Street
Jersey City, New Jersey

Attention: Mr. Johnson Henry, Office Manager

Gentlemen:

The business form of letter is used for correspondence addressed to persons or agencies outside the Department of the Navy. If, however, the outside addressee is familiar with the naval letter, it may be used instead of the business-form letter.

The first page of a business letter is typed on letterhead paper. If printed letterhead is not available, the name and address of the activity are typed on plain bond paper. Continuation pages are typed on plain bond paper. In the absence of the "From" line on a business-form letter, letterhead tissue, printed, typed, or stamped, is used for all copies going outside the originating office. Further instructions regarding stationery and copies are given on page 25 of the Navy Correspondence Manual, a copy of which is sent to you under separate cover.

A business letter of less than one page in length is centered on the page so that it presents a well-balanced appearance. A short letter may be double-spaced and it may be typed with the left and right margins as wide as two inches. Full-page and multiple-page letters are typed with one inch margins.

The signature information, placed below the complimentary close, is typed or stamped in block style or in balanced lines.

Very truly yours,

JOHN E. DOE
Administrative Officer
Severn River Naval Command

Encl:
(1) (SC) Navy Correspondence Manual

ENVELOPES

Business envelopes usually match the paper and are in sizes ranging from 3⅞ by 8⅞ inches to 4½ by 10⅜ inches. They are usually imprinted with the title of an official or company, or the name of the command, with return address in the upper left-hand corner.

Envelopes are addressed in the same manner as inside addresses, and are single spaced and frequently indented. The letter is folded in horizontal thirds and inserted in the long envelope, or folded first in half and then in thirds for the shorter envelopes.

In business, the address may be from two to five lines. Titles are used in the address: "Mr.," "Dr.," "Prof.," "Capt.," etc.

> Mr. John Doe
> Executive Vice President
> Supreme Book Stores
> 115 East 53rd Street
> New York 22, New York

The address could begin with the last three lines and the notation: "Attention Mr. Doe" written in the lower left hand corner. When necessary to signify PERSONAL that word is capitalized above the address.

PERSONAL CORRESPONDENCE

Medium weight paper approximately 6 by 7 inches is customarily used for personal correspondence. A Service crest or insignia, monogram, initials, or name and address may be engraved or printed at the top center or upper left-hand corner of the paper. The conventional colors of white or cream, blue, gray, blue-gray, or light tan are most frequently used, with matching envelopes.

Initials may be engraved, or dye-stamped in color or in simple block form, at the top center or left of the sheet. Initials are usually 3/16 of an inch high, and are spaced to take up no more than ¾ of an inch over all. On large sheets of paper, initials may be ¼ inch high, and may cover about the same amount of space. Initials are preferable to a monogram, but an address is better than either. In the Naval Service, dark blue is customary, but black is frequently used for engraving or printing.

When your full name and address are used on the writing paper or on postcards, printing is more frequently used than engraving—owing to the cost. The best printing is black or dark blue, in plain block letters. The name and address are usually printed at the top center of the page, or they may be printed in a straight line across the top—a form used most often on postcards. A printed address, with no name, is used on single sheets for formal as well as for business correspondence, and is placed in the top center of the page.

Certain types of informal letters may be typed, *but others must be written by hand,* in a legible manner. It is obligatory to hand-write "bread and butter" and "thank you" letters, as well as letters of congratulation, condolence, invitations to small weddings (or their reply), engagements, birth announcements, or letters to prospective sons- or daughters-in-law. *All* formal letters or cards of invitation are handwritten. Answers to engraved invitations are always handwritten.

SOCIAL OR PERSONAL LETTERS

A social or personal letter will follow basic rules. A long letter, or a social-personal letter, will have the date written at the upper right-hand corner of the page. The date may also be written on the last page, or at the bottom of the first page, near the left-hand margin but slightly below the signature. Only very informal letters have abbreviated dates: the more formal the letter, the fewer the abbreviations.

The basic steps are:

1. *Date:*
   Near the top right: "June 15th" (very informal)
   or   Near the top right: "June 15, 1958" (civilian form)
   or   Near the top right: "15 June 1958" (Service form)
   or   Near the lower left: (same form)
   or   Near the lower left: "Saturday" (very formal or very brief).
2. *Salutation:* No inside address, flush with left margin. For example:
   "Dear Mary,"
   or   "My dear Mary,"
   or   "Dear Mrs. Jones," etc.
3. *Body of letter:* Indented paragraphs, or a paragraph, brief note.
   Avoid over-use of the pronoun "I."
4. *Complimentary close:* Start at center of page; occasionally, start at right even with date line. For example:
   "Sincerely,"
   or   "Sincerely yours,"
5. *Signature:* Directly under, or under and slightly at right, of complimentary close. No title or rank, and with first name for close friends —or when the body of the letter gives no clue to the identity of the signer, then write full name, "John Jones." Otherwise, write your name in full.

The conventional salutations and closings for informal or personal correspondence are:

(To a woman)
   Dear Mary,

   ....
   ....

                                    As ever, (or "Yours ever,")
                                    John (or "John Jones")

(To a man)

Dear George,

. . . .
. . . .
. . . .

Sincerely, (or "As ever,")
John Jones

In letters to a relative or intimate friend, the closing would probably be "Affectionately," "With love," "Devotedly," etc., with the last name of the person writing omitted from the signature. Last names are added to the signature in informal letters when the body of the letter does not give a clue to the identity of the writer.

The date is usually written at the upper right-hand corner of the paper, with no address. On a short note, the day instead of the date may be written at the bottom left of the page, two spaces lower than the signature. On an informal note, the month is sometimes abbreviated; otherwise, it is written out.

BREAD-AND-BUTTER LETTERS

"Bread-and-butter" letters are written within 48 hours after you have spent a night or more in someone's house, and are addressed to the hostess.

THANK-YOU LETTERS

"Thank-you" letters should be written within a week after you have received a gift or a favor. Such a letter is also written following a bereavement, in reply to letters of condolence. Although the envelope is addressed to the hostess, there is no inside address and mention must be made of the host. (See Chapter 17, *Invitations and Replies*.)

A basic form to follow in both the "bread-and-butter" letter or the "thank-you" letter is printed herewith, with parts as indicated:

May 15, 1958

Dear Mrs. Doe,

(A) "Thank you for . . . (the gift or occasion, etc.)"
(B) A sincere comment concerning the occasion or gift; an expression of appreciation; a comment concerning something of mutual interest.
(C) A looking-forward-to-seeing-you-again (soon) sentence.
(D) A "thanks again," and a request to be remembered to the host and/or to any other member of the family.

Sincerely,
John Jones

"MAD" OR "LOVE" LETTERS

It is a wise man who will observe certain rules in writing very personal letters:

- Never state anything that can be used against you.
- Be careful of making direct promises or of stating familiarities.
- Never write anything which might damage another's reputation or harm him in any way—for the person who might eventually be harmed most might be yourself.

You should guard against writing angry or abusive letters. If you must write a letter of complaint, wait several hours or overnight, and then re-read the letter before mailing it.

Letters of apology are sometimes required of even the best of us. Brief and sincere notes of explanation are always advisable when you are unable to keep a certain appointment, or when there has been some other misunderstanding.

RESERVATIONS

When you write a hotel or motel for a reservation, give brief but full information.

For example:

45 Redwod Avenue
San Diego 11, Calif.
March 23, 1958

The Manager
Carvel Hall
Annapolis, Md.

Dear Sir:

Will you please reserve a room with bath for my wife and myself, from June first for one week?

If such accommodations are not available at present, please let me know the earliest date you can take us.

Yours truly,
JOHN JONES
Ensign, U. S. Navy

A telegram to a hotel would include the title or rank in the signature:

PLEASE RESERVE SINGLE ROOM WITH BATH FOR ONE WEEK STARTING SATURDAY 8 JUNE. WIRE CONFIRMATION COLLECT.

ENSIGN JOHN JONES USN
45 REDWOOD AVENUE
SAN DIEGO 11, CALIF.

A man or wife may wire reservations ahead to a bus, plane, or train terminal, in this form:

UNITED AIR LINES
NATIONAL AIRPORT
WASHINGTON D C

PLEASE RESERVE TWO SEATS TO STOCKHOLM WIFE AND SELF
FIRST AVAILABLE JUNE. REPLY COLLECT.
ENSIGN JOHN JONES

For reasons of clarity, other than in telegrams, use the terms "my wife and myself." Upon arrival at the hotel or motel, you will register, "Ensign and Mrs. John Jones" *not* "Ensign John Jones and wife."

LETTERS OF CONDOLENCE

One of the most difficult letters to write is a letter of condolence—but no letter is more appreciated than the one expressing sympathy at a time of sorrow. Respect and obligation, affection and friendship are the grounds for writing such letters.

The *brief* letter of condolence has a traditional form; with parts as follows:

1. An expression of sympathy.
2. A kind comment or observation concerning the deceased person.
3. A last word of affection and sympathy.
4. The complimentary close and your signature.

You will always be careful of your choice of words in sending a message following a death which resulted from an accident, suicide, or any catastrophe.

The essentials in writing a letter of condolence are the expressions of sympathy, encouragement, and a desire to help. An example of a letter written to the mother of a classmate killed in an accident, is:

Dear Mrs. Ledbetter,

I have just heard of Larry's fatal accident, and I want you to know that you have my deepest sympathy. Our friendship, which began when we roomed together at the Academy, has always been a solid reality on which I have leaned many times.

Since I am being transferred to Pensacola next month, I plan to stop over in Memphis en route. At that time, I want to call on you and, if possible, be of some service.

Sincerely,
John Jones

Telegrams are frequently sent, and follow this form:

OUR DEEPEST SYMPATHY.

ANN AND JOHN JONES

or

DEEPLY SHOCKED AT YOUR LOSS. ALL MY SYMPATHY.
SINCERELY.

JOHN JONES
(or MARY AND JOHN, for close friends.)

REPLIES TO MESSAGES OF CONDOLENCE

Letters, telegrams, and other messages of condolence, as well as thank-you notes for floral tributes, should be personally answered or acknowledged by the person to whom they were addressed. This brief reply of thanks should be handwritten within six weeks after the message (or floral tribute) has been received, and preferably is written earlier.

A sentence or two will be enough, particularly in cases of ill health or extreme age. In cases of illness, extreme age, or shock, a member of the family may write the note of thanks.

All-white paper is used more frequently for correspondence in connection with bereavement than the traditional black-bordered paper of former years. Mourning paper for men is usually all white, or white with an address or initials engraved in black. Women may use all white, or white with a black or gray border about 1/16 of an inch wide, or with a black monogram or address. A light gray paper is also used.

A reply to a message of condolence may be very brief:

Dear Mrs. Smith,

Thank you so much for your very kind expression of sympathy.

Sincerely,
John Jones

Or, to a long-time friend, you would write a more personal note:

Dear Mary,

Your very kind letter gave me great comfort. Thank you so much for the roses, and for writing. I will call you and Bill as soon as I can.

Very sincerely,
John Jones

In order for the bereaved to acknowledge accurately the messages of condolence, flowers, contributions to charity, etc., an accurate list must be kept by a close friend or a member of the bereaved family when the funeral is held at home. When the funeral takes place at a funeral home, a member of the staff will collect the cards and make a list for the family.

Although social letters of condolence are always handwritten, a letter of condolence may be dictated and typed from a business office to someone related to a person the writer has known mainly in official or business life.

MOURNING CARDS

In case of bereavement, it is correct to send engraved cards of acknowledgment in response to calls, cards of condolence, or floral tributes, where many of the messages of condolence and sympathy are comparatively impersonal but are in the hundreds or thousands. For example:

ADMIRAL AND MRS. JOHN DOE
ACKNOWLEDGE WITH GRATEFUL APPRECIATION
YOUR KIND EXPRESSION OF SYMPATHY

CHRISTMAS CARDS

Christmas cards are sent to close friends and acquaintances, but not to casual acquaintances, or near-strangers. Frequently, in the Services, it is understood that Christmas cards are not sent within an activity or base.

Envelopes of Christmas cards are always addressed to *both husband and wife,* even if you know only one or the other. (A printed card without your name carries the signature at the bottom of the greeting, and you will sign it: "Mary and John Jones.") The rule for signatures is usually "ladies first." But you may sign for both, as: "The John Jones." Because of frequent changes of address in Service life, it is wise to place the return address in the upper left-hand corner of the envelope.

LETTERS OF REFERENCE

When you are asked to write a letter of reference—for example, for someone leaving the Service or your place of employment, you will want to write an honest, straightforward account of that person's ability and character. It is important that the letter be fair both to the future employer and to the employee. The letter should always be dated.

A letter of reference, or any letter written to an unknown reader, needs neither salutation nor closing. The letter is a statement of fact, and is attested to by the signature. The outmoded phrase "To Whom It May Concern" is infrequently used. When you know to whom the letter will be addressed, you of course may use that person's name.

Letters of reference can be typewritten or written by hand. The general points covered in the typical letter of reference are:

- The name of the person or employee.
- The length of his service or employment.

- The nature of his service or work—and *his competence.*
- His honesty and character; his loyalty to the Service or business.
- His sobriety.
- His ability to get along with others.
- The reasons for his leaving the Service or business; an expression of your regret at losing him, if such is the case.
- Your willingness to answer any further questions concerning him, and an expression of your confidence in him in his new field of endeavor.

When a person has been unsatisfactory in his work, or when he has a questionable reputation, omissions in your reference are the best way of indicating it. However, you are under no obligation to give him any reference at all.

FORMAL PAPER

Note paper for formal use is about 6 by 7 inches in size, and is a fine quality paper in a glazed or kid (velvety) finish. The crest or insignia (if used) is engraved, and the paper is always white or cream color, with matching envelopes.

A double sheet with no crest is often used in answering formal invitations, such as weddings, dinners, dances, receptions, etc.

WEDDING INVITATIONS

A heavy white or cream colored paper (vellum) is best for an engraved invitation. The crest or coat of arms should be embossed in the paper without color. The customary size is about 5 by 7½ inches or 5½ by 7 inches, and it is folded in half before being placed in the inner envelope.

A favorite size that does not need to be folded is about 4½ by 6 inches, and is slipped sideways in the envelope. The black lettering on engraved invitations may be the conservative Script or the popular Shaded Antique Roman. Other letterings are Shaded Modified Roman, London Script.

ENVELOPES

Wedding Invitation Envelopes

Engraved wedding invitations are customarily enclosed in two envelopes. The inner envelope is addressed, "Captain and Mrs. Jackson," and is not gummed, therefore it is unsealed. The outer envelope is fully addressed for weddings or other formal occasions:

> Mrs. John Smith Jackson (Name written in full, no initials)
>   39 College Avenue (Avenue or street written in full)
>   Indianapolis (No comma)
>   Indiana (State not abbreviated)

The addresses on wedding invitation envelopes and on all handwritten social correspondence envelopes are written by hand—and the handwriting must be legible.

Before you place any letter in an envelope, check it for corrections, signature, and enclosures. When writing more than one letter, re-check to make sure that the right letter is in the right envelope.

INVITATION CARDS

For formal invitations, fine quality cards are customarily used, about 3½ by 5½ inches, or 4 by 6 inches in size with matching envelopes. The card may be plain or partially engraved with a crest.

The popular *fill-in* cards are white or ivory, with the crest or insignia engraved in dark blue or black at the top center. Your name (or administrative position) is directly under the crest, followed by the line: "request the pleasure of the company of." A few key words complete the engraving. For example:

THE SUPERINTENDENT OF THE

UNITED STATES NAVAL ACADEMY

AND

MRS. JOHN JONES

REQUEST THE PLEASURE OF THE COMPANY OF

AT

ON

AT   O'CLOCK

R.s.v.p.
Flag Lieutenant

The name of the guest and other information is written by hand in blue or black ink. The cards are used for almost any occasion, formal or informal dinners, receptions, cocktails, etc.

When an officer's station will not change for some time and many cards are used, or when a retired officer has a permanent address, the address is engraved in the center of the card directly under the "at . . . o'clock" line. The address is frequently engraved under the R.s.v.p., and the place of entertainment is written by hand under the "at . . . o'clock" line.

Fold-over cards are about 3 by 4 inches in size, and are frequently used for invitations to luncheons, cocktail parties, buffet suppers, etc. These cards are called "informals" and are of smooth heavy paper in white or cream color, with matching envelopes.

Your name is centered on the outside of the card and may be engraved from the same plate used for personal cards. (A name reading "Captain and Mrs. John Jackson Jones" may have the "Captain and" waxed out for a woman's card, and the "and Mrs." waxed out for your personal use.) The invitation is usually written on the lower half of the inside of the card.

An informal flat *message* or invitation card is frequently used in place of the *fold-over* card. This card is about 3½ by 4½ inches in size, and is of heavy white or cream colored paper.

Your name is engraved in the center—or slightly above the center—of the card, with the address in the upper right-hand corner. If desired, a telephone number is engraved at the top left-hand corner of the card.

The message or invitation is written below the name, and an *R.s.v.p.* would be written in the lower left-hand corner. These cards have matching envelopes. They are never used for calling cards.

Since there is more space on this type of card, they are particularly useful to enclose with gifts, when a "thank-you" message may be written on them.

CHAPTER 17

Invitations and Replies

The issuance of invitations, and their replies, follow definite social rules that should be observed. These rules may be considered a framework in which you can extend or answer invitations with maximum advantage and minimum effort for both the guest and the host.

In general, the types of invitations that you will receive are formal and informal. Although most invitations are informal during the early years of a Midshipman, Cadet, or young officer's career, formal invitations are issued by the Superintendent or Commandant at the various Academies. Junior officers, as well as Midshipmen and Cadets, will often receive formal invitations to debutante dinners and dances; official occasions as well as informal parties are encountered during the annual summer cruises to foreign countries. Senior officers will receive many invitations to state, official, and social occasions throughout their Service careers.

Informal invitations may be given in person, over the telephone, or by informal note or calling card. When invitations are extended in person you must be alert and be prepared to accept or refuse without advance notice. When the invitation is one that you will enjoy accepting, there is no difficulty in expressing pleasure. But when you do not care to accept the invitation, your feelings must be concealed.

When you refuse any invitation, your answer should be plausible. Do not fumble with generalities, such as, "Well, I may have the duty that night so I don't know whether I can come or not. . . ." Instead, you may say, "I'm sorry, I'm not free that evening—but thank you."

When you are not sure if you are free to accept the invitation, be frank with the person extending the invitation and say why you cannot commit yourself at the moment; for example, you can truthfully say that you believe you have the watch, etc. You may ask if a delayed reply will be inconvenient, and that if not, you will check your schedule immediately and let the hostess know as soon as you can. If a delay is inconvenient, you should refuse at once, but graciously.

Telephone invitations follow the same pattern as those given face-to-face. The information concerning the time, date, and place, should be repeated in order that no mistake will be made. It is wise to write the information in an engagement book or on a pad, immediately; it would be embarrassing later if you forget and arrive at the wrong hour or day.

Oral invitations usually are issued for smaller occasions, including luncheons, dinners, cocktails, teas, children's parties, christenings, informal dances, picnics, morning coffees, etc. Invitations by card—either calling card or the folded informals or larger message cards—are used for large informal parties such as cocktails, receptions, etc., including both afternoon and evening occasions, buffet suppers, teas, children's parties, dances, at-homes, etc.

Written invitations are also extended to those who cannot be reached by telephone, or when the location of the house or place of entertainment is difficult to find. Pertinent information concerning the location of the party is sometimes illustrated by charts or clever sketches either drawn or imprinted on the card.

When you receive an informal invitation for a time when a friend will be visiting you, you may state in your answer that you are sorry that you cannot accept the invitation because a classmate or houseguest will be with you at that time. Common sense will dictate whether you should do this, however, since you do not want to place the hostess in the position of *having* to invite your guest.

When it is convenient to your hosts, the hostess probably will invite you to bring your classmate or houseguest with you. Otherwise, she may say something like "I'm sorry; we're only having ten guests, and the dinner isn't buffet—but perhaps another time?" Because, as anyone will realize, when mixed guests are to be seated at the dining table, an extra guest would upset the table arrangement.

INFORMAL INVITATIONS, REPLIES

An invitation given by a married couple is usually extended by the hostess. An oral invitation, given in person or by telephone, may be stated in a simple manner: "John and I are having a few friends in for supper on Saturday at seven, we do hope that you and Bill can join us. . . ."

An invitation to an older couple might be extended in this form: "This is Mary Jones. I wonder if you and Captain King could have supper with us next Saturday, at seven?"

When the host extends the invitation, it is given in the name of the hostess: "Mary would like you to have supper with us on Saturday at seven."

An invitation written on personal note paper is usually brief, but will give full information. For example:*

84 Bowyer Road

    Dear Mr. Roberts,
      Commander Swanson and I are having as our houseguests next

---

* In this chapter, *italics* are used to indicate handwriting when used in invitations, acceptances, and refusals.

week Betsy Hallam, the daughter of an old friend, and several of her college friends from Mary Baldwin.

We are asking several Midshipmen for dinner at our quarters on Saturday, the fifteenth, at seven o'clock. We sincerely hope that you can join us.

I am sure that you will find Betsy and her friends most attractive.

Cordially,

Mary Swanson

Monday

Your reply should be written on personal stationery, by hand, and must be mailed within a day or two, or as soon as possible. Replies are addressed to the hostess only. For example:

Room 2045, Bancroft Hall
9 April 1958

Dear Mrs. Swanson,

I am delighted to accept your kind invitation for dinner at your quarters on Saturday, the fifteenth, at seven o'clock.

The occasion will be of added pleasure since I met Miss Hallam at the Army and Navy Club in Washington several weeks ago. Thank you for including me.

Sincerely,

John Roberts*

When your reply is a regret, you should explain the refusal:

Room 2045, Bancroft Hall
9 April 1958

Dear Mrs. Swanson,

I sincerely appreciate your invitation to dinner on Saturday, the fifteenth, but unfortunately I am not able to accept since I have the watch on that day.

It was very kind of you and Commander Swanson to include me, and I regret very much that I will not have the opportunity to meet Miss Hallam and her friends.

Sincerely,

John Roberts

"Thank You" Letter

After you have been entertained in a home, it is customary that you write—or sometimes you may telephone—your hostess and thank her for the occasion. A "thank you" note is brief, but must be genuine in expressing appreciation. The reply is addressed to the hostess, but will take note of any member of the family:

* Sign your full name only; it is not proper to add your title or any other information.

Room 2045, Bancroft Hall
17 April 1958

Dear Mrs. Swanson,

 Thank you very much for a wonderful evening at your quarters on Saturday night. Without a doubt your houseguests were as attractive a group of girls as I have ever met. It was a pleasure to see Miss Hallam again.

 Your dinner was superb, and the memory of the ice cream pie will last a long time, while I am eating Navy chow. All of us enjoyed seeing the film which Commander Swanson took on his last cruise. Thank you again, for having me.

Sincerely,

John Roberts

Invitations for luncheons and dinners may be sent on calling cards, informals, or the newer large flat message cards with engraved names. When an *R.s.v.p.* is written on the cards, an answer is mandatory. Your acceptance or refusal of the invitation may be made on your calling card, by brief note, or by telephone. A bachelor's invitation to a stag luncheon could be written on his personal card, as follows:

Lunch
Saturday, 7 May, 1 P.M.

Captain Stephen Sidney Preble

Officers' Club   **United States Navy**

An invitation to a dinner could be written on the hostess's calling card, as follows:

Dinner
Saturday, March 2, 8 p.m.

Mrs. Henry George Dickinson

R.S.V.P.   *11 Porter Road*

When accepting or refusing an invitation, you may draw lines through the lettered engraving on your personal card, and write in your acceptance or refusal as follows:

The *fold-over informal* has the name of the host and hostess fully engraved on the outside, with invitations or replies handwritten on the inside. These cards are about 2¼ by 3¼ inches in size, or a little larger. (See Chapter 16, Correspondence)

Example (1). Invitation.

(Outside)

Captain and Mrs. John Henry Jones

34 Upshur Road

(Inside)

Cocktails
Wednesday, June 9th
5-7 P.M.

Example (2). A reply to the invitation is also written on the informal card.

> *Sorry I cannot join you on the ninth, for I will*
> *be in San Diego! Thanks for thinking of me.*
> > *Jack**

The larger flat informal, or *message* card, has more space for the writing of invitations, replies, notes, etc. In the case of married couples the full names of both may be engraved higher than on the informal, and the address is at the upper right-hand corner of the card. The title and surname of a flag officer may be used, but a rear admiral, brigadier general, and officers of less rank customarily use their full names.

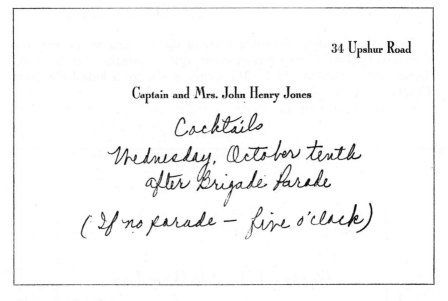

34 Upshur Road

Captain and Mrs. John Henry Jones

Cocktails
Wednesday, October tenth
after Brigade Parade
(If no parade — five o'clock)

Afternoon Receptions

Informal invitations to an official afternoon reception are usually issued on the semi-engraved cards, with the word "informal" or the uniform of the day written by hand at the lower right-hand corner. An admiral's or general's flag, or other insignia customarily centers the top of the card as illustrated at the top of the next page.

The reply to any engraved invitation should be written in the third person. Personal note paper may be used.

---

* Since the name of the writer is printed or engraved on the outside of the informal card, it is not necessary to sign one's name. However, a more personal touch is added in signing a first name.

To meet the officers of   *Her Majesty's Canadian Ship Huron*

The Commandant, Fourth Naval District

and Mrs. Brown

request the pleasure of the company of

Lieutenant and Mrs. Smith

at a reception

on Sunday, the fifteenth of December

at 6:30 to 8:30 o'clock

R.s.v.p.
Flag Lieutenant
Naval Base

Service Dress

Invitations to receptions, garden parties, teas, and at-homes do not require an answer unless a response is requested. Replies to an at-home follow the general form for an afternoon reception, but the words "at-home" are not used in the reply.

FORMAL INVITATIONS

Invitations to formal occasions preferably are fully engraved or partially engraved, or they may be handwritten on white or cream colored note paper, in the third person. Invitations are issued between two and three weeks in advance of the occasion, but wedding invitations and other invitations, where an advance notice is necessary, may be sent out four weeks in advance.

Invitations to very important functions may be fully engraved, and will carry the phrase "request the honor (or pleasure) of your company." An admittance card to be shown at the door is frequently enclosed.

Although it is against protocol and the best social usage, invitations to very large general receptions and parties (but *never* wedding invitations) are sometimes printed rather than engraved, owing to the great expense of engraving.

An admiral's or general's flag may be used on his invitations, and official seals and insignia in gold or color are often used on invitations for such occasions as inaugurations, dedications, ship christenings, and commissionings. The family crest or coat of arms may be embossed without color at the top of wedding or other important invitations.

The Chief of Naval Operations and Mrs. Green
request the pleasure of the company of

at

on

at   *o'clock*

R. S. V. P.
Liberty 5-6700
Extension 53122

                                      Admiral's House
                                      Naval Observatory

Honor guests are customarily designated by the phrases, "In honor of—", which is used mainly for prominent personalities, and "To meet—," which is usually used for new arrivals and houseguests, etc.

The person or persons issuing or acknowledging invitations refer to themselves by their full names: "Ensign and Mrs. John Jones, junior." (When your name is very long, "Jr." is correct.) Their guests or hosts are designated by their last names only: "Captain and Mrs. Brown."

Service rank, titles, and names are written in full: "Lieutenant, junior grade," "Lieutenant Commander," "First Lieutenant," "Second Lieutenant," "Rear Admiral," etc. This does not apply to the Army and the Air Force.

Abbreviations and initials are to be avoided, but there are some established exceptions: "Mr.," "Mrs.," "Dr.," "R.s.v.p." (or "R.S.V.P."), and "p.p.c." etc. When an initial is customarily used in place of a first or middle name, that initial may be used: "Ensign J. Marshall Jones."

In formal invitations, the date and hour are always *spelled out,* but only the day and month are *capitalized:* "Thursday, the seventh of January." "Half after eight o'clock" is preferable to "eight-thirty," although the latter is correct.

A very formal invitation will be indicated in the lower right-hand corner of the card by "white tie." "Decorations" (small medals) mean evening dress, military or civilian. Unless a card states otherwise, a formal and usually a semiformal evening occasion will be "black tie." The dress for official occasions should always be indicated.

The partially engraved card is customarily used for formal and semi-formal functions. It is less expensive than the fully engraved card and is mainly used for large receptions, dinners, luncheons, at-homes, etc.

Replies to formal invitations should be written as soon as possible after you receive them. Dinner and luncheon invitations should be answered within 48 hours, which, in case you can not attend, will give your hostess time to invite another guest without his feeling like a "fill in."

Your reply must be handwritten, on white or cream colored note paper, in the third person. An acceptance will include the names of the host and hostess, time, date, and place (if not the host's address). The reason for this repetition is that the hostess may make corrections if the prospective guest has made a mistake. A regret includes the same information except that it makes *no reference to the time or place.*

Replies are customarily addressed to the hostess, or to an aide or social secretary if so indicated in the R.s.v.p. In some official circles, the envelope is addressed to the host *and* hostess.

A formal invitation to a married couple must be refused when either one or the other cannot accept. The rule here is *both* or *none.*

After accepting a formal invitation—or almost any invitation, for that matter—you are committed to the occasion over all other occasions—except duty—with the exception of your receiving a White House invitation which takes precedence over all other invitations. In case of a conflicting invitation from the White House, you must withdraw any previous acceptance you have made to another occasion.

There are a few reasons for withdrawing an acceptance which are valid: serious illness, a death in the family, or prospective absence occasioned by a transfer of duty, or very important business elsewhere.

Telephone invitations are nowadays correct even for formal functions. Such invitations, however, are more usual for smaller affairs, and the hostess frequently make the calls herself. The guest may accept at the moment, or if absent when the message was received, may reply by writing a note later or by telephone.

An aide will call for his chief, or a secretary for a man or woman. In quarters, a steward or maid may call for the hostess.

When the steward or maid receives the call, the conversation may be somewhat as follows:

"Commander Smith's quarters."
"I'd like to speak to Mrs. Smith, please."
"May I ask who is calling, please?"
"This is Mrs. Jones."
"I'm sorry, but Madam is not at home. May I take a message?"

"Would you please say that Mrs. Jones would like to know if Commander and Mrs. Smith could dine on Saturday, the fifth of March, at eight o'clock, at quarters 'M'?"

"To dine with Mrs. Jones on Saturday, the fifth of March at eight o'clock at quarters 'M' . . . very good. Thank you."

"Thank you."

To confirm invitations, a hostess may send engraved or handwritten reminder cards. The cards may be a regular invitation with "To Remind" written in the upper left-hand corner. The semi-engraved card is frequently used for this purpose.

Semi-Engraved Dinner Invitation

The most favored form of invitation is the semi-engraved card, which is adaptable to any date or occasion. This type of invitation is less expensive than a completely engraved card, and is used mainly for very large occasions, including dinners and dinner dances.

The method of issuing formal invitations at the various Service Academies is slightly different, because of the large number of Midshipmen and Cadets involved. The "machinery" that would be necessary to find out the name of the young lady each Midshipman or Cadet will invite would be so time consuming that a different form is followed in regard to replies to the invitation:

In honor of the *Winter Sports Teams*

The Superintendent of the
United States Naval Academy
and
Mrs Smedberg
request the pleasure of the company of
Midshipman Abbott and Young Lady
at *dinner*
on *Saturday, the thirtieth of March*
at *seven-thirty* o'clock

R.s.v.p.
Flag Lieutenant

Black Tie

Replies at the Service Academies

If you are a Midshipman or Cadet at the Service Academies, you must reply to a formal invitation on your best conservative note paper, hand-written in the third person, or you may write "Escorting Miss—(first and last name)" across the top of your personal card.

It is permissible, and correct, to write the name of your young lady, then your name, across the top of the Flag Lieutenant's reply card, which is always enclosed with the invitation extended by the Superintendent of the Service Academy. You will enclose this card in an envelope, and return it to the Flag Lieutenant. If you are not escorting, you will write "Not escorting" across the top of the card. The card will serve as your reply.

Such a card is:

> Please furnish the Flag Lieutenant the name and address of the young lady you will escort, or indicate if you are not escorting.

When a general invitation is extended by the Commandant of Midshipmen at the Naval Academy, you may indicate your acceptance or regret by initialing appropriate lists in Bancroft Hall.

Handwritten Reply

A Midshipman or Cadet, or any officer of the Services, must remember to answer a formal invitation promptly—but you must first check previous commitments to be sure that you are not accepting something which you will later have to cancel. Once you have accepted an invitation, you are duty bound to accept. If you *must* cancel, do so without delay. In case of cancellations, it is better to use the telephone, regardless of the formality of the occasion. As a member of the Services, you often have official duties which take precedence over social functions.

Your formal handwritten acceptance might state:

> *Midshipman John Johnson*
> *accepts with pleasure*
> *the kind invitation of*
> *Lieutenant and Mrs. Brown*
> *to dinner*
> *on Saturday, the sixth of April*
> *at eight o'clock*
> *Arundel Estates*

or:

> *Cadet William Smith*
> *regrets that because of his*
> *absence from town*
> *he will be unable to accept*
> *the kind invitation of*
> *Colonel and Mrs. Lee*
> *for Saturday, the sixth of April*

Handwritten Invitations

The formal invitation does not have to be engraved but may be written by hand, on white or cream colored note paper, in the third person. The wording and spacing follow the engraved form. The address or place of entertainment is usually centered underneath the line indicating the time, but may be written at the lower right-hand side.

Captain and Mrs. John Smith
request the pleasure of the company of
Rear Admiral and Mrs. Jones
at dinner
on Saturday, the third of March
at eight o'clock
Quarters "M", Naval Base

R.s.v.p.   *Black Tie*

A sample acceptance would be:

Rear Admiral and Mrs. William Jones
accept with pleasure
the kind invitation of
Captain and Mrs. Smith
to dinner on Saturday, the third of March
at eight o'clock
Quarters "M", Naval Base

A regret would say, ". . . regret that they are unable to accept," or, ". . . regret that because of a previous engagement they are unable to accept . . ." etc.

An invitation to a formal reception:

IN HONOR OF THE PRIME MINISTER OF PATRIA
AND
MRS. CAESAR
THE AMBASSADOR OF PATRIA AND MRS. LEGATE
REQUEST THE HONOR OF THE COMPANY OF

AT A RECEPTION
ON SATURDAY, THE FIFTH OF MAY
AT TEN O'CLOCK

R.S.V.P.   WHITE TIE
2698 CALIFORNIA STREET, N.W.   GRAND BALL ROOM, MAYFLOWER HOTEL

The acceptance would be something like this:

Vice Admiral and Mrs. James Smith
have the honor to accept
the kind invitation of
The Ambassador of Patria and Mrs. Legate

for Saturday, the fifth of May
at ten o'clock
Grand Ball Room, Mayflower Hotel

The regret would be somewhat as follows:

Vice Admiral and Mrs. James Smith
regret that because of their absence from the city
they will be unable to have the honor of accepting
the kind invitation of
The Ambassador of Patria and Mrs. Legate
for Saturday, the fifth of May

Formal Afternoon Reception

A fully engraved formal afternoon reception may have a separate card stating the prescribed uniform:

In honor of
The Secretary of the Navy and Mrs. Spencer
Admiral and Mrs. William John Mann
request the pleasure of your company
at a reception
on Wednesday, the fifth of July
from five-thirty until seven-thirty o'clock

R. s. v. p.
Navy Department
Extension 55313

Officers Club
Bethesda Naval Medical Center

UNIFORM

White Dress

Ship Commissioning Invitation and Reception Card

THE COMMANDANT, FIRST NAVAL DISTRICT,
THE PROSPECTIVE COMMANDING OFFICER AND SHIP'S COMPANY
REQUEST THE HONOR OF YOUR PRESENCE
AT THE COMMISSIONING OF THE
USS JOHN S. MC CAIN (DL-3)
AT THE BOSTON NAVAL SHIPYARD, BOSTON, MASSACHUSETTS
ON MONDAY AFTERNOON, THE TWELFTH OF OCTOBER
NINETEEN HUNDRED AND FIFTY-THREE
AT TWO-THIRTY O'CLOCK

PLEASE PRESENT THIS CARD
AT THE HENLEY STREET GATE   CAMERAS NOT PERMITTED

THE COMMANDING OFFICER AND WARDROOM OFFICERS
OF THE USS JOHN S. MC CAIN (DL-3)
REQUEST THE PLEASURE OF YOUR COMPANY
AT A RECEPTION AT THE
COMMISSIONED OFFICERS' MESS
BUILDING 5, BOSTON NAVAL SHIPYARD
IMMEDIATELY FOLLOWING THE COMMISSIONING

R.S.V.P.
COMMANDER, BOSTON NAVAL SHIPYARD

The Partially Engraved At-Home Invitation

*Decoration of Colors by the
Brazilian Marine Corps at six fifteen o'clock*

THE COMMANDANT OF THE MARINE CORPS
AND MRS. HENDERSON
AT HOME

R.S.V.P.   *Service Dress White*
LIBERTY 5-6700   COMMANDANT'S HOUSE
EXTENSION 7683   MARINE BARRACKS

Dance Invitations

A formal, fully engraved invitation to a debutante dance would follow the form below:

CAPTAIN AND MRS. JOHN SMITH, JUNIOR
REQUEST THE PLEASURE OF
THE COMPANY OF
Midshipman Ricketts

AT A DANCE IN HONOR OF THEIR DAUGHTER
MISS MARY MARTHA SMITH
ON SATURDAY, THE FIFTEENTH OF FEBRUARY
AT ELEVEN O'CLOCK
ARMY AND NAVY CLUB

R.S.V.P.
300 FIRST STREET

An afternoon debutante reception would be stated:

CAPTAIN AND MRS. JOHN SMITH, JUNIOR
MISS MARY MARTHA SMITH
AT HOME
SATURDAY, FEBRUARY FIFTEENTH
AT FIVE O'CLOCK
DOGWOOD HILLS

R.S.V.P.
DOGWOOD HILLS
ARLINGTON

The acceptance would be in the following form:

Midshipman John Fork Ricketts
accepts with pleasure
the kind invitation of
Captain and Mrs. Smith
Miss Smith
for Saturday, the fifteenth of February
at five o'clock
Dogwood Hills

Your refusal would be somewhat as follows:

Midshipman John Fork Ricketts
regrets that having the watch
he will be unable to accept
the kind invitation of
Captain and Mrs. Smith
Miss Smith
for Saturday, the fifteenth of February

A semi-engraved form frequently used for formal dances:

CAPTAIN AND MRS. JOHN SMITH, JUNIOR
REQUEST THE PLEASURE OF THE COMPANY OF
Midshipman Ricketts
AT *a small dance*
ON *Saturday, the twenty-third of December*
AT *half-after ten o'clock*
Army and Navy Club

R.S.V.P.
300 FIRST STREET   *Black Tie*

A less formal invitation may omit the name of the guest:

CAPTAIN AND MRS. JOHN SMITH, JUNIOR
MISS MARY MARTHA SMITH
REQUEST THE PLEASURE OF YOUR COMPANY
at a small dance
on Saturday, the Fifteenth of February
at ten o'clock
Dogwood Hills

R.S.V.P.
DOGWOOD HILLS
ARLINGTON

In replying to invitations that carry the names of several persons on the invitation—such as co-hosts at a dinner or reception, or the names of the parents with that of their daughter written directly underneath, or the names of the sponsors of the event—these names also appear in your reply.

In answering an invitation to a "small dance," your reply omits the word "small."

POSTPONING OR ADVANCING INVITATIONS

If Captain and Mrs. Smith must postpone the dance, the announcement to that effect would follow the same form as the invitation:

CAPTAIN AND MRS. JOHN SMITH, JUNIOR
WISH TO ANNOUNCE
THAT THE DANCE IN HONOR OF THEIR DAUGHTER
MUST BE POSTPONED UNTIL
SATURDAY, THE TWENTY-SECOND OF FEBRUARY

PLEASE RESPOND TO
300 FIRST STREET

When it is necessary to postpone or advance the date of a formal invitation, an engraved notice (or printed notice, when time is short) is sent out in a form similar to the original invitation, with this information:

BECAUSE OF THE
IMMINENT DEPARTURE OF
THE CHIEF OF NAVAL OPERATIONS
THE RECEPTION IN HONOR OF
ADMIRAL AND MRS. WARD
WILL BE ADVANCED FROM
THURSDAY EVENING, THE TWENTIETH OF JUNE
TO
FRIDAY EVENING, THE FOURTEENTH OF JUNE
AT NINE O'CLOCK
GRAND BALL ROOM, MAYFLOWER HOTEL

R.S.V.P.

WITHDRAWING AN ACCEPTANCE

As mentioned earlier, an invitation from the White House takes precedence over all other invitations. In such cases, if you have already accepted an earlier invitation to a conflicting occasion, you would have to cancel your previous acceptance in words something like these:

> *Rear Admiral and Mrs. John Smith Hampton*
> *regret that because of an invitation*
> *to the White House*
> *they must withdraw from*
> *Captain and Mrs. Jones' dinner*
> *on the third of May*

RECALLING AN INVITATION

It is better to postpone than to cancel an invitation, once you have extended it, but when unavoidable circumstances warrant, a formal invitation must be recalled. When the occasion was small and the guests would know the reason for the withdrawing of the invitations—such as a bereavement or a serious accident—none need be stated for the withdrawing of the invitations:

> THE INVITATIONS OF
> CAPTAIN AND MRS. JOHN SMITH
> FOR SATURDAY, THE FIFTEENTH OF MAY
> ARE RECALLED

But when it is an official occasion involving guests who might not know the circumstances, the reason for recalling the invitation would be stated on printed forms, since engraving takes too long:

> CAPTAIN AND MRS. JOHN SMITH
> REGRET EXCEEDINGLY
> THAT BECAUSE OF THE RECENT DEATH OF
> FLEET ADMIRAL OWENS
> THE INVITATIONS TO THE RECEPTION IN HONOR OF
> THE SECRETARY OF DEFENSE
> AND
> MRS. WINGATE
> MUST BE RECALLED

GUEST OF HONOR

It is contrary to custom to invite those of higher rank to meet those of lower rank. However, when this is unavoidable, the following rules may be employed:

- Ask the ranking guest to waive his right for the occasion in favor of the guest of honor.

- Seat the guests according to precedence, even if it places the guest of honor well down the table. When ambassadors and very high ranking guests are present, this plan must be followed.
- Make the senior guest the co-host if it is a stag party and if he is of the same nationality as the host.

When the party or dinner is informal, you may have a guest of honor of lower rank than other guests—but not at official or formal affairs. In extending the invitation to someone to be a guest of honor, you may say, "I would like so much to give a dinner for you,"—and when the person is married, ". . . for you and your wife (or husband)," for the invitation must include both.

A letter to a prospective guest of honor may be written in this form:

> *Dear Mrs. Jones,*
>   *Will you and Captain Jones dine with us on either Thursday, the third of October, or Saturday, the twelfth at eight o'clock?*
>   *We want to ask some friends to meet you, and hope very much that we may be fortunate enough to find you free on one of those evenings.*
>   *Very sincerely,*
>   *Mary Smith*
>
> *September seventeen*

When invitations to guests are issued over the telephone, you do not use the phrase "in honor of" as this phrase is used only on engraved invitations. The hostess may say instead, "We are giving a dinner next Saturday, the tenth, for Admiral and Mrs. Jones . . ." etc.

WEDDING INVITATIONS

The traditional wedding invitation is engraved on white or cream colored vellum or kid finish paper. The size most customarily used is a double sheet, 5 by 7½ inches, that is folded across its length and then enclosed in the inner of one of two envelopes. If a smaller invitation (usually 4½ by 6 inches) is used, it is not folded but is placed sideways in a single matching envelope.

In case of invitations using the double envelopes, the inner one will have the guest's rank or title and last name written on it in black or dark blue ink. The tissue protecting the engraving on the invitation is not removed before placing in the envelope. The inside envelope is faced toward the back of the outside envelope when inserted, in order that the names will be face up when the envelope is opened.

As a general rule, abbreviations, initials, numerals, are to be avoided, whenever possible, in wedding invitations. The hour is always written out in full. However, Roman numerals may denote a second or third generation: John Paul Truxtun, "II" or "III." The designation "Junior" applies to the next in direct line of descent. The numbers "II," etc., indicate the sequence in the use of the name.

The groom sends a list of his friends' names and addresses to his mother, who in turn will send the list of names and addresses of friends and relatives of the family to the mother of the bride. Invitations are mailed by the bride's mother between three and four weeks before the event. If all guests are not to be invited to the reception or breakfast following the wedding, this should be designated on the list by an R for reception, and C for ceremony. If the parents of the bride are deceased, the invitations would be issued by a close and older relative.

Invitations to church weddings do not carry the "R.s.v.p.," therefore they do not require an answer. When a card is included in the invitation, inviting you to the reception or breakfast following the ceremony, the card customarily has an "R.s.v.p." and must be answered.

The home address of the bride's family is usually engraved on the reception or wedding breakfast card, so that replies will be sent to that address and *not* to the place of the wedding.

Commissioned officers of the Navy, Merchant Marine, and Coast Guard who rank *below* commander, or lieutenant colonel in the Army, Air Force, or Marine Corps, should *not* use their titles before their names on the invitation.

The traditional engraved wedding invitation reads as illustrated on the following page.

There are a number of variations in the wording of parts of the invitation:

1. When the bride's parents are deceased, and a relative is giving the wedding:

MR. GEORGE OLIVER SMITH
REQUESTS THE HONOR OF YOUR PRESENCE
AT THE MARRIAGE OF HIS SISTER
MARY MARTHA
etc.

2. If the bride's grandparents give the marriage:

DR. AND MRS. OLIVER BRANCH
REQUEST THE HONOR OF YOUR PRESENCE
AT THE MARRIAGE OF THEIR GRANDDAUGHTER
MARY MARTHA SMITH
etc.

3. When the bride's father is dead or divorced, and her mother has remarried:

Commander and Mrs. John James Smith

request the honor of your presence

at the marriage of their daughter

Mary Martha

to

Donald James Adams

Lieutenant, United States Navy

on Monday, the first of May

at four o'clock

The Navy Chapel, 3801 Nebraska Avenue, Northwest

Washington, District of Columbia

MR. AND MRS. PAUL LEWIS DORN
REQUEST THE HONOR OF YOUR PRESENCE
AT THE MARRIAGE OF HER DAUGHTER
MARY MARTHA SMITH
etc.

4. Or the invitations may be issued in the mother's name only:

MRS. PAUL LEWIS DORN
REQUESTS THE HONOR OF YOUR PRESENCE
AT THE MARRIAGE OF HER DAUGHTER
MARY MARTHA SMITH
etc.

This form also applies to the bride's mother when she has not re-married following death or divorce of the bride's father. If the bride's father is a widower, the same form is used, with the exception of the word "his" instead of "her" before the word daughter.

5. If the bride's mother is dead and the father has married again, the form usually is:

COMMANDER AND MRS. JOHN JAMES SMITH
REQUEST THE HONOR OF YOUR PRESENCE
AT THE MARRIAGE OF HIS* DAUGHTER
MARY MARTHA
etc.

6. When a young widow is married, the married name of the widow is given, and the form is:

COMMANDER AND MRS. JOHN JAMES SMITH
REQUEST THE HONOR OF YOUR PRESENCE
AT THE MARRIAGE OF THEIR DAUGHTER
MARY MARTHA ADAMS
TO
JOHN DOE BLANK
SECOND LIEUTENANT, UNITED STATES ARMY
ON SATURDAY, THE FIRST OF JUNE
AT FOUR O'CLOCK
SAINT ANNE'S EPISCOPAL CHURCH
ANNAPOLIS, MARYLAND

Or: When the widow gives her own wedding, the form (in part) is:

THE HONOR OF YOUR PRESENCE
IS REQUESTED AT THE MARRIAGE OF

* When the relationship is close, "their" would be used instead of "his" which would be inclusive of the stepmother.

MRS. DONALD JAMES ADAMS
TO
JOHN DOE BLANK
etc.

7. Engraved invitations are rarely sent to the wedding of a divorcée. A divorcée's wedding is usually a small ceremony, but when invitations are sent, the above forms may be used with the divorcée's given name used with the last name of her former husband: "Mary Martha Smith Adams" or "Mrs. Smith Adams."

8. When there are no close relatives or friends, the bride may send out her own invitations, with the wording (in part) as follows:

THE HONOR OF YOUR PRESENCE
IS REQUESTED AT THE MARRIAGE OF
MISS MARY MARTHA SMITH
TO
DONALD JAMES ADAMS
etc.

9. When sisters are married at a double wedding, the name of the older sister is given first:

COMMANDER AND MRS. JOHN JAMES SMITH
REQUEST THE HONOR OF YOUR PRESENCE
AT THE MARRIAGE OF THEIR DAUGHTERS
MARY MARTHA
TO
DONALD JAMES ADAMS
LIEUTENANT, UNITED STATES NAVY
AND
SARAH JANE
TO
FRED PERRY HAAS
ENSIGN, UNITED STATES COAST GUARD
ON MONDAY, THE FIRST OF JUNE
AT FOUR O'CLOCK
THE NAVY CHAPEL, 3801 NEBRASKA AVENUE, NORTHWEST
WASHINGTON, DISTRICT OF COLUMBIA

10. At a double wedding, when the brides and bridegrooms are very close friends, but are not related, the invitation may be written according to the rank of the fathers or bridegrooms, or in alphabetical order.

11. When the bride's parents are separated but not divorced, the fact of the separation is frequently ignored, and the invitations are engraved in the customary form.

INFORMAL WEDDINGS

A very small, informal wedding does not require engraved invitations. The mother of the bride may write short notes of invitation, or may telegraph or telephone the relatives and friends who are to be invited to the ceremony or to the reception, or to both.

The notes are written on conservative paper, usually white or cream color, giving the time and place of the ceremony. If the invitation is only for the reception, the time and place are all that is necessary. Informal invitations may be sent on short notice, but the usual two weeks in advance is customary.

The typical informal note would read something like this:

59 Southgate Avenue

Dear Mary,

Janet is being married here at home to Ensign John Jones, USN, who was graduated from the Naval Academy last week. The wedding will take place Monday, June 9, at four-thirty. We do hope you will be with us and will stay for a very small reception, afterwards.

As ever,
Bess Smith

Answers to invitations to small weddings (even answers to invitations received by telegram) are made by letter—if you have time. A brief, sincere note on your personal paper would be correct.

RECEPTION INVITATIONS

There are several ways of sending an invitation for a wedding reception. If the wedding takes place in the morning or early afternoon, a wedding breakfast card is enclosed along with the invitation itself.

1. A small card about 3 by 4 inches, engraved on the same type paper as the wedding invitation, is included *inside* the invitation. There is no crest or coat of arms on the card, and the protecting tissue is not removed before mailing. The phrase "pleasure of your company," is used, since this is now a social occasion:

COMMANDER AND MRS. JOHN JAMES SMITH
REQUEST THE PLEASURE OF YOUR COMPANY
AT THE WEDDING BREAKFAST
FOLLOWING THE CEREMONY
AT
DOGWOOD HILLS
ARLINGTON

R.S.V.P.

2. The conventional invitation to a reception is:

COMMANDER AND MRS. JOHN JAMES SMITH
REQUEST THE PLEASURE OF YOUR COMPANY
AT HALF AFTER EIGHT O'CLOCK
THREE HUNDRED FIRST STREET, SOUTHEAST

R.S.V.P.

Or:

THE PLEASURE OF YOUR COMPANY
IS REQUESTED AT THE RECEPTION
AFTER THE CEREMONY
AT
THREE HUNDRED FIRST STREET, SOUTHEAST

R.S.V.P.

3. When a wedding is very small, with *no* wedding invitations to be issued, but with a large reception planned afterwards, the *reception invitations* are engraved on paper about the same size as the traditional wedding invitation:

CAPTAIN AND MRS. JOHN JAMES SMITH
REQUEST THE PLEASURE OF YOUR COMPANY
AT THE WEDDING RECEPTION OF THEIR DAUGHTER
MARY MARTHA
AND
DONALD JAMES ADAMS
LIEUTENANT, UNITED STATES NAVY
ON MONDAY, THE FIRST OF JUNE
AT FOUR O'CLOCK
DOGWOOD HILLS
ARLINGTON, VIRGINIA

R.S.V.P.

4. The invitation to the reception may be included in the wedding invitation when all guests are invited to *both* the wedding and reception. The following information is added at the bottom of the wedding invitation, following the name and address of the church:

AND AFTERWARDS AT
DOGWOOD HILLS
ARLINGTON, VIRGINIA

R.S.V.P.

ACCEPTANCE AND REFUSALS

When you are invited to the ceremony and to the reception, or to the reception alone, the R.s.v.p. is usually requested and *must* be answered. Your reply will follow the form of the engraved invitation, or of the informal letter. You will write in longhand, on cream colored or white note paper, and the form for the acceptance or regret is similar, except for the lines of acceptance or regret.

A simple but desirable form of answering the invitation to the wedding, to both the wedding and the reception, or to the reception only, is:

Lieutenant and Mrs. William Blank
accept with pleasure
the kind invitation of
Captain and Mrs. Smith
for
Monday, the first of June
at four o'clock

The same general form is used to regret as to accept an invitation. You will remember that in all refusals of invitations, the hour of the occasion and the address are always omitted. When the refusal is for an invitation from a close friend, the reason why is frequently added in the second and third lines, such as: "regret that their absence from the city prevents their accepting."

A more detailed form for answering the invitation is shown in the following regret for a reception only:

Lieutenant and Mrs. William Blank
regret that they are unable to accept
the very kind invitation of
Captain and Mrs. Smith
to the wedding reception of their daughter
Mary Martha
and
Donald James Adams
on Monday, the first of June

A reply to a small or informal wedding invitation is usually sent in the same form in which it was received. If by telephone or telegram, the answer may be sent in the same way to the sender of the invitation. If time is not short, it is preferable that your reply be a handwritten note. An acceptance could read:

Monday

Dear Mrs. Smith,
I am very happy about your daughter's forthcoming marriage to my classmate, Dick Brown, and am pleased to be included. I'll fly in and will be staying with friends.

Sincerely,
John Jones

MARRIAGE ANNOUNCEMENT

Engraved marriage announcements are issued on the same type paper used for wedding invitations, and are sent out *after* the marriage has been performed. The announcements are sent by the bride's parents or by a person designated to do this.

Wedding announcements are sent to less intimate friends and acquaintances who were not invited to the wedding, or to all friends and acquaintances following a ceremony when no guests were invited. The year is customarily written out in the invitation:

CAPTAIN AND MRS. JOHN JONES SMITH
HAVE THE HONOR OF ANNOUNCING
THE MARRIAGE OF THEIR DAUGHTER
MARY ANN
TO
MR. GEORGE CARL WILSON
ON SATURDAY, THE SEVENTH OF JUNE
NINETEEN HUNDRED AND FIFTY-EIGHT*
TREASURE ISLAND CHAPEL†
SAN FRANCISCO, CALIFORNIA

RECALLING WEDDING INVITATIONS

Because of illness, change of orders—or a change of mind!—wedding invitations may have to be recalled, or postponed, after they have already been issued. Notices must then be sent to all those who had received invitations. The best form for recalling a wedding invitation is:

DR. AND MRS. WILLIAM SMITH
ANNOUNCE THAT THE MARRIAGE OF THEIR DAUGHTER
MARY ELLEN
TO
ENSIGN JOHN LEE JONES
WILL NOT TAKE PLACE

When the wedding invitation is recalled because of a bereavement in the family, the engraved or printed card may state the reason:

DR. AND MRS. WILLIAM SMITH
REGRET EXCEEDINGLY
THAT BECAUSE OF THE RECENT DEATH OF
THE FATHER OF ENSIGN JONES
THE INVITATIONS TO THE MARRIAGE OF THEIR DAUGHTER
MARY ELLEN
TO
ENSIGN JOHN LEE JONES
MUST BE RECALLED

* A departure from the conventional wording of the wedding invitation is the use of the year, written out, in wedding announcements. In some cases, the year is not specified.

† The name of the church may, or may not, be added. The hour of the wedding is not specified.

Or:

MRS. WILLIAM SMITH
REGRETS THAT THE DEATH OF
DR. SMITH
OBLIGES HER TO RECALL THE INVITATIONS
TO THE WEDDING OF HER DAUGHTER

The recalling of the invitations in case of a death in the immediate families does not always mean that the wedding may not take place on the scheduled day. If the families agree, a very quiet ceremony may be held on the original day of the wedding, with perhaps only one attendant each for the bride and groom.

When members of the bridal party have already arrived, and some have come from a distance, or when the bridegroom is in the Service and has only a few days' leave, or has new duty that will take him some distance, the wedding may be held as scheduled, but with no guests other than members of the families and the bridal party.

POSTPONING INVITATIONS

When it is necessary to postpone a wedding, a form similar to this may be followed:

CAPTAIN AND MRS. JOHN JONES SMITH
ANNOUNCE THAT THE MARRIAGE OF THEIR DAUGHTER
MARY ANN
TO
MR. GEORGE CARL WILSON
HAS BEEN POSTPONED FROM
SATURDAY, THE FIRST OF JUNE
UNTIL
SATURDAY, THE TWENTY-SECOND OF JUNE
AT FOUR O'CLOCK
TREASURE ISLAND CHAPEL
SAN FRANCISCO, CALIFORNIA

"AT HOME" CARDS

When you want friends to know your new address, and when you know where you will be living long enough to make the cards worth while, "at home" cards are often enclosed in the same envelope with the wedding announcement.

The cards are similar to a large calling card—about 3 by 4 inches—and are the same color as the wedding announcement. One form is:

ENSIGN AND MRS. JOHN JONES
310 REDWOOD AVENUE
AFTER THE FIRST OF JUNE   SAN DIEGO, CALIFORNIA

Or: A smaller card, about the size of the usual calling card, may be used:

AFTER JUNE 1ST
310 REDWOOD AVENUE
SAN DIEGO, CALIFORNIA

WEDDING ANNIVERSARIES

The announcements of wedding anniversaries, the year of the wedding, and the year in which the invitation is issued are customarily stamped or engraved at the top of the anniversary invitation or announcement. The couple's initials or monogram, coat of arms, or a seal, may be engraved in gold or silver, or in black or dark blue ink. Such invitations may be sent out by the couple (or by their children). An example in the first case would be:

1908   1958

ADMIRAL AND MRS. JOHN JAMES SMITH
REQUEST THE PLEASURE OF
Captain and Mrs. George Ballou's
COMPANY ON THE FIFTIETH ANNIVERSARY
OF THEIR MARRIAGE
ON FRIDAY EVENING, MAY THE THIRD
FROM SEVEN UNTIL NINE O'CLOCK
DOGWOOD HILLS
ANNAPOLIS, MARYLAND

Or:

1908-1958
ADMIRAL AND MRS. JOHN JAMES SMITH
AT HOME
FRIDAY, THE THIRD OF MAY
FROM FIVE UNTIL SEVEN O'CLOCK
DOGWOOD HILLS
ANNAPOLIS, MARYLAND

SECTION VI

EASY CONVERSATION

CHAPTER 18

Introductions and Farewells

It is fortunate that the mechanics of making introductions are simple and natural, because you probably will be introducing people to each other for the rest of your life. In the majority of cases, the purpose of introductions is that two or more persons may know each other. The simplest form of introduction is illustrated by a young child who introduces a hero-worshiped older child by announcing, "Mommy, this is Johnny!"

Brevity and accuracy are the two requirements that must be kept in mind when introducing people. The person making the introduction is completely in charge of the situation for the length of time that it takes to effect it. When you are that person, you are momentarily the ringmaster who must be sure not only of what you are going to say but how you are going to say it.

INTRODUCTIONS

When making introductions, all names must be clearly and correctly stated. You must know instantly whose name is stated first. There are a few simple rules you should remember:

- A man is always presented *to* a woman—with the exception of the president of any country, a King, or a dignitary of the Church (Pope, Bishop, etc.).
- The honored or higher ranking person's name is stated first, then the name of the person being presented.
- Young people are presented *to* older people of the same sex.
- A single person is introduced *to* a group.
  To illustrate these rules, you should introduce these persons in this manner:
  "Mr. President, may I present Mrs. Jones?"
  or: "Mrs. Jones, may I present Admiral Smith?" or, "May I present Admiral Smith . . . Mrs. Jones."
  "General Smith, may I present Colonel Jones?"
  "Mrs. Jones, this is my daughter Ann," or "Mrs. Jones, Miss White."
  "Miss White (or, This is Miss White—)—"Ensign Fields, Miss Lewis, Midshipman Brown, Miss Smith, Cadet Long," and so on, irrespective of rank or sex. In this case, when you wish to indicate individuals in the Services, junior rank is stated.

SERVICE INTRODUCTIONS

In the Navy, junior officers are those of the rank of lieutenant commander and below, including Midshipmen and Coast Guard Cadets. They are introduced and addressed as "Mister" at both social and official occasions—with the exceptions of certain military, state, official, or social occasions when the designation of title is necessary.

In all other Services, commissioned officers are introduced by rank, starting with the grade of lieutenant, including both first and second grades; officers of both grades are introduced and addressed as "Lieutenant."

Cadets at the U. S. Military Academy are introduced and addressed as "Mister," except at certain occasions when the designation is necessary. Cadets at the U. S. Air Force Academy are introduced as "Cadet—" and addressed thereafter as "Mister." (See Chapter 19, *American Forms of Address*.)

WHAT TO SAY

In making introductions, the easiest way is simply to state the names of the two persons concerned: "Miss White, Mr. Jones," or "Commander Brown, Mr. Smith." The phrase, "May I present," is more formal, but it is always correct to say, "Miss White, may I present Mr. Jones?" You may then add, "Jack is a Second Classman."

Midshipmen and Cadets may introduce fellow classmates in this manner: "Mary, this is my roommate, John Jones—Miss White." If the friendships are less intimate, the introduction my be "Miss White, Mr. Jones." When you introduce your sister or your best girl friend (or your fiancée) to your roommate who knows her name well, you may say, "Mary, this is John Jones." If she knows your roommate's name equally well, you may simply say, "Mary, this is John"—but this latter form is reserved for intimate friends only.

Although it is proper to use first names in introductions, it is important that those being introduced are contemporaries or are on equal footing. When a very close friend or relative is introduced to a stranger, the last name must be worked into the introduction: "Mary, may I present Midshipman John Jones . . ."; then turning to Midshipman Jones, you add, "—Miss White." Otherwise he will have no idea who "Mary" may be.

You should be careful about making personal comments when introducing people. Biographical data or human interest stories that are too long may cause embarrassment rather than establishing the topic of conversation for which they were intended. However, a brief comment can be very helpful in breaking the ice between strangers, and can be the start of a lasting friendship. "Mrs. Wilson, may I present Mrs. Smith? Her husband, as you know, served with General Wilson at Iwo Jima."

To introduce a newcomer to a group, the easiest way is to announce to all present, "This is Miss Brown." Then the names of those present are stated in rotation around the room. Should part of the group be actively engaged in a game or conversation at the time of your arrival, introductions should be made only to those closest to you and the newcomer, and other introductions are made later.

When you yourself are being introduced to a large group of people, you do not need to make the rounds and shake hands with everyone present; but you may shake hands with each man near you—and to any woman who offers her hand first. When a woman is introduced to such a group, she is not always taken around the room. If the group is small and the room not crowded, however, the host or hostess may take the newcomer around and introduce him or her personally to everyone.

FAMILY INTRODUCTIONS

When introducing a member of your family, usually you omit the last name of the person you are introducing. A Midshipman may say, "Mother, this is my roommate, James Smith." If your father is dead and your mother has remarried, you would say, "Mother, this is my roommate, James Smith"; —then turning to Midshipman Smith, you would add, "—Mrs. Northrop."

A married man refers to his wife as "My wife" to people who do not know her, and by her first name to people who do know her. You would introduce your wife in this manner: "Mrs. Smith, may I present my wife?" If you want to encourage the friendship, you may add your wife's first name: "Mrs. Smith, may I present my wife, Ruth?"

You would introduce your wife to a man in this manner: "Ruth, this is Captain Jones . . . my wife." You *never* refer to your wife as "Mrs." at a social occasion, except when you are going through a receiving line at a reception when you present your wife as "Mrs. Brown."

When speaking with very junior officers, enlisted personnel, tradespeople, servants, etc., however, you do refer to your wife as "Mrs.———."

When a wife introduces her husband, she says, "Mrs. Smith, this is my husband," and refers to him as "husband"—not as "Mr."— or "The lieutenant." She will only refer to him as "Mr. Brown" with tradespeople, servants, etc.

When introducing or referring to your wife, you should never use humorous forms such as: "Jim, I want you to meet the missus," or, "Meet the greatest little wife in the world."

When introducing your mother- or father-in-law, you may use the term "My mother-in-law" or "father-in-law," but it is preferable that you say, "Mother (or whatever she is called), may I present Lieutenant John Smith?" Then turning to Lieutenant Smith you add, "Mrs. Woods is Mary's mother"

—Mary being the name of your wife. A stepparent would be introduced, "My stepfather, Mr. White," but the relationship need not be mentioned unless you care to.

Half-brothers or sisters are usually introduced as brothers and sisters even though their last name is different from your own. You must give their names, however, when these are different from your own. "Mary, this is Cadet Smith—my sister, Miss White." Relatives, such as cousins, uncles, etc., are so designated at the end of the introduction, rather than in the body of the introduction.

FORGOTTEN INTRODUCTIONS

When you are presented to someone you have met previously but who apparently has forgotten that introduction, you may say: "I believe that I met Miss Lewis at the Ring Dance last year," or make other reference to the place of introduction. But do not blurt out, "Oh, I've met Miss Lewis—don't you remember?" It is obvious that she does not remember, and such a remark only causes embarrassment.

The fact that a junior officer, Midshipman or Cadet is not remembered by a senior officer does not imply that the senior officer is rude, or that you, the junior, did not make a good impression. A senior officer meets many people in his career, at many places, and the person who "never forgets a name or face" is a rarity in this accelerated world of today. Introductions made at large social functions, or made long ago, are easily forgotten.

When someone momentarily forgets your name when introducing you, help him out by giving your name, "John Jones." This momentary lapse of memory sometimes happens to even your best friends, and, in reverse, to you. When someone seems to have forgotten you, you may say, "How do you do, Mrs. Smith—I'm John Jones. We met at the station Christmas party."

If a person appears deliberately to forget you were introduced previously, you should not mention having met before. But do not be too quick to take offense at a forgotten introduction.

When a person joins a group and his last name is unknown—or you have forgotten it—it is best to say, "I'm sorry, but I have momentarily forgotten your last name," before attempting introductions.

ACKNOWLEDGMENTS

The customary answer to an introduction for both persons concerned is, "How do you do?" You may add, "So nice to see you." If you want to be certain that you understand the name correctly, say "How do you do, Mrs. Smith." You are *not* expected to answer, "I'm fine, how are you?"

It is good training to listen carefully when introductions are made so that it will not be necessary to have the name repeated. To acknowledge an introduction with a flip remark or with an attitude of indifference is not only improper, but insulting. Introductions should always be treated with the respect that they deserve; they invariably constitute first impressions, and first impressions should be good ones.

Young people frequently answer, "Hello," following an introduction. Although the expression "How are you?" is frowned on, it is correct and is used to some extent in certain sections of the country. The temptation, however, is to answer the query, which makes for an awkward situation.

Some men acknowledge another man's introduction by saying, "It is nice to know you," which phrase the other man may repeat, or he may merely say, "Thank you."

You should always avoid such acknowledgments as, "I am pleased to make your acquaintance," or, "Pleased to meet you." But—a hostess will cordially greet a guest's friend who is a stranger by saying, "I am so pleased you could come." And when you are introduced to someone who is an intimate friend of a friend of yours, you will probably say that you are pleased to know him!

Never use such trite phrases as, "Cadet Jones, shake hands with Jim Brown," or, ". . . I want you to make the acquaintance of. . . ." Embellishments on introductions can be confusing; it is best to keep introductions as simple and as direct as possible.

SELF-INTRODUCTIONS

Self-introductions are sometimes necessary, but they should be treated with care. Too often, the self-introduction has been used by presumptuous persons, with the result that others are wary of the custom.

There are occasions, however, when self-introductions can not be avoided. For instance, when you are a stranger at a large reception or cocktail party and the host and hostess are busy elsewhere and cannot introduce you into a new group—then you may introduce yourself.

When you introduce yourself at a social or non-official occasion, you do *not use your rank or title.* Say, "My name is John Jones" or, "I am John Jones." When your name is mispronounced and it seems advisable to correct it, say "Excuse me, my name is Jones (or John Jones)." You do not say, "Lieutenant Jones" or "Mr. Jones."

When you are telephoning someone who is your senior, you should introduce yourself: "Captain Brown, this is John Jones." If it is an official conversation, you would state your rank or title. A woman would say to the Captain's wife, "Mrs. Brown, this is Mary Jones. My husband is Lieutenant John Jones, who is serving under Captain Brown. . . ."

INTRODUCTIONS IN GROUPS

Introductions made in large groups must be handled in an efficient way, with the person or persons presented *to* the group. It is impossible to introduce everyone at a large function, but do introduce all guests at small gatherings of a dozen or so. A host and hostess should introduce a guest into a small group upon his arrival, and to the others later, when it is convenient. Otherwise, after the first introduction, the guest is on his own.

WHAT TO DO

When introduced to a man or woman, you, of course, rise if you are seated. You shake hands with another man when being introduced—but you will wait for a woman to extend her hand before offering yours. If you should forget and extend your hand first, it is no breach of etiquette since you are showing friendliness, but you will feel more comfortable if you remember to wait. You may bow slightly, when presented to a woman, but do not bob your head.

When you are at an inconvenient distance from a person to whom you are being introduced, you may nod or bow slightly. At a crowded table in a restaurant, you may half-rise when a person stops at your table and introductions are made. But if you are the one *making* the introductions, you always stand.

Outdoors, in uniform, the hand salute is customary when you are introduced to a man or woman, and you do not remove your hat. In civilian dress, you remove your hat and leave it off, weather permitting. However, if you should be the only man in uniform in a mixed group, you may feel more comfortable by deferring to civilian practice, and accordingly remove your hat when introduced to a woman.

Usually, you do not lift your hat to and among men when women are not present. It is awkward to attempt to lift your hat, and then shake hands. But if you are presented to a dignitary or very high ranking man outdoors, when you are in civilian dress, you may as a matter of courtesy remove your hat with your left hand before shaking hands.

If you are wearing gloves when introduced to a man or woman, remove your right glove—that is, if you have time. But do not keep a person waiting while you peel it off. When ushering at a wedding or funeral, or when attending a formal dance where white gloves are worn, do *not* remove your glove when introductions are in order. At no time do you need to apologize for leaving gloves on.

In Europe, you will shake hands with anyone presented to you. The gallant custom of kissing the hand of a Continental woman is not expected of American men visiting in a country where this custom prevails—or when the woman is visiting here.

A woman does not rise when introduced to another woman of about her own age, but she will stand when introduced to an elderly woman or the wife of a senior officer. She will remain standing until the elderly or senior woman is seated. A woman may shake hands with another woman, when convenient. But the younger or junior woman usually waits for the elderly or senior officer's wife to offer her hand first.

A woman does not rise when introduced to a man—unless he is the President, a King, or a dignitary, such as a Pope or Bishop. When a young woman is in the presence of a very high ranking officer or dignitary, she may rise. A woman customarily extends her hand first to a man of *any* age or rank except to heads of State or members of royal families. Children and teenagers should stand when introduced to an adult, man or woman.

THE PRESIDENT OF THE UNITED STATES

If you should have the good fortune to present someone to the President of the United States, you would stand straight, look directly at the President, and probably say, "Mr. President, may I present Admiral Brown?"

If you should be the person being presented, you would wait for the President to offer his hand, and you will bow as you shake hands. A woman being presented to the President also waits for him to offer his hand first. But most men—regardless of rank or title—usually prefer the customary form of a woman offering her hand first.

If you are called upon to make a formal presentation of the President at a banquet, you will give his full title: "Ladies and gentlemen—the President of the United States." In conversation, you address him as "Mr. President."

The Vice President is addressed and introduced in the same way as the President. The wives of Presidents and of Vice Presidents are introduced and addressed as "Mrs." When introduced and when in conversation, a former President is called "Mr." Though he is never so called while in office, an ex-President is given the courtesy title of "The Honorable."

FAREWELLS

After an introduction, the first person to move away might say, "I hope that I see you again soon." The other person will probably answer, "Thank you." He may wish to add such a comment as, "I hope so, too," but this tends to cause a slight awkwardness.

In taking leave of a group of strangers, it makes very little difference whether a person has been introduced all around or merely included in certain conversations. The most courteous action is to bow "goodbye" to anyone who happens to be looking at you. No attempt should be made to attract the attention of those who are apparently unaware that you are leaving. When saying goodbye to an acquaintance, you may say, "Goodbye, it was so nice to meet you." or "I hope we can meet again soon."

It is impossible to say goodbye to all guests at a large party, but you can do so to those with whom you were most recently talking. You will say goodbye to all guests at a very small party, such as a dinner, and you *always* say goodbye to your host and hostess.

When saying "goodbye," both men and women stand. A hostess rises to her feet when she sees that a guest is ready to leave. A woman guest makes the first move to leave, and her husband or escort immediately rises and joins her. The hostess and host shake hands with their guests on departure the same as on arrival.

A departing guest should make some appreciative comment to the hostess, and then the host: "It's been a very pleasant evening, thank you so much." The hostess might answer, "Goodnight, I'm so glad you could be with us."

At a formal dinner, the hostess would remain standing inside the living room when saying goodbye to guests, and the host would walk to the door of the living room or into the hall with a high ranking guest. The high ranking guest is always the first to leave. A steward or butler would open the door for guests and say, "Goodnight, Sir." A guest would answer, "Thank you, goodnight."

At informal parties, or when the host lives in the country, the host usually walks with guests to their cars—and always makes certain that everyone has a way to get home.

CHAPTER 19

American Forms of Address[*]

WRITTEN ADDRESS	SPOKEN ADDRESS	INTRODUCTIONS

A. *NAVAL SERVICE:* Full rank *precedes* the name of commissioned officers; customarily, rank may be abbreviated in official correspondence, but is *written out* in social correspondence. The rank also precedes the names of warrant officers, midshipmen, Coast Guard cadets and Merchant Marine cadet-midshipmen. The rating *follows* the name of non-commissioned officers.

WRITTEN ADDRESS	SPOKEN ADDRESS	INTRODUCTIONS
Rear Admiral John Jones, USN Superintendent United States Naval Academy Annapolis, Maryland	Admiral Jones	Admiral Jones (or, formal) Admiral John Jones, Superintendent of the United States Naval Academy
(or) LCDR John Jones, USN USS Catfish c/o Fleet Post Office New York, N.Y. (social) Lieutenant Commander and Mrs. Jones	Mr. Jones	Mr. Jones (Commissioned officers of the rank of lieutenant commander, and down, are addressed and introduced as "Mister" except for certain official or social occasions when the designation of rank is necessary.)
(or) CWO-2 John Jones, USN USS Catfish c/ Fleet Post Office New York, N.Y.	Mr. Jones	Mr. Jones
(or) Midshipman John Jones Room 3654, Bancroft Hall United States Naval Academy Annapolis, Maryland	Mr. Jones	Mr. Jones (Upon certain occasions, midshipmen and cadets are addressed and introduced as "Midshipman Jones" or Cadet Jones" for purposes of designation.)
(or) Mr. John Jones, Sn 1-C, USN USS Catfish c/o Fleet Post Office New York, N.Y.	Jones	Mr. Jones

[*] Adapted from *Etiquette* by Frances Benton. Copyright 1956 by Random House, Inc.

WRITTEN ADDRESS	SPOKEN ADDRESS	INTRODUCTIONS

B. *ARMY, AIR FORCE AND MARINE CORPS:* Although the Marine Corps is an integral part of the Naval Service, the rank is similar to that of the Army and Air Force, and therefore is included with these Services. In written correspondence, both official and social, full rank and ratings precede the name and are written out. In conversation, all Generals are "General—"; all colonels are "Colonel—"; and all privates and sergeants are "Private—" and "Sergeant—."

Brigadier General John Doe, USA Commandant of Cadets United States Military Academy West Point, New York	General Doe	General Doe (or, formal) General John Doe, the Commandant of Cadets at the United States Military Academy
(or)		
Lieutenant Colonel John Doe, USAF 335th Bomb Squadron Langley Air Force Base, Va.	Colonel Doe	Colonel Doe
(or)		
First Lieutenant John Doe, USMC Marine Corps School Quantico, Va.	Lieutenant Doe	Lieutenant Doe
(or)		
Cadet John Doe Company C, Corps of Cadets United States Military Academy West Point, New York	Mr. Doe	Mr. Doe (For purposes of identification or designation, the title "Cadet Doe" is used upon certain official or social occasions. *A cadet at the Air Force Academy is introduced as "Cadet Doe" and addressed thereafter as "Mr. Doe"*)
Chief (or Warrant Officer) John Doe, USMC c/o Fleet Post Office San Francisco, California	Mr. Doe	Chief Warrant Officer Doe (or Warrant Officer Doe)
Technical Sergeant John Doe, USAF Tinker Air Force Base Oklahoma City, Oklahoma	Sergeant Doe	Sergeant Doe

American Forms of Address—continued

WRITTEN ADDRESS	SPOKEN ADDRESS	INTRODUCTIONS

C. *UNITED STATES—Federal, State* and *Local Dignitaries:* "The Honorable" is the preferred form for addressing most American officials in office or retired, and is always written out. The phrase is always used with the full name—and *never* with any other title such as "The Honorable Admiral Jones," or "The Honorable Mr. Jones". In the salutation and close of a letter to the President, you would say, officially or in business, "Dear Mr. President:" and socially, "My dear Mr. President:"; and, officially and in business, "Respectfully yours," or, socially, "Very respectfully,". In writing to all other American officials, the official or business closing is, "Very truly yours," or socially, "Sincerely yours,". Wives of American officials are addressed and introduced as "Mrs.—."

The President

The President	Mr. President	The President
The White House		(or, formal)
Washington, D.C.		The President of the United States

(or, social)		
The President and Mrs. Doe		(abroad, add)
The White House		. . . of America
Washington, D.C.		

The President's Wife

Mrs. John Doe	Mrs. Doe	Mrs. Doe
The White House		
Washington, D.C.		

The Vice President

The Vice President	Mr. Vice President	The Vice President
United States Senate	(or)	(or, formal)
Washington, D.C.	Mr. Doe	The Vice President of the United States

(or, social)		
The Vice President and Mrs. Doe		(abroad, add)
(home address)		. . . of America

The Vice President's Wife

(home address)	Mrs. Doe	Mrs. Doe

The Chief Justice of the Supreme Court

The Chief Justice of the Supreme Court	Mr. Chief Justice	The Chief Justice
Washington, D.C.	(or)	(or, formal)
	Mr. Doe	The Honorable John Doe, Chief Justice of the Supreme Court of the United States

American Forms of Address—continued

WRITTEN ADDRESS	SPOKEN ADDRESS	INTRODUCTIONS
(or, social) The Chief Justice and Mrs. Doe (home address)		(abroad, add) . . . of America
Associate Justices Mr. Justice Doe The Supreme Court Washington, D.C.	Mr. Justice (or) Mr. Justice Doe	Mr. Justice Doe (or, formal) The Honorable John Doe, Associate Justice of the Supreme Court of the United States
(social) Mr. Justice and Mrs. Doe (home address)		(abroad) . . . of America
A Cabinet Officer (man)* The Honorable John Doe Secretary of State Washington, D.C.	Mr. Secretary (or) Mr. Doe	The Secretary of State, Mr. Doe (or, formal) The Honorable John Doe, Secretary of State
(social) The Secretary of State and Mrs. Doe (home address)		
A Cabinet Officer (woman) The Honorable Jane Doe Secretary of Labor Washington, D.C.	Madam Secretary (or) Miss (or) Mrs. Doe	The Secretary of Labor, Miss (or Mrs.) Doe (or, formal) The Honorable Jane Doe, Secretary of Labor
(social, when married) The Secretary of Labor and Mr. Doe	Mrs. Doe	
The Attorney General The Honorable John Doe Attorney General Washington, D.C.	Mr. Doe	The Attorney General, Mr. Doe (or, formal) The Honorable John Doe, Attorney General

* All Cabinet Officers except the Attorney General and the Postmaster General use the title of Secretary. Although the Service secretaries do not have Cabinet rank, they may be addressed and introduced as "Mr. Secretary," or, "The Secretary of the Navy." The Secretary of Defense has cabinet rank.

American Forms of Address—continued

WRITTEN ADDRESS	SPOKEN ADDRESS	INTRODUCTIONS
Secretaries of the Army, Navy and Air Force (Under Secretaries and Assistant Secretaries)		
The Honorable	Mr. Doe	Mr. Doe, or The Secretary
John Doe	(or)	of the Navy, Mr. Doe
Secretary of the Navy	Mr. Secretary	(or, formal)
Washington, D.C.		The Honorable John Doe, Secretary of the Navy
(social)		
The Secretary of the Navy and Mrs. Doe		
(home address)		
The Speaker of the House of Representatives		
The Honorable	Mr. Speaker	The Speaker, Mr. Doe
John Doe	(or)	(or, formal)
Speaker of the House of Representatives	Mr. Doe	The Honorable John Doe, Speaker of the House of Representatives
The Capitol		
Washington, D.C.		
(social)		
The Speaker and Mrs. Doe		
(home address)		
American Ambassador (men)*		
The Honorable	Mr. Ambassador	The Honorable John Doe,
John Doe	(or)	the American Ambassador
American Ambassador	Mr. Doe	(when he is not at his post,
London, England		the name of the country to which he is accredited must
(social)		be added: "to—")
The American Ambassador and Mrs. Doe		
American Embassy		
London, England		
(or)		
His Excellency	Your Excellency	His Excellency the American
The American Ambassador	(or)	Ambassador
London, England	Mr. Ambassador	
H. E. The American Ambassador and Mrs. Doe		

* When a woman is a United States Ambassador, or a United States Minister, the word "Madam" is substituted for "Mr." in the spoken address.

American Forms of Address—continued

WRITTEN ADDRESS	SPOKEN ADDRESS	INTRODUCTIONS
American Ministers (men)		
The Honorable	Mr. Minister	The American Minister
John Doe	(or)	(or, formal)
American Minister	Mr. Doe	The Honorable John Doe,
Dublin, Ireland		the American Minister
(social)		(or, not at his post)
The American Minister and		"... to—" (name of country)
Mrs. Doe		
American Charge d'Affaires and		
Consular Officers		
John Doe, Esquire	Mr. Doe	Mr. Doe
American Charge d'Affaires		(or, formal)
(or Consul General, or Vice		Mr. John Doe, the American
Consul)		Charge d'Affaires
Paris, France		
(social)		
Mr. and Mrs. John Doe		
(home address)		
United States Senator		
(or State Senator, with ap-		
propriate State address)		
The Honorable	Senator Doe	Senator Doe
John Doe	(or)	(or, formal)
United States Senate	Senator	The Honorable John Doe,
Washington, D.C.		Senator from Oklahoma
(social)		
Senator and Mrs. Doe		
(home address)		
United States Representative		
(or Assemblyman)		
The Honorable	Mr. Doe	Mr. Doe
John Doe		(or) Representative Doe†
House of Representatives		(or, formal)
Washington, D.C.		The Honorable John Doe,
		Representative from South
(social)		Carolina
The Honorable and Mrs. Doe		
(home address)		

† The title "Congressman" seems to be widely used in informal introductions by the Representatives themselves and by others when introducing them. It is not incorrect to call a Congresswoman "Congressman."

American Forms of Address—continued

WRITTEN ADDRESS	SPOKEN ADDRESS	INTRODUCTIONS
Governors*		
The Honorable	Governor Doe	Governor Doe (or) The Gov-
John Doe	(or)	ernor
Governor of Maryland	Governor	(or, formal)
Annapolis, Maryland		The Honorable John Doe,
		Governor of Maryland (or)
(social)		. . . of the State of Maryland
The Governor and Mrs. Doe		
(or, outside the State)		
The Governor of Maryland and		
Mrs. Doe		
(or)		
His Excellency the Governor		
and Mrs. Doe		
Mayors		
The Honorable	Mayor Doe	Mayor Doe
John Doe	(or)	(or, formal)
Mayor of Boston	Mr. Mayor	The Honorable John Doe,
Boston, Massachusetts		Mayor of Boston
		(or) . . . Mayor of the city of
(social)		Boston
Mayor and Mrs. Doe		
(or, formal social)		
The Honorable and Mrs. John		
Doe		
(house address)		
Judges		
The Honorable	Judge Doe	Judge Doe
John Doe		(or, formal)
Judge of District Court		The Honorable John Doe,
(or whatever court)		Judge of the District Court
Wheeling, West Virginia		
(social)		
Judge and Mrs. Doe		
(or, more formal)		
The Honorable and Mrs. Doe		
(home address)		
Head of a Federal Agency		
The Honorable	Mr. Doe	Mr. Doe
John Doe		(or, formal)
Administrator, Federal Works		The Honorable John Doe,
Agency		Administrator of the Federal
Washington, D.C.		Works Agency

* The Governor is given the title "Excellency" in many states, but the title *Governor* is the one used by the Department of State.

American Forms of Address—continued

WRITTEN ADDRESS	SPOKEN ADDRESS	INTRODUCTIONS
(social) Mr. and Mrs. Doe (or, more formal) The Honorable and Mrs. John Doe (home address)		

*Head of a Division or Bureau
  of a Department*
Mr. John Doe
Chief, Federal Bureau of In-
  vestigation
Washington, D.C.
	Mr. Doe	Mr. Doe
		(or)
		Mr. John Doe, Chief of the
		Federal Bureau of Investiga-
		tion

(social) Mr. and Mrs. John Doe (home address)		

D. *AMERICAN CLERGY AND CHURCH DIGNITARIES*

WRITTEN ADDRESS	SPOKEN ADDRESS	INTRODUCTIONS

*The Presiding Bishop of the
  Protestant Episcopal Church
  in America*
The Most Reverend John Doe,
  D.D., LL.D.
Presiding Bishop of the Protest-
  ant Episcopal Church in
  America
(local address)
	Bishop Doe	Bishop Doe
		(or)
		The Most Reverend John
		Doe, Presiding Bishop of the
		Protestant Episcopal Church
		in America

Protestant Episcopal Bishops The Right Reverend John Doe, D.D., LL.D. Bishop of— (local address)	Bishop Doe	Bishop Doe (or) The Right Reverend John Doe, Bishop of—
Roman Catholic Cardinal His Eminence John Cardinal Doe Archbishop of New York New York, N.Y.	Your Eminence	His Eminence (or) Cardinal Doe (or) His Eminence, Cardinal Doe

American Forms of Address—continued

WRITTEN ADDRESS	SPOKEN ADDRESS	INTRODUCTIONS
Roman Catholic Archbishop (or *Bishop*)		
His Excellency, The Most Reverend John Doe, S.T.D. Archbishop (or Bishop) of Chicago Chicago, Illinois	Archbishop (or Bishop) Doe	Archbishop (or Bishop) Doe (or) His Excellency, The Most Reverend John Doe, Archbishop of Chicago (or) His Excellency, The Archbishop of Chicago
Methodist Bishop*		
The Very Reverend John Doe, D.D., LL.D. Bishop of Denver Denver, Colorado	Bishop Doe	Bishop Doe (or) The Very Reverend Bishop Doe, Methodist Bishop of Denver
Roman Catholic Monsignor		
The Right Reverend Monsignor John Doe, S.J. (local address)	Monsignor Doe	The Very Reverend (or Right Reverend) Monsignor John Doe (or) Monsignor Doe
Protestant Episcopal Archdeacon		
The Venerable John Doe, D.D.* Archdeacon of— Diocese of Virginia	Archdeacon Doe (or) Doctor Doe	Archdeacon Doe (or) Doctor Doe (or) The Venerable John Doe, Archdeacon of— in the Diocese of Virginia
Deans and Canons		
The Very Reverend John Doe, D.D. Dean (or Canon) of Washington Cathedral Washington, D.C.	Dean (or Canon) Doe (or) Doctor Doe	The Very Reverend John Doe, Dean (or Canon) of Washington Cathedral

* All Protestant clergymen with Doctor's Degree may be addressed and introduced as "Dr. Doe," and "The Reverend Dr. Doe," respectively. Without such a degree, they are addressed and introduced as "Sir," and "The Reverend Doe," respectively.

American Forms of Address—continued

WRITTEN ADDRESS	SPOKEN ADDRESS	INTRODUCTIONS
Priests, who are Addressed as "Father"		
The Reverend John Doe, S.J. St. Mary's Church Washington, D.C.	Father Doe	Father Doe (or) The Reverend John Doe
Rabbi		
Rabbi John Doe Kneseth Israel Congregation Annapolis, Maryland	Rabbi Doe (or) Rabbi (or, with scholastic degree) Dr. Doe	Rabbi Doe (or, with scholastic degree) Dr. Doe
Mother Superior		
The Reverend Mother Mary (and the initials of her order) The Convent of— (address)	Reverend Mother	Reverend Mother
Sisters		
Sister Mary (and initial of her order) (local address)	Sister Mary	Sister Mary
Brothers		
The Reverend Brother John Doe Fordham University Bronx, New York	Brother John (or) Brother	Brother John
Cantors		
Cantor John Doe Kneseth Israel Congregation Annapolis, Maryland	Cantor Doe	Cantor Doe

E. *INDIVIDUALS*

Professors and Doctors		
Professor (or Assoc. Professor or Asst. Professor) John Doe (or, with Doctor's Degree) Dr. John Doe Columbia University New York, N.Y.	Mr. Doe (or) Professor Doe (or) Dr. Doe	Professor Doe (or) Dr. Doe

American Forms of Address—continued

WRITTEN ADDRESS	SPOKEN ADDRESS	INTRODUCTIONS
Divorcées		
Mrs. Smith Doe	Mrs. Doe	Mrs. Doe
(the maiden surname is followed by the ex-husband's name)		
(local address)		
Widow		
Mrs. John Doe	Mrs. Doe	Mrs. Doe
(the same as when her husband was alive)		
(local address)		

RÉSUMÉ OF DIFFERENCES IN THE FORMS OF ADDRESS

In the Navy:

- All grades of admiral are addressed and introduced as "Admiral"—with the exception of a formal presentation when the full grade would be stated.
- All chaplains are addressed and introduced as "Chaplain Jones."
- Medical and dental officers are addressed and introduced by rank including and above the grade of commander; including and below the rank of lieutenant commander they are called "Doctor."
- In a mixed group it is customary to introduce a captain in the Navy as "Captain, United States Navy," since the rank of captain in the Navy corresponds to the rank of colonel in the Army, Air Force, and Marine Corps—and the rank of captain in these Services corresponds to the rank of lieutenant in the Navy.
- A woman officer in the WAVES is addressed and introduced in the same way as a male officer in the Navy. For example, a lieutenant commander in the WAVES is "Miss Jones"; a commander is "Commander Jones," etc.
- Navy enlisted WAVES are also addressed in the same manner as the men, excepting a warrant officer is "Miss."
- Marine servicewomen, officers and enlisted, are addressed and introduced by rank or rating.
- Aboard ship, the captain of the ship is *always* "Captain"—regardless of his rank.

In the Army, Air Force, and Marines:

- All officers are addressed and introduced by rank.
- It is not correct in a spoken address to use the title by itself, such as "Colonel." It is correct to say, "Colonel Doe," etc.
- At a social occasion, the various ranks are not necessary to mention (for example, all generals are "General"), but at a formal presentation the full title is stated: "Brigadier General" etc.
- Warrant officers are addressed and introduced as "Mister" (except for formal occasions, or reasons of designation when the full rating is stated).
- Non-commissioned officers are addressed and introduced by their rating, such as "Private Doe," etc., not "Doe" or "John."
- Servicewomen, both officers and enlisted, are addressed and introduced by rank or rating.

In civilian life:

- "The Honorable" is the preferred form for addressing most American officials, in office or retired. The phrase is always used with the full name—and never with any other title.
- "His Excellency" is used in addressing a foreign ambassador but his wife is *not* called "Her Excellency."
- Some of the American officials addressed as "The Honorable" are American ambassadors and ministers, governors of States and Territories, cabinet officers, senators and congressmen, the secretary to the President, assistant secretaries of executive departments, judges (except judges of the Supreme Court), commissioners of the District of Columbia, American representatives on international organizations, heads of independent federal agencies, and mayors of cities.
- High officials such as presidents, ambassadors, and cabinet members are addressed by their titles only, never by name.
- In addition to the above mentioned persons addressed as "The Honorable" you should remember that "Once an Honorable, always an Honorable," and that a person out of office may be addressed in writing as "The Honorable."
- The word "Honorable" is never used by the person who holds this distinction in issuing or answering invitations, or on personal or calling cards—or in any other way.

CHAPTER 20

The Art of Conversation

For many people, the art of conversation is of little importance. In some walks of life this may be true—but not for you as an officer in the Service, or for anyone who chooses to become a professional leader of men.

The general public considers an officer in the Services to be a man of position and so renders judgment upon this basis. You must, therefore, devote significant thought and effort to the development of proficiency in general conversation, since you are, so to speak, "on the spot."

The first thing you must do in order to be a good conversationalist is to *have something to say;* second, you *must be able to say it well.*

MANNER OF CONVERSATION

Poor grammar, rude or vulgar talk, and the persistent use of improper and uncouth phraseology are representative of careless personal habits that can be corrected if you take sufficient interest. There are officers who perform their duties acceptably—occasionally, excellently—despite their inability to express themselves clearly and in good taste. But this is the exception rather than the rule.

Errors of a gross nature in conversation are particularly noticed by those officers junior to the speaker—and, paradoxically enough, even by those juniors who themselves use poor grammar.

Juniors, despite shortcomings of their own, expect high standards in their superiors, and justly so. Such use of careless speech will inevitably result in the loss of prestige. The juniors are likely to suspect that a senior who tolerates carelessness in his own speech may well tolerate carelessness in other phases of his official behavior. Such a suspicion is something that every officer wishes to avoid, so it is well that a Cadet or Midshipman recognize this fact and cultivate the habit of proper speech in everyday conversation.

OFFICIAL AND SOCIAL CONVERSATION

"The tongue is but three inches long, yet it can kill a man six feet high." This old Japanese proverb can, too often, be only too true.

In the Service, the essential difference between official and social conversation is one of situation. Conversation in an *official situation* requires that the conversationalists recognize differences in rank even while carrying on their conversation. Regardless of how pleasant and congenial such con-

221

versation may be, the speaker should always remember that such congeniality is never any excuse for not giving due deference for rates.

Social conversation means general talk between men—or in mixed company—in which no conscious recognition of rank, as such, is made. Social conversation is more informal and is made up of considerable "small talk." This is pleasant talk that is not important—and not at all harmful. But small talk that is fitting and proper at a dinner party is not carried on during an official conversation.

In both types of conversations, the objectives are the same: to create a personal relationship without tension in which thoughts and ideas may be exchanged. The tone of official conversation is generally more serious, but not necessarily so. Senior admirals and generals are only midshipmen and cadets grown older, and they, like anyone else, often enjoy a light conversation that does not concern career or business problems. Official business, of course, should never be discussed at social gatherings.

When talking with a senior or very high ranking officer, a junior officer shows deference and allows the senior to take the lead in the conversation—but should never freeze up while desperately trying to think of something brilliant to say. At a social occasion, the Service officer should be attentive—but not "at attention."

FAMILIARITY

Official conversations between seniors and juniors follow a basic principle: Seniors may call you, the junior, by your first name, but this does not grant you similar privileges. It is a gesture of friendly consideration on the part of the senior to call a junior by his first name, and this should be accepted as approbation by the junior.

Upon occasion, a senior will ask a junior to call him by his first name—but such informality must be handled with care on your part, and it must be clearly understood that the familiarity of the first name is *not* to be used in official conversations. Neither does the privilege of calling a senior by his first name automatically carry with it a "back slapping" familiarity—in fact, quite the opposite. The senior must have expected you to exercise the utmost propriety, or he would not have lowered the bars in the first place.

In talking with your contemporaries in the mess, or anywhere else—you must be on guard against telling your personal affairs. Your mess mates and station friends will become very good friends in time, but they are not the same as your parents or your immediate family. When you talk "just a little" with others about your personal affairs, a "little" quickly becomes "too much," and you will find that constraint and unease begin to develop in your formerly easy relationship.

When on duty, conversations between seniors and juniors, and between commissioned and non-commissioned officers, should always be kept on the official and impersonal level. This does not mean that you should resemble Captain Hornblower when talking with men of junior rank, but it does mean that you should avoid undue familiarity either afloat or ashore.

Enlisted men appreciate your consideration for their welfare and your interest in their interests, but they do not appreciate—or want—familiarity. They know that familiarity in manner tends to cause an officer to forfeit his status as an officer; they distrust an officer who talks as though he wants to "join the gang" one moment, and then shortly thereafter issues even a minor reprimand in his official capacity. Any such occurrences hurt the sensibilities of the junior who is reprimanded.

The necessity for reprimands is not frequent, but the same situation will hold when you must make even minor criticisms: their significance is clouded over by the personal element. In positions of command, "Familiarity breeds contempt."

DISSENSIONS

Be careful of dissensions! You will find that you can disagree in your mind completely, and furthermore, can express that disagreement in conversation with a group without "leaving the sea strewn with burning wrecks." It merely takes tact. But there are those who cannot disagree with any expressed opinion without seeming to launch a personal attack on the person who stated the opinion. A good rule to follow is, "Never talk about a senior unless you have something nice to say about him."

An effective way to disagree with an expressed conversational opinion is to make no return comment at all—or, to make a rather roundabout comment which tends to veer the conversation away from the offensive statement without being obvious about it.

When you feel it necessary, however, to go on record as disagreeing with something that has been said, you may do so in a number of polite ways. For example, you may say, with a pleasant smile, "I'm afraid that I do not agree with that," or, "I have given the matter considerable thought and have come to an entirely different conclusion." A light but disarming remark could be, "I'm from too far South to agree with such a Yankee idea." In brief, learn how to disagree without being disagreeable.

You may politely, but with firmness, express disagreement by obviously changing the subject. Since this maneuver is not in the best social taste, it should be reserved for situations which require drastic treatment—as when a person enters upon a tirade concerning a religious sect, and you know there is a member of that sect present. In such cases you are within the safest grounds of propriety to change the subject swiftly and decisively in order to avoid an unfortunate situation.

There may come a time, however, when a senior officer states an opinion which is radically against your own convictions. Unless some action on your part is imperatively called for, you naturally avoid comment, out of deference for your senior's greater age and experience. But if your senior then asks you to give an opinion, you may say "I have not entirely made up my mind, Sir," or "I'm not too well versed in that subject, Sir."

When the senior officer persists in an answer, you must state your honest opinion, or you will not be true to your own convictions and risk being labeled as a "yes man." With due respect, you may say "Sir, that is a matter of opinion, but my experience has been to the contrary."

IMPORTANCE OF REMEMBERING

Names are important to remember. You do not like your own name forgotten or mispronounced—so do not forget or fumble another's. Some people have excellent memories for names and faces, others must work at remembering. Most memory courses depend upon associating the name with an object, or repeating a name over and over in your mind after an introduction. If you miss the name on first being introduced, you can quite properly ask to have the name repeated.

When you cannot remember a person's name, and yet it is your duty to make the introduction to a conversational group, it is better to admit your lapse and say, "I'm sorry, but I will have to ask you your name." or "Please tell me your name again." The question should be asked with poise and no embarrassment.

In conversations, it is complimentary to remember another's personal concerns: a birthday or wedding anniversary, or an accomplishment by a member of the family. Any pleasant occurrence—an award, or the recent promotion in grade—that has happened to an individual, often serves to provide a background for conversation.

TABOOS

Controversial subjects—such as religion, race, creed, and frequently, politics—are to be strictly avoided. Unpleasant subjects are not discussed at social functions, and are treated carefully at any time. Examples of such topics to be shunned are death, disasters, accidents, battle losses, serious illness, etc.

Off-color stories and the subject of sex should never be discussed in mixed groups—and the discreet gentleman avoids them as topics at any time.

Never discuss a person's age in his or her presence. Elderly people do not enjoy being considered decrepit, neither do young people want to feel immature and inadequate. Both the very young and the very old are frequently sensitive about their ages.

EASY CONVERSATION

An essential part of your everyday living is the art of simple, easy conversation. A good conversationalist always has something interesting to talk about, is not overbearing in his attitude, and never irritates his listeners.

In general, plain words are preferable to ponderous phrases, and trite expressions are tiresome. The topics for conversations are endless: newspapers, books, magazines; television personalities and news analysts can always be discussed, and art, music, and concerts appeal to the artistic. Any sports event in season is of interest to most men.

A topic of conversation may be discussed as long as the listeners find it of interest, then new ones must be introduced. When you are talking, look at your listeners and observe their reactions. No monologue is of interest—except possibly to yourself. When you are the listener, pay attention to what is being said. It is extremely discourteous to openly show obvious disinterest—such as allowing your glance to wander off to other people or things.

A good conversationalist does not interrupt or contradict another. He learns to draw out the shy person by finding out his interests, then adroitly asks leading questions concerning that hobby or interest. When talking with a horticulturist, you could ask him about a rose spray; an author would be interested in a new book.

When you want to start a lively conversation, ask a question which presents a challenge: "I hear the Army is strong—who do you think will win the Army-Navy game?" or, "Would it be better to return to the Three R's than to continue with progressive education?"

When you desire a certain subject to be discussed without directly asking about it, you should bring up a related subject or experience that will open the door to the desired subject of conversation. For example, if you wish to hear a man who wears the Navy Cross talk about his experiences, you might pave the way by saying, "Captain, how many patrols did you make during World War II?"

In order to talk intelligently on a certain subject to a person of authority, it is well to brief yourself on that subject beforehand. In this way you can converse easily with the personage about his work or accomplishment and at the same time increase your own store of knowledge.

In your desire to make a good accounting of yourself, however, do not be so obvious in expressing your interest that you are considered "greasy."

It is an insult to your seniors, or to anyone else, to express more interest than common courtesy allows.

POISE AND GOOD MANNERS

When you talk, do you keep your hands and feet quiet, or do you gesture widely and shuffle your feet? Do you drum on a table with your fingers, or tap your feet on the floor? If you do—stop it. To shift from one foot to the other, when standing, makes you appear ill at ease and detracts not only from your appearance, but also from what you are saying. Finger or foot tapping draws attention to what you are *doing,* rather than what you are saying.

A good conversationalist is always a considerate one; he will reflect upon a new thought before blurting out a remark which may be regretted later. He is tolerant of other's ideas, and does not ridicule or laugh at an unfortunate remark, or tell an amusing story to the discredit of anyone.

Poise in conversation includes the ability to time a conversation—to know when to talk and when to be silent. Relaxation is an essential ingredient for a poised conversationalist; an incessant chatterer will soon exhaust his listeners.

Sometimes, without anyone intending it, two people start talking simultaneously. Such a situation generally happens when there has been a lull in a conversation and both persons attempt at once to relieve the situation. In such cases, if you are one of the two, you should give way amiably and quickly. To fail to do so makes you seem rude and domineering.

A skilled conversationalist can be compared to a ship's captain, he can steer thoughts and ideas into interesting conversational channels; but when necessary, he can also chart the course of an unfortunate subject away from the reefs to the safety of a harbor.

TONE OF VOICE

A well modulated voice is an asset to anyone. Words should be enunciated clearly, in a pleasant tone which is pitched neither too high nor too low. There are over eight tones in the average voice range, and with practice you can develop a tone best suited to your personality or to the occasion.

If you aren't aware of how your voice sounds to others, try speaking naturally or reading a news item into a recording machine; then play it back. Do your words run together? Do you bark them out? Are you too loud? The range of your voice is always important; speaking in a monotone makes any topic dull and monotonous.

With some effort on your part, you can control your voice by breathing from your diaphragm and developing a range in tone which will improve both your voice and your conversational appeal.

NAMES AND TITLES

Sometimes it's hard to know just what to call a person when he is very junior or senior to you. A senior officer and his wife may call a junior officer and his wife by their first names in an informal and friendly manner —but they are still "Captain and Mrs. Smith" to you, the junior officer, unless you are requested to call them by their first names.

Officially, senior rank is always observed when speaking with or referring to an officer, regardless of how well you know him. Socially, close friends call each other by their first names regardless of age or rank.

You do not call a woman by her first name until she takes the initiative, such as calling you by your first name or asking that you call her by hers. Then, you are free to use her first name.

You do not refer to a man or woman of your own background as a "gentleman" or "lady" unless they are elderly. You would say, "He is a fine man" or "She is a good woman." It is patronizing to say, "My dear John!"

ASKING FOR FIRST DATES

Although the majority of young men attending the Service Academies are experienced in asking girls for dates, there are some who have had little time or inclination to date before entering the Academies.

Upon first meeting a girl, a rather shy young man usually "talks around" the problem of asking her to drag for the first time. If you are that young man you might say something like, "Do you like sports?" If she replies in the affirmative, you might mention the Army-Navy game or any specific occasion when you can drag. She will usually give you some kind of a lead indicating whether or not she has been asked to the occasion, and in her manner or answer will be a clue to tell you whether or not she would like you to ask her.

If she seems favorably interested, then you can say, "How would you like to meet me after the game and go on to the Brigade Cotillion?"—or to the movies, or whatever the occasion might be. In the case of a Plebe, you would ask the girl to meet you at the place or occasion limited to your rare opportunities of meeting young ladies.

Some young men are afraid that a girl will turn them down, thus hesitate to ask for a date. In turn, the girl may be afraid to seem over-eager when you show interest, and what appears to be coolness on her part may be a bit of stage fright. So *ask*.

If a girl, however, refuses you twice, then you should hesitate to continue the pursuit. But do learn to take an occasional refusal with poise—she may have a very sound reason why she cannot accept your invitation.

RULES TO REMEMBER

Do:

- Have something to say—and say it well. Brief amusing stories, a news item, unusual incidents, a TV personality—all are conversation starters.
- Be a good listener.
- Develop the art of small talk; this is pleasant talk about nothing in particular, but does *not* include official or harmful subjects.
- Learn to remember names and faces; nothing will make you more popular.
- Put a shy person at his ease by getting him to talk about his hobbies, pets, children, or known interests.
- Put yourself at ease—by thinking of the *other* person.
- As a host, act as moderator and intervene in a monologue, a "dead" group, or a controversial discussion, by changing the subject.
- Talk in a moderate tone of voice.
- Keep your eyes and ears open—and, occasionally, your mouth *shut.*

Do not:

- Gossip. Say nothing about a person that you would not want him to hear.
- Talk business at a social gathering.
- Substitute sarcasm or ridicule for wit.
- Interrupt or contradict others.
- Monopolize any conversation.
- Talk over anyone's head, or "talk down" to anyone.
- Be "greasy"; insincere flattery is unwelcomed.
- Talk endlessly; silence, at times, *is* golden.
- Allow a guest to be stranded with a conversational bore.
- "Clam up"; a shy guest is a burden to a host, who thereupon must force conversation.
- Exclude anyone from a conversational group.
- Use effeminate expressions such as *"perfectly darling,"* or *"so sorry."*
- Give the state of your health when someone says, "How are you?" This is simply a polite expression, generally used in greetings or "small talk."

CHAPTER 21

Good Manners Before an Audience

Any officer in the Services must be able to speak effectively in any situation. At the Naval Academy, the need for public speaking is considered so important that Midshipmen receive formal classroom instruction in speech, and after-dinner speaking is required of the First Class. In this course, small formal dinners are held at the Academy, with each First Classman delivering a certain number of brief speeches during the year. The dinners are complete with toastmaster, guest of honor, and an instructor who gives helpful criticism. The dinners are prepared under conditions approximating those which can be expected later.

A third method of helping the Midshipmen converse and speak effectively is their participation in such extra-curricular activities as the Forensic Activity, Foreign Relations Club, the Masqueraders, and the Political Economy Club.

After graduation from the Academies, or Officer Candidate Schools, an officer will find that one of the most important aptitudes which he can possess is skill in addressing a group. From the very beginning of his career, he will find himself called upon to address a division aboard ship—or a company ashore—to enter into general meetings in the wardroom or mess—and to discuss professional matters before groups of other officers at critiques, etc.

Later on he will find himself drawn into the public life of his community. He will be called upon to deliver speeches upon patriotic occasions, to present proposals in public meetings, and to be an active member of service clubs and civic organizations.

Preparedness for such a role is one of the responsibilities which you will assume as a man in public life, where the general public expects experienced leadership from officers in the Services. The responsibility for group leadership may not be something that you desire—but it may be something that you must assume.

When you are asked to be president of a PTA or chairman of Service Night at Rotary, you cannot plead inability to speak in public, or ignorance of parliamentary procedure. The public knows better. They know that you had the opportunity to learn these things, and they expect to find you, if not an expert, at least well grounded in the fundamentals. The best grounding that any officer can have is a clear understanding of the proprieties of public speaking, and the forms of courtesy to be followed when addressing a group.

The purpose of this chapter is not to lay down rules for public speaking except where they fall under the heading of good manners before an audience.

APPEARANCE

The *appearance* of the speaker is the first thing an audience notes; then his *mannerisms,* and next his *voice.* A speaker in uniform should be at his best—his uniform immaculate, his posture perfection. A man in civilian dress should be conservatively dressed, his tie in order, suit pressed, and hands out of pockets. A speaker should not stand or sit ramrod-stiff; neither should his hands or feet be in constant motion.

An audience expects the speaker to recognize and address properly the leader or chairman of the meeting. It also expects him to use correct forms of address when speaking to the group as a whole, or to an individual member. A speaker can be as polite—or as impolite—to a group of people as he can be to a single person.

PERSONAL CONDUCT IN SPEAKING

You should always avoid "talking down" to a group, or "over their heads." It is insulting to an audience to address them as though you are the only one who knows anything about a given subject—even when you are an expert in that particular field. You should avoid the over-use of the first person pronoun: "*I* think—," "*I* know—," or "*I* did—." Simplicity and ease of speech are as important as your subject matter.

Your yardstick in speaking (or writing) is: Can people understand what I mean? A familiar word is better than a "show off" word or phrase; a short word is preferable to a long one.

No audience likes to hear a speaker apologize for himself or for what he has to say. Any apology puts the speaker on the defensive. Apologetic and self-conscious gestures such as clearing the throat, jutting the chin up and down, straightening a tie, rebuttoning your coat, shifting from one foot to another—all such gestures make an audience as uneasy as the speaker.

Although most words spoken in private conversation are just words, some of these same words may set up a chain reaction against you when used in a speech or before an audience. Experience will teach you what these words and expressions are—either yours or another's—and they should be mentally catalogued "fighting words" and not used again.

From various viewpoints, such *fighting words* could be: "We of the intelligentsia—," or, "You military dictators—," or, "You civilians couldn't understand our Service."

To the listener, such words and expressions indicate a disregard for his personal feeling—regardless of whether he is merely one of hundreds in the audience and has never seen you before. The listener may merely consider you high-handed for some expression—but you will still be unpopular. A joke which seemed so amusing to one may seem like ridicule to another—if the shoe fits, so to say.

You should be respectful of others' opinions at a meeting, and should attempt to look at various viewpoints from all sides before making up your own mind on a subject. You must always be fair—but firm.

Always give credit whenever credit is due, but be careful of the timing in expressing a compliment made in public. An ill-timed compliment may embarrass the recipient as well as give an impression of "fawning" upon him.

THE FUNNY STORY

A brief amusing story of reminiscence, a good joke, or a good quotation are all ice-breakers at the opening of a meeting. Such stories must be *good,* however, or the speaker will lose his audience and will have to try harder than ever to win them over.

The first rule in telling a story is that it must be amusing to you, the speaker, or you cannot expect it to be funny to your audience—unless you presume them to be of lower intelligence than yourself. In this case, you have played down to your audience.

The second rule is that a joke sparkles best in brevity.

You must, of course, be fully aware of the type of audience you will address when speaking before a club or organization: large or small, mixed or stag, rural or cosmopolitan. You should take into careful consideration the racial, religious, political, and age groups involved. The type of club or organization will determine the tone of your talk, and you must make certain that your material is in keeping with the spirit of the occasion.

An off-color story is a dangerous story to tell before an audience at any time. Such a story told in a locker room or in a foursome may seem to be hilarious to those few—but when the same story is brought out at a public or private gathering, particularly before a mixed group, the one telling the story may be marked as a crude, vulgar, or uncouth oaf.

Lastly, at no time and place must you ever allow your sense of humor to desert you. A good sense of humor will protect you from the barbs of others—intentional or otherwise—and you will also be protected from becoming "too full of yourself."

CONDUCT AT MEETINGS

In effect, public speaking is based upon one's ability to treat courteously the group at hand. Your first problem is to "get over" to the group. A speaker, as he rises, must ingratiate himself with his listeners by his manner, his appearance, a smile—himself. It is a general axiom in public speaking that your first and most important objective is to create in your audience a favorable impression of yourself before attempting to deliver your message. The impression which you leave with an audience is almost as important as the message which you have delivered.

Dale Carnegie recognizes the relative importance of this relationship of a speaker to his message in the title of his book on public speaking: *How to Win Friends and Influence People.* You will note that "friendship" ranks ahead of "influence."

When you attend a meeting you usually are:

- A member of the group, or of the audience
- Making a report, or delivering an address
- Chairman of the group, or presiding officer.

When you attend a meeting, you may do little more than listen attentively, form an opinion, and vote when called upon. When the occasion arises, you may wish to address the Chair and be recognized so that you may present an opinion or petition, or make a nomination.

You *obtain the floor* by rising after the floor has been yielded, and you courteously address the Chair by saying, "Mr. Chairman," or "Madam Chairman," not by saying, "Mr. Jones," or "Mrs. Jones." There are various forms of address, including "Mr. President," or "Mr. Moderator," or at Service conferences where you address the senior officer present; for example, "Admiral—."

After addressing the chairman in a voice sufficiently loud to be heard, you await recognition by the Chair. If a person continues to proceed in a discussion without recognition, thereby disrupting the meeting with improper procedure, he may be ejected from the meeting.

You usually will find yourself recognized by the Chair (presiding officer), who may call you by name or address you by a formal title such as "Mr. Member," or "The gentleman in the rear of the room." At very large meetings, such as conventions, the member will probably be called upon to identify himself by giving his name and the organization which he represents. In this situation the chairman makes recognition of a member by a more formal method, such as "The gentleman from Indiana."

To insure your courteous conduct in requesting recognition from the Chair, you must always bear in mind that control of the meeting is vested in its chairman, and it is his prerogative to refuse recognition when he considers the member or the motion out of order. If the meeting is to be properly conducted, each member will be recognized in his turn, and the individual and collective welfare is best served by patience and recognition of the importance of proper procedure on the part of each member.

Having been recognized, the member should address the chairman and say clearly and distinctly: "I move that—" or "I nominate—" etc. It is not in good form to say, "Shouldn't we do so and so—." Improper introduction of a motion is not a serious breach of etiquette, but it does detract from your major objective of getting across what you need to—and it shows up your poor manners.

It is in good order to preface a motion or nomination by a few introductory remarks, but it is wholly out of order to launch into a full discussion of the motion prior to its being placed before the assembly by the chairman for discussion. The rights of a member do not extend beyond introduction of a motion. The Chair will ask for a second to the motion, and if there is none, the motion is not in order.

It is always best to formulate your ideas clearly and have them in mind before you attempt to state them. It is tiresome as well as confusing to give a lot of background information not pertinent to the subject.

MOTIONS

The business of an assembly or organization is brought before it by the motion or resolution of a member, or by the presentation of a communication. A *motion* is a proposal that the assembly or organization take certain action; a *resolution*—which should be in writing—is a more important or lengthy main motion. Customarily, motions begin with the words "I move that—" and resolutions begin with the words *"Resolved,* That—."

Before any subject is open for discussion, *a motion must be:*

1. Made by a member who has obtained the floor
2. Seconded (with a few exceptions)
3. Stated by the Chair.

As a general rule, every motion should be seconded. The Chair should immediately ask, "Is the motion seconded?" A member should say, "I second the motion," or "I second it." At a small meeting the member seconding the motion need not rise; in large assemblies, he should rise, and without recognition from the Chair, say, "Mr. Chairman, I second the motion."

Certain motions are not seconded, including (a) questions of order (pertaining to the way the business is being handled); (b) objection to the consideration of a question; (c) leave to withdraw a motion; (d) inquiries of any kind; and (e) nominations. However, there are many types of business—usually unimportant and noncontroversial business—where the formality of a motion is not needed to carry it out.

There are many types of motions, including *privileged motions,* which are of such importance as to require them to take precedence of all other questions. Such motions are undebatable and include, in the order of precedence, such questions as:

1. Fix the time to adjourn
2. Adjourn (if not for the effect to dissolve the assembly)
3. Take a recess (if made when another question is pending)
4. Raise a question of privilege
5. Call for orders of the day (a demand that the assembly conform to its program or order of business).

Next in importance are *incidental motions,* which are:

1. Points of order and appeals
2. Objection to consideration
3. The reading of papers
4. Withdrawal of motions
5. Division of a question
6. Request for information
7. Suspension of rules.

Subsidiary motions are those applied to other motions for the purpose of more appropriately disposing of them. An original motion may be modified, or action postponed, or it may be referred to a committee for investigation. Such motions must be decided before the main motion can be acted upon.

Subsidiary motions, in the order of precedence, are:

1. Lay on the table (undebatable)
2. The previous question
3. Limit or extend limits of debate
4. Postpone definitely, or to a definite time
5. Commit or refer
6. Amend
7. Postpone indefinitely.

To *lay on the table* means a motion to delay action on a question until a more suitable time during the same or the next meeting, or at a future time.

If a motion to lay on the table has been made and lost, it shows that the assembly wants to consider the question *now.* The value of such a motion is that the assembly may attend to more urgent business; the danger of the motion is that a member, or members, may wish to suppress action on the question by avoiding an immediate vote.

The form in making such a motion is: "I move to lay the question on the table," or " I move that the question be laid on the table." Such an action is in order when a motion is pending and no one has the floor, but after the introducer of the original motion has had an opportunity to claim the floor and debate the question.

A request to *withdraw a motion* may be made by the introducer at any time *before* voting on the question has started. Such a request may be made even after an amendment has been made to the motion. It does not need a second.

When the introducer requests permission to *modify* the motion (or to withdraw it), the Chair will ask if there is any objection, and, if there is none, the Chair will announce the result. If someone should object, the Chair puts the question on granting the request to the assembly or a motion may be made to grant the request.

STATE THE QUESTION

When a motion has been introduced and seconded, it is the duty of the presiding officer to state the question (the motion) to the assembly so that it is thoroughly understood. During this restatement of the motion, the Chair should give careful attention to the introducer of the motion to insure that his own restatement is accurate.

A general discussion by the members starts immediately after the restatement of the motion by the Chair, and the various members address the Chair to obtain the floor and proceed with their remarks. Once the floor is given to a member, the Chair permits the speaker a reasonable length of time to talk and should avoid interruptions whenever possible.

When the chairman feels that a member is imposing on the group and is demanding too much time, he must call time on that speaker. The chairman must always be able to sift out discussions and motions that are not pertinent to the subject, and permit only a limited amount of time for discussion of any question.

When a member wants to be heard on the subject, he will rise to his feet or raise his hand and request to be recognized by the Chair. But when another member has the floor, you should never interrupt his speech with a request to be heard, and you never indicate restlessness or attempt to "gag" another speaker in order that you may be heard. The floor belongs to the speaker until this privilege is terminated by the Chair.

When you have been recognized by the Chair, however, you should remember the virtue of brevity. In using ten minutes of the time of a large group—say, of 60 persons—you have used up the equivalent of ten hours of discussion time. Upon completing your remarks, *sit down.* You have no right to jump up again—even if you have a gem of an afterthought—without further recognition by the Chair.

The Chair will close the discussion by some remark such as, "Is there any further discussion?" This is a signal that it is time to end the discussion. When the debate appears to have closed, the Chair asks again, "Are you ready for the question?" Since silence indicates the assembly is ready to vote, the Chair proceeds to *put the question* (take the vote), first calling for the affirmative and then for the negative vote. The result of the vote is *always* announced by the Chair.

If the question has not been stated recently, or if the question is on the adoption of a resolution, or a lengthy motion, *the motion should be read again before asking for the vote.*

When the vote is called for, members customarily say *"aye"* or *"no."* Shouting, cheering, or "cat-calling" to influence the vote and discredit the speaker is in the worst possible form.

Although the usual method of taking a vote is *viva voce* (by the voice), when the result of the vote is in doubt the Chair will have the vote taken by "raising the right hand" or, by rising. He cannot, however, have the voting taken by ballot or roll call unless so authorized by the rules of the assembly, or by a vote of the assembly.

The forms usually followed when calling for a vote are:

- "Those in favor of the motion say *aye*"; (then, after the ayes have responded), "those opposed say *no*. The ayes have it, and the motion is adopted." Or, "The no's have it, and the motion is lost."
- "As many as are in favor of agreeing to the resolution will rise." (The count is then taken.) "Be seated; those opposed will rise." (The count is again taken.) "The affirmative has it and the resolution is adopted (or carried)," etc.
- "It has been moved and seconded that an invitation be extended to Captain Jones to address our section at its next meeting. Those in favor of the motion will raise the right hand." (Count.) "Those opposed will signify it in the same way." (Count) "The affirmative has it (or, "The motion is carried") etc.

A majority vote (a quorum present) is sufficient for the adoption of any motion that is in order. Other motions may require a two-thirds majority, including such motions as suspending the rules, or the amendment (or annulment, repeal, or the rescinding) of any part of the Constitution, By-laws, or Rules of Order previously adopted by the assembly.

The *Rules of Order* are the general rules by which the assembly is run. A call for the *Order of the Day* (or "Point of Order") means a demand that the assembly keep to its program or order of business. Such a call can be made at any time when no other privileged motion is pending, and when the correct order of business is being changed—but only then. It needs no second.

However, when the Chair follows the business to come before the assembly in its proper order, there will be no occasion for such a calling for order.

When you, yourself, are the chairman, you must have a good understanding of the rules of order. Any chairman should have a copy of *Robert's Rules of Order, Revised.* This book on parliamentary procedure, incidentally, was written by a West Pointer, a general in the Army.

Tact and forbearance are important attributes for a chairman to acquire. There are situations that require diplomacy to handle: when the subject is controversial; when a member is out of order or vague in stating issues; when motions must be re-stated. A good chairman is not a dictator, but he is nevertheless charged with the progress of the meeting.

A chairman must sense when a motion is presented merely as a delaying tactic, introduced to annoy or delay the Chair or the assembly. And he *always* must be in control of the situation, be impartial, be fair—and know the rules of procedure.

In electing officers of an organization, the nominating committee usually consists of five members, but a small group may have only three. No vote is taken on accepting a nominating committee's report. Other nominations may always be made from the floor, however, and these are then added to those submitted by the nominating committee.

ORDER OF BUSINESS

Any presiding officer should have a well planned agenda in order to control his meeting. The following *order of business* may be adapted to fit almost any type meeting:

1. Reading of minutes and approval of same.
2. Treasurer's report.
3. Report of Boards and Standing Committees.
4. Reports of Special Committees.
5. Unfinished business.
6. New business.
7. Program.
8. Announcements.
9. Adjourn (a motion to adjourn, if the meeting is a business session, with no program).

RÉSUMÉ OF PARLIAMENTARY PROCEDURE

For The Presiding Officer:

- Open the meeting, *on time*.
- Ask for the roll call, if any, and the reading of the minutes separately.

- Say, "You will please listen to the reading of the minutes of the last meeting."
- Upon publication, sign the minutes beneath the signature of the secretary, and thus share responsibility for the accuracy of the record.
- Call for *narrative* reports by groups: officers, standing committees, and special committees, etc. Narrative reports are those which detail the work; those containing recommendations are put to the vote.
- A financial report should be audited before it is adopted by vote— frequently at the close of an organization's yearly meetings.
- Speak of yourself as "The Chair" or "Your President"—and not as "I."
- *Stand* to introduce business, but *sit down* during its transaction.
- Say "The Chair will entertain a motion," not "Do I hear a motion?"
- Say, "Is there a second to the motion?" or "Is it seconded?" Ask only once. If there is no reponse, you should announce: "The motion is lost for want of a second."
- The acceptance of an amendment must come *voluntarily* from the one who made the original motion. The Chair should not ask the member who made the motion to accept the amendment.
- When a business meeting is concluded with a program and a social hours, it adjourns automatically. Before adjourning a business meeting the Chair should ask if there is any further business to come before the assembly.
- Say that "Captain Jones *will take charge* of the program," not, "We will now turn the program over to Captain Jones."
- At large meetings, the officers may sit together behind a table facing the assembly, with the Vice President to the right of the President, the Secretary to the left of the President, and the Treasurer to the left of the Secretary.
- Call the Vice President to the Chair when making your reports, either as President or as Chairman of the Executive Board. The President's report should be considered *last* under the group of officer's reports, and the Board report last under the category of Standing Committees.
- The President has no right to appoint a member to preside in his place. In the absence of the Vice President, or Vice Presidents, the Recording Secretary should call the meeting to order, and conduct the election of a Chairman pro tem, and then resume his station.
- Only *two* amendments can be pending at the same time to a motion.

Any number, however, may be offered, as long as previous amendments have first been disposed of by vote. All amendments to a motion must be voted on before the main motion itself is put to vote. For instance, you put the second amendment to vote first, then the first amendment as amended, and lastly the motion as amended. You declare the final result by saying "The *ayes* have it, and the motion, as amended, is carried," or, "The *no's* have it, and the motion, as amended, is lost."

- You *reconsider* a vote, but you *rescind* an action.

For the Recording Secretary:

- When the Chair says, "You will please listen to the reading of the minutes of the last meeting," the Recording Secretary rises and reads the minutes.
- The Secretary signs the minutes with his given name, and omits the words, "Respectfully submitted."
- The Secretary sits by the side of the President in order to quietly confer with him without disturbing the members. He keeps two minute books—one for Executive Board meetings which is read *only* in Board meetings, and one for the meetings of the organization itself.
- The minutes are corrected informally, with the Chair directing the Secretary to make the necessary corrections. When there is a difference of opinion as to the proper correction of the item recorded, a vote is required to settle the question.
- When an error is noted in the minutes, it may be corrected informally, with the Chair assuming the unanimous consent of the assembly. Minutes may be corrected regardless of the time elapsed.
- All members have access to the minute book if they desire, but this must be done in the presence of the Secretary.
- Record in substance enough of the reports to be explanatory, but do not go into descriptions. Minutes are the record of business transacted, and nothing else.
- A unanimous vote is required for the Secretary to cast the unanimous vote of the assembly.
- The Secretary reminds the President of *unfinished* business (not of old business).
- Place the words "Minutes Approved," with the date of approval, at the end of each set of minutes. If the minutes have been corrected, place the words "Approved as corrected," and the date, at the end.

GENERAL PROCEDURE AT MEETINGS

For Members:

- Always answer *"present"* to a roll call; do not say "Here."
- Say "I move that," not "I make a motion."
- Say "Mr. President" (or "Madam President"), "I second the motion," without rising and without awaiting recognition.
- Before you, a member, can present a motion you must obtain the floor by addressing the Chair and must wait for recognition.
- Address the Vice President, or any member who temporarily takes the Chair, as "Mr. Chairman" or "Madam Chairman."
- Read a report straight through. When explanations are necessary, give them briefly *at the close of your formal report*.
- If a report is a narrative report giving the simple details of your work, just hand it to the Chair. No vote is necessary; you do not have to move its adoption. It will be placed on file as information. *If*, however, the report contains a recommendation, you will, immediately after the reading, move that the report be adopted. Sign your report with your given name.
- Wait until the Chair states a motion before addressing the Chair.
- In an election, neither nominations by a committee nor nominations from the floor require a second or an adoption by vote. Nominations are *never* seconded except as an endorsement of candidates not known to the assembly.
- A motion may be made to close nominations, but this motion is not in order until the assembly has been given sufficient time to add further nominations to those already made.
- Calls of "Question! Question!" are disorderly. They should not be recognized by the Chairman.
- Do not say "secret ballot"—"ballot" means secret.

SECTION VII

ON YOUR OWN

CHAPTER 22

Places of Entertainment

MOVIES AND THEATERS

Without taking a poll, it is safe to say that just about everybody has attended a movie. Yet, in general, there is a lack of common everyday courtesy among many movie-goers—including the peanut and popcorn eater, the paper rattler, the loud whisperer, and the big hat wearer. There is always the person who passes back and forth in front of you; then there is the character who lolls in his seat and overflows on the arms of your seat.

Your manners at a movie or theater ought to be the same whether you go alone, in a group, or escort a woman of any age. Common courtesy should be observed at all times.

A man of any age escorting a woman should take her past the first doors into the lobby where she may wait while you buy the tickets. If the line is long and the weather pleasant, she may prefer to stand outside in line and talk with you.

After you have bought your tickets and have given them to the doorman, you take off your overcoat, when wearing one, in the lobby. Your guest may also take off her coat, but women usually prefer to leave their coats on until after they sit down, when they lay them back over their chair backs.

Before going down the aisle, you should ask your guest where she would like to sit—in front, near the center, etc.—then you will tell the usher so that he can seat you accordingly. She will follow the usher to the seats, ahead of you, and enter the row first.

When there is no usher, or when he is busy elsewhere, you may walk *ahead* of your guest and look for suitable seats. After you have found them, you should step aside and allow your companion to precede you into the row. You should take the aisle seat, so that when you need to go after something you will not have to step in front of your guest. Also, if any question should arise, you will be in a better position to discuss it with the usher.

You always want to be certain that your guest is comfortable, and that she can see the screen or stage. When a hat worn by a woman sitting in front of you blocks your visibility, it is your responsibility to ask the person to please remove her hat—but this must be done with courtesy. When those

243

around you are talking so loudly that you cannot hear well, then you must quietly speak to those persons. If anyone will not comply after a polite request, you may ask the usher to take care of the situation.

However, in looking after the comfort of your guest, you must remember that there are others to consider, and any inquiries concerning her welfare must be made quietly in order that you also are not being a nuisance.

On your way to your seats, particularly if these are in the center of a section, you must be careful of the people you are passing. You should pass facing the screen, as quickly as possible, and you may say "Excuse me" or "Thank you" in a low tone. Watch out for the coat you are carrying, for it often sweeps the heads of people in the row in front of you. And, needless to add, you should be careful not to step on anyone's toes. The persons already seated usually draw their feet well under their chairs and out of harm's way.

Once you are in your seats, you should assist your guest with her coat, and will manage to do this without blocking the view of those seated behind you. The best place for your own coat and hat is in your lap, or your coat may be placed over the back of your seat and your hat balanced on your knees or placed in the rack under your seat, when such is provided.

There is little reason for conversation at the movies or theater, but if you *must* talk, then by all means whisper softly. If you are also one who cannot get through a movie without a little snack (which is banned at many movies as well as theaters), then get something that doesn't crackle when the wrapper is removed or when you are eating it.

Fortunately, smoking is forbidden in most American theaters; however, in some European theaters, particularly in London, it is permissible to smoke during the performance and most seats have ashtrays built into their backs.

Although a darkened movie or theater may have romantic music and a sentimental plot in the picture or play, and the over-all feeling is one of accelerated emotion, do not engage in demonstrations of affection. If for no other reason, remember that you paid good money to *see* the show—not *give* it.

After the movie is over, you precede your guest to the aisle, where she will walk ahead of you to the lobby. Do not assist her with her coat until you reach the lobby; there you can also put on your own coat as well.

When you attend a movie in a large group, or when you are the host to such a group, you will tell the usher how many seats you need and ask if it is possible to get them together. You will precede your guests to the seats, following the usher, and see that guests will be seated in mixed order. When you are host, you do not permit anyone else to help pay for the tickets; when you are guest, you do not insist on paying, or helping pay for them.

If the group decided to attend the movie on the spur of the moment, then couples will go "Dutch treat," with the men paying for their drags or guests.

When a lady gives the movie or theater party and asks you to buy the tickets (usually in advance) and gives you the money for the tickets, you should *not* offer to pay or feel any hesitancy in taking the money.

At the regular theater, you are expected to be on time, with curtain time usually 8:30 P.M. for an evening performance. You may check your hat and coat for a quarter, or you may place them in racks under your seat. But a bulky overcoat is always a problem, and checking it is convenient—unless you are in a hurry after the performance. You may buy a program before taking your seats, but this is not necessary, since the theater management issues a plain but sufficient program. If you want a more detailed program, one is enough for two or more persons.

There are always ushers at theaters, and you should wait for an usher to show you to your seats, with your guest preceding you. During intermission, you may want to go to the lobby for a smoke. If your guest does not care to join you, you may excuse yourself and go ahead. If she cares for a smoke and you don't, you accompany her to the lobby and wait for her.

When the lights in the lobby are dimmed, or when a bell rings, the management is signaling that the next act is about to begin and you must return to your seats immediately. Don't linger over the last drag on your cigarette, and then be forced to stumble over someone's feet in a darkened theater.

If for some very good reason you are late at curtain time, you should stand in the back of the theater until the first intermission.

After a particularly well-enacted scene, you may want to applaud the actor—but if your timing is wrong, this can destroy the effect that the actors are trying to achieve. You remain in your seat until the curtain has been lowered for the last time, then you leave.

OPERAS AND CONCERTS

Operas and concerts are other forms of entertainment that you will encounter through the years. If you are a music lover, you will attend such entertainments at an early age. Frequently, you will be invited to attend either function as a guest. Although the opera once was a full dress affair, you will see a few men in "white tie" and some in "black tie"—and quite a few males in dark business suits. Your hostess will indicate what you should wear; otherwise you should ask her.

If your hostess is a patron of the arts, she may have a box. Each box contains chairs which are arranged in pairs from the front of the box—where the most desirable seats are—to the rear. It is customary for the hostess to sit in the first row, on the chair farthest from the stage, with the ranking woman guest seated by the hostess in the seat closest to the stage. The ranking man will be seated directly behind the hostess, with the host seated behind the ranking woman. Unless your hostess especially assigns you a seat, you should take the rear seat farthest from the stage.

At concerts, the conductor of a symphony orchestra will turn around and face the audience at the end of a number—and you should not begin applauding until he does so. At a piano recital, you do not applaud between the movements of a sonata, or a similar piece of work, even though the pianist momentarily stops playing.

If you should have the misfortune to develop a coughing or sneezing fit, you should leave the room or auditorium, since any noise is disturbing to an artist.

Intermissions are plainly marked on the program, and this is the only time that you should leave the auditorium, other than for necessity.

Encore numbers are played or sung after the artist has received a number of curtain calls, or after much applause. He will indicate that there will be an encore, and this cue stops further applause.

If the music at an opera or concert is too classical for your uneducated ear, never fidget or show signs of boredom. Most of the other people there will be enjoying the music, and you should not interfere with their enjoyment.

PRIVATE CLUBS

Private clubs, in one form or another, exist all over the country. The types most familiar are the country clubs, the fraternities and sororities at colleges and universities, and the officers' clubs at military installations.

Civic organizations and service clubs, such as Rotary, the Chamber of Commerce, and the Military Order of World Wars have large memberships, and their goal is civic improvement and national and international good will.

Most young men have belonged to a club of some type in high school or preparatory school, where membership was based upon similar tastes and qualifications. Such clubs may have been the 4-H Clubs, Greek letter fraternities, DeMolay, Boy Scouts, athletic organizations, square dancing groups—and many more. The principles of working together are first learned at such clubs, then in colleges and universities where the activities are more advanced but where the principles of working together are the same.

A country club is more of a luxury club than other type clubs. There is usually a club house, golf course, swimming pool, tennis courts, etc. The membership is by invitation, and there probably will be a large initiation fee and sizable monthly club dues.

When you are invited to be a guest at such a club, you should look upon the invitation in somewhat the same manner as being asked into a home. You will take part in the current activities (customarily, there is a Saturday night dinner dance). On the golf course, you are not expected to pay for anything other than your caddy fee although if you are invited by the same member more than once, you should offer to pay your green's fee. And it is always a mark of politeness to offer to pay your host's caddy fee as well as your own.

Most country clubs have the chit system of signing for services—food, drink, cigarettes, etc.—so that a guest cannot pay for anything. If you are a frequent guest, however, you should suggest some arrangement with your host for sharing expenses; and if he refuses—which he probably will—you should try to repay his hospitality in some way of your own.

The country club may be a very large one, but large or small, you must not take liberties. You should not be careless with cigarette ashes and sprinkle them on the floor, and you do not shove furniture around or roll back the rug when you want to dance. If you must clear a space, you should ask your host or the club manager first; there usually are club rules to this effect.

As a guest, you must remember that your host has accepted the responsibility of introducing you into his club and to his friends, and you naturally do not want to turn this responsibility into a liability. In brief, do not embarrass your host. You will not barge up to a good looking young lady and introduce yourself and say you are Bill Jones' guest—because Bill Jones may not know her either! And if he does know her, he will make the proper introduction—just as he would at home.

Sometimes, when you are stationed in an area where friends of your family or friends of your own are members of a private club, you may be given a guest card for a limited time. The card will be given to you by your friend, or it may be mailed to you by the club. This card must be handled with discretion.

A guest card means that you enjoy the privileges of the club, and that you pay for these privileges—such as food, drinks, and any small fee that accompany the use of the swimming pool or golf course. Sometimes these fees are printed on the card, but, if not, you should inquire at the club's business office concerning such fees. You should realize that there is usually a moderate charge to the member for each guest card which he requests.

When you accept the guest membership, you take the card to the office, where your name is placed on the guest list. You will leave your address where bills are to be sent, and, upon your receiving the bill, you must pay it *immediately*. When you do not pay, your bill is placed on the account of your sponsor—and you may lose a friend. Guest cards do not give you the right to nominate *anyone else* for guest cards in the club. Customarily, a guest card does not give you the privilege of taking guests to the club for meals, etc.

Many private clubs in metropolitan areas have restricted memberships. Some of these clubs have rooms where members live, or rooms where out-of-town members may stay briefly. The atmosphere of such clubs is more home-like than at a country club, and there will be fewer members.

Private clubs are usually located in the city proper, and generally have rooms for entertaining. There will be a dining room, a library, lounge, and bar, besides bedrooms. Members of these clubs are usually friends of long standing. As a guest, your behavior must be circumspect.

The problem of money is the same here as at the country club—you cannot pay for privileges. If you are given guest privileges for a limited period of time, you are charged with these privileges as at the country club. Although the private town club is more intimate, you yourself must not presume to intimacy with the members.

Many older members of private clubs have many little privileges: certain chairs in certain parts of a room may be "theirs." A table by a window at one side of the dining room may always be occupied by a certain man or group at a given hour. It is well to respect such desires of austere members.

Before or just after leaving a tour of duty, you should write notes of appreciation to all clubs, officials, and individuals that have shown you special courtesies. Such a note should be written to the president of the club.

Most private clubs—including country clubs—do not permit tipping. However, the locker room attendant at the country club may be tipped when he has done some special service for you. You may ask your host what is the usual tip for such services in his club.

COLLEGE FRATERNITIES AND SORORITIES

Men's social fraternities and women's sororities will have their own houses on or near the campus of colleges and universities throughout the country. Anywhere from 40 to 100 members make these houses their homes during the academic year, and a housemother is assigned to each.

Membership is by invitation, and the houses are governed by strict rules of manners and conduct. Infractions of rules cause the members to be fined, and a serious infraction may result in the failure of a candidate to be accepted or the expulsion of one who is already a member.

As a guest, you must observe the fraternity's house rules—particularly those concerning drinking and gambling. At most colleges and universities, drinking and gambling may have as heavy a penalty as at a Service Academy.

A national social fraternity is a closed organization, with private weekly meetings, and a guest should not ask questions concerning these meetings. Any questions concerning the history or membership of a fraternity are in order, but not its business.

Lastly, a guest should endeavor to follow any custom of the fraternity or sorority such as singing the fraternity song at the table, and standing while singing it.

At a sorority house, the housemother is more in evidence than at a fraternity house and respect is always shown her. As with "drag houses" in Annapolis, you are not allowed above the first floor in a sorority house. Most sororities have a curfew, also, and you must be careful to get your date back to her house on time. You will not be permitted to stay on at the house after curfew, so don't try. As a rule, most sorority houses do not have male guests for casual meals, but you will probably be invited for more formal dinners.

Although the interest in fraternities and sororities is mainly confined to college days, many national alumni chapters are formed in cities throughout the nation, with active membership participation.

OFFICERS' CLUBS

Officers' clubs will become the most familiar type of club life which you will experience in your own professional life. Most major stations and posts both in the United States and overseas, have an officers' club to which you will automatically be extended the privilege of joining. Some of these clubs have monthly dues and others do not, but every officer should join the club of his station and give it wholehearted support.

The majority of these clubs are located on the station or post proper, and have a dining room, several lounges, and a bar. Each club has its own house rules, and you should be quick to discover what they are. You should always take pride in your club, and treat it with the same respect and thoughtfulness that you would your own home.

Some clubs use the chit system, whereby all services must be paid for with chits from a coupon book that you buy from the office. Others are on a cash basis only, and still others have members sign their orders on chits provided for that purpose. When the club is on the latter system, you will be billed at the end of the month, and, as with all other bills, you should pay your club bill promptly. If you do not—and the last date for payment is usually made known to you by the house rules—you may be placed in the unfortunate position of having your name posted in some prominent place as a delinquent member.

As a member, you may have as many guests as you wish—but a young officer must remember that on the chit system the bill is *yours*. If you are with a group whose male members are not in the Service, you may settle the bill between yourselves later—but do not do this in front of women guests.

Your conduct in any officers' club must be beyond reproach. There may be many senior officers present, who, though, not in your party, may be visiting the club, and loud, boisterous behavior may attract unwanted attention your way. Remember, this is an officers' club, not a boys' club.

Although the question of rank does not assert itself as such at an officers' club, you should show the same courtesies to senior officers there that you would anywhere else. Respect to age and rank will prompt you into the correct approach when greeting and speaking with seniors; you should neither hold back nor forge ahead.

Dress in all clubs is prescribed by the house rules; some clubs permit sport shirts without ties up uptil 6 P.M., other clubs are more formal. When you visit a club at another station—or a club of a different Service—it is wise to find out in advance if there are any big differences in club regulations.

You will find through the years that your officers' club life is an integral part of your Service life, and as a member, it is up to you to help keep the club standards high.

CHAPTER 23

Good Sportsmanship

Good manners at sports contests are synonymous with good sportsmanship. Every officer has taken part in athletics at some time in his past, either as a player in the game or as an observer on the sidelines, and undoubtedly will take part in many future games.

The impression of a lady or gentleman is frequently gleaned from behavior at sports events. In the world of sports, there is a saying to the effect that, "If you want to find out what kind of a man he is, play golf with him when he is off his game, or go fishing with him when they aren't biting."

Good sportsmanship embodies the ideals of fairness, self control, support of the team, and performing to the best of one's ability and honor. Qualities of this nature are expected of anyone, anywhere.

It is good sportsmanship for Midshipmen and Cadets to cheer when it is announced that another Service Academy is winning a game. You want the other Academy to win every game—except, of course, the one with your own Academy!

The spectator is always very much a part of any game. The player reacts to the roar of the crowd as much as the fan thrills to the exploits of the player. The officials of the contest are also aware of the spectators and must always be on the lookout for the person who attempts to interfere with the rules of the game, or who tries to intimidate the official by heckling him.

OFFICALS

An official is empowered to eject from the stands anyone who abuses the rules of the game and he may stop the contest when discourteous actions continue after due warnings. Thus a penalty may be invoked on a team, or, when the action is serious, the game may be forfeited—which means that one or more spectators can be responsible for the loss of the game by their favorite team.

Officals of amateur or professional contests are selected after passing rigid examinations and trials in a particular sport. They are the best qualified personnel available for the task. The rules of the contest which they enforce have been adopted after intensive study by national sports associations, and they spell out the conduct of play that will insure fair play and good sportsmanship for all concerned.

The decisions made by officials are frequently matters of judgment and are subject to vantage point, interpretation, and stress of the moment. When a spectator becomes enraged over a ruling, he should realize that officials have been carefully screened and are calling the rule as they see and interpret it. Very few spectators know *all* the rules of any game.

You should always remember that you must abide by the decisions of the official in charge of the contest, whether you agree with them or not.

BOOING

The American baseball fan is a peculiar brand of individual of intense loyalty to the home team and at the same time its most severe critic. He knows better than the manager when to bunt, hit, and run. The "bum" of the previous inning may become the hero of the day by a timely hit. The fan seems to be a maze of contradictions, and is consistent only in his inconsistencies.

The baiting of umpires at baseball games may be a trend of the times— but it is very poor manners. And throwing debris on the field or at the players and umpires, running onto the field of play, or the use of abusive or profane language are most flagrant displays of bad manners.

While enthusiastic cheering for your favorite athlete or team is expected, booing a decision or play which goes against your team is not only crude but unsportsmanlike.

Although no one likes to lose, a good loser will compliment the winner on his skill, and a good winner will commiserate with the loser's ill luck.

SPORTS ETIQUETTE

The most common breaches of good manners at sports events are excessive noises made by spectators or players in an effort to divert the opponent. This interference includes shouting, whistling, clapping of hands, dropping of objects, sudden movements of the arms or legs, or any other distraction.

The sports program at the Service Academies covers the proper behavior of Midshipmen and Cadets at all sports events, both from the participant and spectator viewpoint. Almost twenty sports are covered. Among the rules of courtesy discussed are those of keeping quiet when an opponent or a member of your own team is attempting a free throw in basketball, a putt in golf, a strike in bowling, or a rally in tennis. Any game of skill demands concentration by the player.

Displays of temper, such as obscene language or fighting, defeat the purpose of the game. Spectators at football games should conduct themselves in such a manner that they do not reflect discredit upon their Academy or college. This includes conduct during liberty periods following the game as well as at the game itself, and is particularly important for uniformed personnel, as the entire Service may be judged as rowdy by the isolated indiscretions of a few individuals.

Since many football games are played during inclement weather, there is a problem of personal comfort versus good manners. An umbrella may keep the rain from your head—but it may also block the view of someone behind you. Also jumping up with an umbrella during an exciting play is not without its hazards for those sitting nearby.

Football games are frequently played in weather that is uncomfortably cold for the spectator. A number of persons use this as an excuse for consuming alcoholic beverages in the stands. This is not only illegal in many stadia, but is a reflection upon the individual. The uniformed member of the Armed Forces has a special responsibility to conduct himself in a gentlemanly fashion.

In golf matches, no one should move, talk, or stand close to or directly behind the ball or hole when a player is making a stroke. Attention should be paid to the casting of shadows between the hole and a ball about to be played. Players should leave the putting green immediately upon determining the result of a hole.

When a ball is lost, or when your twosome or foursome is taking excessive time to play, you should signal other players behind you to go through you and should wait until this second group has played past you and is out of range before continuing play.

When a woman is in your group, you need not carry her golf bag—this is her responsibility. Presumably, she is in good health and able to carry her own bag or she wouldn't be on the course.

The fast-moving game of tennis requires good manners by the spectators in that players are distracted by moving objects in their range of vision. A tennis ball in flight moves with great speed and any unexpected movement in the neighborhood can throw a player off his game. Any movement at the opposite end of the court, especially, should be held to an absolute minimum.

If you should be sitting in a stand that faces more than one court, you should not move from one match to another until play is over. You do not applaud during a rally, but you may when the point has been played out. Errors such as a shot that goes out of court or into the net should not be applauded even if it gives the point to your favorite player. You only express approval for *good* strokes.

A number of specific sports have not been mentioned—not because they are less important, but because the good manners at other sports are similar to those already discussed. The basis of the rules in any sport is the creation of a spirit of fair play. The line between the rules and good manners is a fine one. The distinction might be set in this manner: the rules prescribe penalties to be invoked when there is a violation, whereas there generally is no penalty for a breach of etiquette *except* the censure of your neighbors or the public.

YOUR ALMA MATER

Every Service or college man is proud to hear the song of his Alma Mater played or sung. Midshipmen and Cadets stand at attention when their own Alma Mater is played or sung, therefore it is good manners that you stand when the song of your opponent's Academy or college is played or sung.

PAYING YOUR WAY

When you are invited as a guest to play on the golf course at a country club, you will want to pay your own way whenever you can. Usually, your invitation is a privilege extended to you by a member, and you should be prepared to pay all other costs—or as many as your host will permit. Such expenses include greens fees, caddies, food, drink, etc.

In making sure that you do the proper thing without embarrassing your host, you must be alert to size up the situation correctly. First, you should find out if the club runs on a cash or a chit basis. Where everything is paid for in cash, the guest has no problem. In such cases, when the member host signs you in, you will have your greens fee ready. If your host *insists* that he takes care of the fees, you will accept and thank him. When he pays for the greens fee, however, you should pay for both caddies.

In some clubs, the greens fee of members and their guests is billed to the member at the end of the month. In this case, you cannot pay your fee, and you should be careful about offering money to your host—unless he is a good friend, and you have made arrangements ahead of time.

When everything is by chit service, you can pay for nothing, and it is useless to insist. Then, you should return your host's hospitality by inviting him to your ship or station, or to some other function of comparable degree.

Sometimes you will be entirely upon your own by virtue of having been introduced by letter or by telephone by your host. In this case you will pay for whatever you can, and make certain of keeping a record of any charges that you have signed on your host's bill, so that you can send him a check promptly. Since you have signed chits in his name, you will generally know how much the charges are.

It is a custom at some clubs for everyone to go "Dutch treat." When a guest of yours is not aware of this custom, you may make a comment about "chipping in" or "going Dutch treat." And when you yourself have been the recipient of considerable hospitality in which you have not financially participated to your full share, you should unobtrusively press upon the main provider of the group a bill large enough to cover any expenses incurred in your behalf.

Certain customs often prevail at clubs, and everyone should be aware of them. For example, the winner of the money at golf is often expected to stand the group to a round of drinks. As a guest of the club, you may wonder how to go about this. The best way is to step forward promptly and say that you want to buy this round—or you may ask your host what is customary at his club. But in any case, you should *make the offer.*

As an officer (sometimes as a VIP) you may run into occasions when you are not expected to pay for anything, and where offering to do so might be in very poor taste. In such cases you usually are the guest of a man who is wealthy or someone who has known your family for a long time—or, perhaps, the host is an older man who desires to extend full hospitality to you as a young officer.

When you go on a boating trip with friends, you may volunteer to split the expenses or to bring a carton of drinks and some food. There must be an understanding beforehand, however, otherwise you may show up with a lot of provisions that merely duplicate your host's preparations. On the other hand, you may find yourself an empty handed co-host.

In game fishing, the Dutch treat kind of situation is customary, with a group chartering a boat and splitting expenses. Game fishing is luxury fishing at its best, and is expensive. Prices vary for chartered boats at different ports, but twenty dollars and up per rod per day is not unusual.

The problems encountered with a skiing party are slightly akin to those of a safari—you usually travel a distance to get to your destination, and you stay a weekend or overnight at least. When unmarried women are in the group, dormitory-style lodging is customary, and the ladies usually pay for their own lodging. Tipping is similar to that in any hotel.

On a hunting trip, guests are expected to bring their own clothing, gun, and ammunition—unless the host has specifically said that he has equipment for all hands.

When you are a guest at a private game preserve or hunting camp, you may be assigned a guide. You should tip the guide anywhere from two to five dollars, depending upon the length of your stay and the services you received. This tip, of course, is in addition to the share of the guide's wages which courtesy or custom would assign to you.

PAYING A WOMAN'S WAY

It was once considered gentlemanly for a man to offer to pay for a woman's expenses, no matter what. When accompanying a woman on a train or subway, or while on a casual shopping trip, a man offered to pay for the transportation, meals, magazines, or whatever she fancied—within reason.

Today, a well-mannered woman who may only be a casual acquaintance will refuse to permit you to pay for such items. She will not object if you buy a magazine or a soft drink, and perhaps even pay a taxi fare—but usually, when the taxi fare is high, she will offer to pay for her own share.

When young people find themselves traveling together to the same destination, by chance or by pre-arrangement, there is no need for a man to pay a woman's expenses, other than for small trifles.

CHAPTER 24

The Overnight Guest

As the host or as the guest, you will frequently extend or receive an invitation to stay overnight. As the guest, you may be invited to stay with a friend when you are passing through his city. A Midshipman or Cadet will be asked to spend the holidays with a roommate, for example, or to attend a house party. Usually, your friends are in about the same moderate circumstances as yourself, and you will act in their home as you would in your own. As the host, you expect a houseguest to be congenial and courteous.

THE WEEKEND GUEST

The weekend guest is probably the most frequent type of overnight guest. The invitation to stay for a limited number of days is extended in person, by telephone, letter, telegram, or any convenient way. The guest should answer immediately, and his reply must be definite.

When accepting the invitation, the guest must make it clear when he expects to arrive and how—whether by car, plane, or train. In the latter cases, the guest may need to be met by his host, thus the time of arrival is important. When refusing the invitation, the guest must always say *why*.

The host will give advance information concerning the weekend so that a guest will know what to bring with him. When something special is planned—a formal dance, a boating trip, golf, tennis, etc.—the host should suggest the necessary clothes or sports equipment needed. If the hosts do not mention anything in particular, the guest may take for granted that the weekend is informal—but it is better to *ask* than to be caught unprepared.

A guest is always concerned about what luggage to take—what is necessary, what he can get along without. Most guests bring too much luggage, rather than too little, which is cumbersome to all hands. The proper amount is frequently decided by the method of travel—plane, train, or car—but a "two-suiter" with perhaps a small bag, and a shaving kit, takes care of an average weekend. As the name implies, a "two-suiter" bag is just large enough for two suits and the necessary changes of clothing for a few days.

It is a good investment for any officer to have presentable luggage. Although good luggage is expensive, you will need it for the rest of your life, since you are a traveling man. It is wise to invest in good quality luggage as soon as you can afford it.

THE HOUSEGUEST

A houseguest is a guest who stays a longer length of time than an overnight or weekend guest. When you are the houseguest, you may have a suite of rooms and a private bath, or you may fall heir to a small room and share the bathroom with members of the family. But as long as you are a guest in the house, you *must not* complain.

HOUSEPARTIES

As a member of a houseparty, you can expect to room with other male guests—but this dormitory-style life should be no problem for you. You must be pleasant with all other guests, many of whom you may never have met before. It is important that you get all names straight at the beginning of the visit—it is a compliment to a stranger that you remember his name. On any houseparty, the hosts always try to have guests who will be congenial company for each other.

WHAT TO TAKE

In this day of "drip-dry" or nylon shirts and pajamas, dacron slacks, and "stretchie" socks, you can take less clothing—which packs easier—than ever before. What you will need depends upon where you will visit—the climate, type of community (a summer colony or a city apartment), etc.—but no matter where you go, travel as light as possible.

Usually, you need a dark or conservative suit, shoes, a sport jacket, and slacks—which you will probably wear on the trip—and an extra pair of slacks; one pair of pajamas, two changes of shirts a day, socks, changes of underwear, and house slippers (soft and crushable ones that will take little room in a bag).

For an informal weekend, you will need more sport shirts, a sweater, Bermuda shorts, extra pair of slacks, and swimming trunks, rather than dress clothes. If you are driving, you may take your golf clubs and shoes, tennis racket, or anything else. When your hosts plan a special occasion—such as deep sea fishing, you need not worry about fishing gear, since your hosts will undoubtedly have all necessary equipment or they would not plan such an occasion.

When formal entertaining is planned by your hosts, you will need your dinner jacket. If you do not own one, take your blue uniform with black bow tie, or your summer whites.

After you have packed everything you need, re-check your luggage—particularly your shaving kit. Some officers who travel on short notice should have a check-off list taped on the inside of the shaving kit. You should include in your luggage such items as toothpaste, aspirin, cigarettes or cigars, smoking tobacco, etc.

DUTIES OF GUESTS

The duty of any guest is to be congenial at all times. If you are the guest, then you will not want to be hard to please, a person who contributes little to the pleasure of others. When you take part in a game, try to join in the fun, whether you happen to prefer tennis, quoits, or charades. When you truly can't participate in the activity, then you must give a valid reason.

In a servantless household, a guest will not make himself a burden to his hosts. It is important that you be on time for meals. Your hostess usually tells you at what time meals will be served—so be there. The matter of being on time holds for any activity in which you may engage—a boat trip, a golf game, or any planned event. If anything, be a little ahead of time.

The hour for breakfast may be a minor problem in a household: the host may go to work early, the family may be early or late risers, the children may get off to school in the usual early morning confusion. A hostess may find it easier to send a tray to a guest's room when a guest needs to sleep late. If you do not care for breakfast, or eat lightly, say so and relieve your hostess of extra work.

A considerate guest will be alert to the household routine, particularly in small quarters. If you sleep on the sofa in the living room, then remember that that part of the house cannot be occupied until you are dressed. If you are adept at making beds—and you *do* know how—then it is helpful for you to make your own bed.

When a bathroom is shared by the family and guest, you should be careful not to overstay your fair time or use all the hot water. Try to leave the bathroom as neat as when you entered it. Do not leave damp towels on the floor, or your razor in the wash basin. Always hang up your clothes in your room, and do not leave your hat or gloves on the living room furniture.

You will want to offer to help your hosts when there are no servants, but do not insist if your hostess says "no." Try to be helpful, but don't get in the way.

A thoughtful guest will take a small gift to his hostess. Nowadays the old standby of a box of candy is *not* appreciated by a diet-conscious hostess. A small inexpensive gift that is always acceptable is a little bottle of good perfume such as many foresighted officers buy when on foreign cruises. It is a wise officer who buys many small and inexpensive gifts while in foreign countries—gifts that cost only a dollar or two there, but much more in this country.

A guest may choose to take the children of the family he is visiting a gift each, rather than taking a gift to the hostess. In this case, candy or a toy is a good choice. When a guest does not takes gifts to his hostess or the children in the family, however, he may send something after his departure. Upon any occasion, flowers are always in good taste.

The rule of thumb concerning gifts is: They should never be expensive, but must always be of *good quality*.

OVERSTEPPING HOSPITALITY

When a guest is visiting in a town or community where he has other friends, he must be careful of using the house where he is staying as a springboard for renewing these other acquaintances.

When you are the guest, you must also remember not to talk endlessly on the house telephone. Your hosts may urge you to have your friends visit you in their home, and you are free to do so, but you must guard against overstepping your host's hospitality.

And if your friends are strangers to your hosts, you must make certain that such a visit would not inconvenience the household where you are visiting. It is better to visit or telephone your friends at times when your hosts have other obligations—or, better still, to save such visits until your own stay in your host's home is over.

ACCIDENTS IN HOMES

When something unexpected happens—such as your breaking a valuable object, or becoming suddenly ill—common sense will tell you what to do. In case you broke something which you can replace, you should replace it at your earliest convenience. If you cannot do so, you may send a gift which you feel your hostess will enjoy, such as flowers or a nice potted plant which can give pleasure for some time.

You will say how sorry you are for such a mishap at the time of the accident, and after your departure you will briefly state on your personal card, enclosed with the replacement or flowers, that you are sorry concerning the incident.

If you should become ill while on your visit, you will let your hosts know—and call a doctor. Any host would be distressed to learn that his guest was ill, but foolishly said nothing about it. Of course, the guest pays for all doctor fees or medicines especially bought for him.

DEPARTURE

When you leave the house—or any place—after a visit, be sure that you have not forgotten anything. A check-off list is handy to avert forgetting. It is a bother for your host to wrap and mail your razor or any other object, so don't forget it.

When you have said that you plan to leave at a given time—do so. Don't be persuaded to take a later bus; your hosts may be sincere in their invitation that you stay longer, but usually a family has other plans or obligations. Anyway, it's *time to leave!*

On the other hand, don't forget to let your hosts know well ahead of time when you expect to leave. It is not good manners to bring your packed bag into the living room and say *thanks* and *goodbye,* then leave. This is inconsiderate, because your hosts will probably wonder if you are hurt or angry, to leave so suddenly.

When there is a servant in a household, you will want to tip her or him something. In the South, many homes have the family cook who is an integral part of the family and whom you undoubtedly met during your visit. Before you leave, stop in the kitchen and give her a dollar or so, depending on the length of your stay. You do not hand the money to your hostess and ask her to give it to the cook—*you* hand it to the cook in person. And you should add something complimentary, such as, "Yours is the best spoon-bread I've ever eaten!"

In a large home, unless your hostess asks that you do not give the servants a tip, you should give something to the valet or butler if they performed any services for you. Usually a dollar or so is sufficient, but this is determined by the length of your stay. (See Chapter 10, *Tipping Charts.*)

As soon as you arrive home, or at your station, you will write a note of thanks to both your host and hostess (but addressed to the hostess). (See Chapter 16, *Correspondence.*) You should express your sincere appreciation for their hospitality, and mention some incident or party of note. Your letter should be on its way within two days after you have been entertained.

VISITS TO CIVILIAN COLLEGES

In visiting a civilian college, a Midshipman or Cadet should not be too surprised at the differences he will find—particularly the lack of regimentation of the students. Every college campus has its rules, regulations, and conventions, however, and you will discover that these actually differ but little in spirit from those to which you are accustomed.

Informality of dress is the rule at colleges, just as formality of dress is stressed at the Academies. You will further find that there are a few special rules by which the college community lives, and by learning them, you will establish yourself in a congenial friendship with people whose purposes in life are surprisingly similar to your own.

You may be a guest on a college campus, either as a member of an athletic team or as a social guest for the weekend. In either case, your Academy will be judged by your actions. A Midshipman or Cadet member of an athletic squad should follow the special instructions of the officer representative and coach during his stay on the campus.

As a social guest, the normal rules for a weekend guest apply here. You must be alert to observe the local ground rules, and follow them conscientiously. At all times, you must be congenial.

The rules for visiting a girl's college are necessarily more strict, but the weekends have been planned for the entertainment of men like yourself, and you will have a good time if you are a good sport and observe certain regulations—such as:

- Do not violate rules concerning drinking on or off campus.
- Get the arrangements straight concerning the time of your arrival, departure, transportation, clothes, etc. (You will be facing the same problem every "drag" faces when she comes to your Service Academy.)
- Remember that you have a hostess—and do not play wolf to the entire campus.
- Your hostess may reserve and pay for your room during your stay —and sometimes your meals and tips. But you will pay for taxis, flowers, refreshments, snacks, and all other such supplementary expenses.

CHAPTER 25

Hotel and Motel Manners

Unless you are an experienced traveler, there may be a moment of unease when you step up to the desk clerk in a hotel or motel to register. If you are newly married, you may wonder what is the best way to sign your name—and your wife's—and you may wonder how much, and whom, you should tip.

Before you started your trip, however, you may have wondered where you could obtain the best information concerning hotels and motels in general. There are a number of reliable sources of information concerning places to stay in each state; such sources as the AAA, Tour Aids, and special books and pamphlets put out by various organizations and individuals.

When you know where you will be at a certain date, and approximately what hour, you should write or wire the selected hotel or motel for a reservation, and if time permits you should ask that the reservation be confirmed. In your letter or wire, you should specify the price of the room that you want, the number of people who will be occupying the room or rooms, what type of accommodations you need (a single room with bath, for example), and the expected length of your stay and the approximate time of your arrival. (See Chapter 16, *Correspondence*.)

Should your request be confirmed, be sure that you do not lose the confirmation; this little piece of paper can be very important when a busy clerk has bungled your reservation.

Any good hotel in any city in the country has a doorman who greets guests upon their arrival. When you are a guest and are arriving by car, you will tell the doorman that you would like a porter to come for your bags—unless you are smart enough to travel light and can carry your bag yourself.

If you plan to use the hotel's garage, tell the doorman and he will arrange to have your car taken to the garage. If you are not using the hotel garage, you may ask the doorman where you can park your car. Unless he does some special service for you, it is not necessary to tip him at this time. If you should arrive at the hotel by taxi, the doorman will open the taxi door, but no tip is required.

When you do not travel light and the porter has taken your bags to the lobby, he will direct you to the desk. If you have a reservation, you tell the desk clerk your name and say that you have a reservation. When you do not have a reservation, tell the clerk that you would like a room with bath—or whatever you want—and ask if such a room is available.

You will undoubtedly want to know what the price of the room will be, so ask. Say, "What is the price of the room?" If the price is more than you can pay, ask the clerk if he has something less expensive. When there is nothing else—you stay or you leave.

REGISTERING

If the price of the room is satisfactory, you will sign the register. It is necessary in all states and in all countries that you sign the hotel or motel register, and it is only necessary to sign your name and your home town, or your ship or station. Occasionally, the desk clerk asks for a street address, but usually this is not required.

When you sign the register, you may write, "Midshipman John Smith, Annapolis, Maryland," or, "John Smith, Annapolis, Maryland." In the case of married couples, you sign the register, "Ensign (or Captain) and Mrs. John Smith, Annapolis, Maryland (or West Point, New York)," *never* "Ensign (or Captain) John Smith and wife."

After you have registered, the bell boy will precede you to your room with the keys. After he has deposited your luggage, turned on the lights, and asked you if there is anything else that you will need, you are expected to tip him. If you have one or two bags, 35 to 50 cents is adequate—provided that the luggage is not extremely heavy and that the bell boy has not done some service other than carrying your luggage. When there are several pieces of luggage, your tip should be increased, about 10 or 15 cents per bag.

SPECIAL SERVICES

All hotels offer many personal services, and these services are usually spelled out somewhere in the room, along with the prices. In a big hotel, it is often perplexing to know to whom you should make your request. The easiest way is to pick up the phone and ask for "Room Service," telling whoever answers what it is that you want. Sometimes you will be referred to the "valet" (pronounced " val-lay"), in which case you ask for "Valet Service." Large hotels will have a central clearing house for service and "Room Service," and will tell you whom to call, or else will take your order directly.

For any special services, you can pay at the time they are received, or you can have the charge put on your bill by signing the check that accompanied the service. Should you need extra towels or blankets, call the "Housekeeper." She will have a maid bring you the necessary items, but you must be specific in what you need. If you need one blanket and three towels, say so. In most hotels, the housekeeper also is in charge of lost and found articles.

Should the luxury of having breakfast in bed appeal to you, remember that food served in the room is always subject to a substantial extra service charge. If you must be economical, the coffee shop to be found in most hotels will have the fastest service at about half the cost.

ROOMS WITH—OR WITHOUT MEALS

European plan means that the price of the room does not include any meals. *American plan* means that the price of the room does include all, or some, meals. The latter plan is usually found in resort hotels, and has one disadvantage: You must take all your meals at the hotel or else you will be losing money. If you want to take your meals when and where the fancy strikes you, it is best that you select a hotel that does not operate under the American plan.

When you prefer the American plan, you will find that you are given a specific table in the hotel dining room which you will occupy at each meal—if the table meets with your approval—during your entire stay. In Europe, this same system is practiced at some hotels under the title of *pension*. When you register at a resort hotel, it is well that you inquire into the practice of serving meals.

HOTEL MANNERS

As a guest, you must be considerate of employees in a hotel, but you should always be impersonal. An important rule to follow in addressing service people in a hotel is to look at them, know what you are going to say, speak clearly and distinctly, and say it as though you mean it.

When a guest appears uncertain or ill at ease, some hotel employees become careless with that guest's requests. A guest should be quiet but firm when making requests—and, equally, should make no requests that are not reasonable.

You should tip in accordance with your income, the hotel's reputation— and the service rendered. If the service has been poor, you will tip accordingly. While you may not want to under-tip, it is just as bad taste to over-tip —particularly when you cannot afford it.

MOTELS

Motels are a boon to the traveling man or family. The average motel differs basically from a hotel in that there are almost no services provided, no garage problems, and no tipping. There is little fuss and bother; you arrive and leave without delay.

Before you register or pay out any money at a motel, you should ask the motel operator to show you the room that you expect to occupy. This firsthand inspection gives you the opportunity to make sure that the room is clean, in order, and that it meets your standards. If not, you may ask to see another room—or not accept it at all, and go on your way.

Most motels are approved by various qualified organizations whose business it is to inspect them at regular intervals. You will soon learn to recognize these organizations, for all motels are anxious to advertise the fact that they are approved courts.

Motels require that you pay in advance of your occupancy in order to facilitate early morning checkouts, so be ready to pay promptly upon registering. When you are driving cross country and know where you will be the following day or night, it is advisable to make advance reservations. In summer months and in resort areas, motels are generally full by late afternoon. When you find a motel chain that you like, it is well to stay with it on your whole trip. The various managers will assist in solving the advance reservation problem.

MOTEL MANNERS

Although you are paying for the motel room, you are to treat it with the same respect that you would the belongings of another person. Before taking ashtrays and towels as souvenirs, stop and consider how much it would cost you if guests in *your* home carried off ashtrays and towels.

SECTION VIII

STRICTLY SERVICE

CHAPTER 26

Wardroom Life

Wardroom country aboard ship is the officer's seagoing home—a home in which he should be proud to entertain his relatives and friends. It is also his club where he may gather with his fellow officers for moments of relaxation, such as a discussion of the daily problems, enjoying a movie, radio, musical or TV program, or just a game of acey deucey, or bridge over a cup of coffee. Whatever the event, it is a place where members should conduct themselves within the ordinary rules of propriety, common sense, and good manners, in addition to observing the rules of etiquette founded on naval customs and traditions.

All members of the wardroom mess have a collective responsibility for the wardroom's appearance, the stewardsmen's attention to duty, the service of food, and the cleanliness of officer's rooms and the wardroom country in general. Punctilious performance of duty by the stewardsmen can only be assured by the close and personal attention of all officers and the exaction of high standards of service at all times.

The stowage, cleanliness, preservation, and appearance of the wardroom, galley, pantry, staterooms, and heads and showers set the pattern for the ship. All these details should be accorded the meticulous attention that such pace-setting examples deserve. In the Navy the expression is so often heard: "The standards set in wardroom country are the standards found throughout the ship."

UNIFORM

The uniform of the day is the uniform in the wardroom, and it is also the uniform for dinner except on formal occasions. When khaki is the uniform of the day, the requirements for the wearing of the coat for meals is relaxed on some ships, depending upon the informality of the occasion and the desires of the commanding officer. When special guests or ladies are present, however, it is generally considered that the formality of the occasion demands that the coat be worn. Except when at sea, the tie should be worn with the khaki uniform. When at sea, the wearing of the tie, particularly for meals, is considered to be subject to the desires of the commanding officer. Short sleeved shirts are worn with some uniforms.

Officers should not loiter or remain in the wardroom in civilian attire. An exception to this is when you are waiting temporarily for a liberty boat, or because of some similarly sound reason. Whenever civilian clothing is worn, it is expected to be in keeping with the dignity of the officer as well as of the occasion.

STATEROOM

An officer's stateroom should be neat, orderly, and clean at all times so that it presents an exemplary appearance to anyone that might enter. This involves an orderly manner of living by the officer himself as well as an adequate performance by the stewardsman assigned.

The stewardsman is responsible for cleaning the room, making the bunk, tending to the uniforms and belongings, and placing the stateroom in order at least once each day—and normally as soon after breakfast as practicable. It should be remembered, however, that stewardsmen have other staterooms assigned and wardroom duties to perform, and your cooperation is necessary to maintain your stateroom in shipshape order. The requirement for a neat and orderly stateroom is obligatory for all ranks.

A stewardsman is assigned to attend to the quarters and general belongings of the officer occupant. Officers normally stow their own clothes and put out what must be cleaned. Slovenly habits of not stowing clothes are a frequent source of complaint against junior officers. If an officer improperly insists on doing some chores—such as tending to his laundry, carrying his chair to the movies, and jumping up from the table to help himself—you can rest assured that the stewardsman will not stop him. However, if you, the officer, furnish a good example in the orderliness of your living habits, and are reasonable and patient in making your requirements known, the stewardsman will normally respond.

MEALS

The hours for wardroom meals are designated by the President of the Mess, subject to the approval of the commanding officer. (On small ships—destroyers and smaller—the president of the mess is usually the commanding officer.) Breakfast hours may be shifted from time to time to conform to daily routine. In any event, except for Sundays and holidays, the wardroom should be cleared by 0800.

Lunch is usually served at 1130 underway and 1200 in port. Dinner normally will be served at 1730 underway, 1800 in port or 1830 when in foreign ports. The custom of serving dinner at 1830 provides for time to make calls during prescribed calling hours, and the more leisurely dinner hour also permits the unhurried arrival of invited guests and allows sufficient time for officers returning from shore to shift into the uniform of the day prior to dinner. Punctilious arrival at meals is expected.

When troops or other officers not attached to the ship are embarked, it may be necessary to adjust meal hours in order to insure maximum convenience and service for all concerned. On small ships, when the establishment of a wardroom mess is not possible because of the lack of personnel and facilities, officers may be subsisted from the general mess in accordance with the pertinent article from the *Manual of the Bureau of Supplies and Accounts*. In such cases, consideration should be given to adjusting the officers' meal hours to those of the general mess.

SEATING

Seating arrangements in the wardroom depend upon Navy tradition and custom, and are usually set up by the mess treasurer and approved by the executive officer. If there is any chance for confusion, a seating diagram should be posted on the wardroom bulletin board. The president sits at the head of the senior table with the mess treasurer at the opposite end. Members are seated at the right and left of the president in order of seniority. This system is also followed in seating officers who are aboard for temporary duty or for transportation.

It is important that guests be seated properly. Guests of senior officers usually sit at the senior table, with the honored lady on the right of the presiding officer, the host officer second, and other guests taking precedence over regular mess members. In large ships with a number of mess tables, the guests are seated next to their officer hosts and as close to the place of honor as possible. It is important that members be prompt to give way or to fill in a vacancy at the table with a minimum of confusion. The space next to a guest should never be left unoccupied.

At formal dinners, use of place cards is desirable to avoid confusion in seating. Names may be printed or written on the cards, which are then placed on the table according to the seating diagram that has been approved by the mess treasurer.

COMMON COURTESIES

The senior officer should be punctual in seating himself by the time the meal is scheduled to begin. In the event he is delayed, he should inform the next senior officer whether or not to proceed with the serving of the meal. Other members of the mess should arrive in the wardroom from three to five minutes prior to meals, in order to be present for introductions and to be seated at the same time that the senior officer sits down.

You never sit down to meals before the senior officer takes his seat. If you are *late* for the meal, you make apologies to the senior member at your table. If business *unduly detains* you, notify the senior officer present and ask the steward to save a ration for you; then eat later with the officers coming off watch. When you are to be *absent,* notify the chief steward in advance. This not only will permit him to arrange the seating but will enable him to do better planning and thereby reduce the messbill.

During the serving of the meal, demands upon the stewardsmen for personal service should be kept to a minimum. However, you may ask the steward for a second helping if you desire it.

The senior officer present usually makes any announcements. If you have something you wish to bring before the members, request his permission and brief him on your subject. Officers going on watch should eat before regular meal hours and be clear of the wardroom prior to the regular meal.

All officers should promote a cheerful atmosphere at the table. This does not mean boisterous conduct, but rather a contribution to the conversation. A pleasant atmosphere promotes digestion and cultivates good will. A good rule to follow is: "Don't talk shop during mealtime, but save it until after dessert and coffee."

You should never discuss religion or women in the mess. Also, try to be discriminating when you discuss politics and debatable issues of the day.

It is wise to avoid unfavorable comment about the food. If you have constructive criticism to make, privately advise the mess treasurer or mess caterer—he is interested in doing a good job, and will appreciate your comment.

It is not polite to gulp your food and then leave the table precipitately. If you must leave the table before the meal is over, you may ask to be excused by those in your immediate vicinity—and if practicable (depending on the size of the mess), you should ask to be excused by the head of the table and/or by the senior officer present.

Only under unusual circumstances should an officer be disturbed by professional matters during a meal. If the business is urgent, the officer should excuse himself from the table and conduct the business outside the wardroom.

The practice of smoking throughout the meal has never been sanctioned by Navy custom. You should wait until coffee is served before you light up, and should always give consideration to the convictions and smoking habits of your neighbors—especially any ladies who are present.

If two seatings at the table are required, you must avoid unnecessary loitering at the table that may delay the second service. And you should never ask for meals to be served in your stateroom except in case of sickness or when especially authorized by the commanding officer.

The quality of food and the service will depend largely upon the interests and efforts of the members of the mess. You will observe good table manners as a matter of course—there is nothing that condones bad table manners. The mess president will privately counsel those whose deportment brings down the tone of the mess.

All officers will remember to remove their caps when passing through *any* messing compartment at meal times and in sick bay.

GUESTS

The mess should have a written policy in regard to guests—which will insure coverage of the following items: (a) How guests of any individual are to be distinguished from guests of the mess; (b) What charge, if any, is to be made for guests; and (c) What proportionate charge should be made for children as compared to adults.

Officers should be encouraged to bring their guests aboard ship for dinner, but not repeatedly. Each guest that enters the mess should be treated as the guest of the entire mess, and it is the duty and privilege of each member to carry out his social obligations as co-host.

To insure a pleasant occasion for all parties, an officer bringing guests into the wardroom will comply with the following procedure:

- Inform the mess president beforehand of any plan to have guests.
- Give the mess president advance background facts about guests.
- Notify the mess treasurer and steward of the number and names of the guests in order that place cards and seating may be arranged.
- Make certain that the guests understand, beforehand, the time the meal is to be served. This will permit them to arrive on time so as not to be embarrassed by either late or early arrival. If the ship is at anchor, the host should be sure that his guests are well informed as to the weather and the boat schedule.
- Insure by advance arrangements that the guests will not be unduly delayed at the naval base gate because of identification.
- Be available on the quarterdeck to welcome guests aboard.
- Take the guests to his stateroom for removal of their coats and hats, if practicable, before mealtime.
- Designate a certain room for the use of women guests.
- Introduce all members present to his guests (each member should come forward to meet them).
- Arrange for the guests to depart at a reasonable hour. Generally, dinner guests leave within an hour after the movie, smoker or party.
- Notify the officer of the deck well in advance as to the boat in which the guests are to depart.
- If possible, accompany the women guests home, or have them accompanied by a fellow officer; otherwise, arrange for the women guests to return to their homes in groups.

WARDROOM HABITS

A smart and neat appearing wardroom depends largely upon the attitude and conduct of the officers who use it. You always remove your cap upon entering the wardroom, and you never appear in the wardroom out of uniform. Never be boisterous or noisy in the wardroom; it is the home of all officers, and their rights and privileges should be respected. You also should show consideration for your fellow officers by moderating the volume when using the radio, phonograph, or television.

When playing cards, you should choose a table location that will not interfere with others.

Don't abuse the use of the duty stewardsman by sending him on long errands—other members are also entitled to a share of his services.

There is no objection to your dropping into the wardroom for coffee, but don't make a practice of lingering there during working hours. Such a practice may mark an officer as being the indolent type.

When you have finished with your coffee, remove the cup and saucer from the table to the pantry shelf or sideboard if there is no stewardsman immediately available. This is a little thing that will help the continual good appearance of the wardroom.

You should also remember that mess tables must be cleared at least thirty minutes before meals, in order to permit the stewardsmen to set up on time.

Wardroom magazines and newspapers should be carefully handled, not left adrift; neither should they be damaged, hoarded, or removed from the wardroom where they have been placed for availability to all members.

When smoking, you will insure that an ash tray is available before lighting up. If ventilation is a problem, you should accordingly reduce smoking or else stop it completely.

You should always remember that obscenity, vulgarity, and off-color tales do not belong in an officer's general conversation at any time—and are, especially, out of place in the wardroom. The junior officer pursues the correct course by being the best listener in the mess, the senior officer by setting the example of dress, manners, consideration, and intelligent conversation.

Unkind and unfavorable comments about other officers, and critical opinions about seniors, are not appropriate *at any time* in the wardroom.

When guests are present—especially when they are seated alongside you —you should take note of their presence, and engage them in conversation when the opportunity presents. Such courteous interest will be appreciated by both the guests and their host. In such conversations, however, matters under discussion should be in keeping with good taste. Personalities and ship talk—subjects likely to be unfamiliar to the guests—should not be discussed in detail. Guests in any walk of life—teenage youth or oldster—

should never be "talked down to" nor treated condescendingly just because they are unfamiliar with Navy customs or matters.

When you send a stewardsman on an errand, such as picking up your dry cleaning, you should be sure and give him the money for the payment, with the request that he return the change. You should not require the stewardsman to furnish his own money for your service.

You should stay clear of the wardroom immediately after breakfast, as this is usually the period for general cleaning. When leaving the wardroom, leave the place you have been occupying neat and orderly, whether you found it that way or not. This will be appreciated by those who follow you.

And remember to keep your feet on the deck, rather than on the furniture. If you wish to sleep, you should retire to your own stateroom.

EXCHANGE OF MEAL COURTESIES

It is courteous for the wardroom occasionally to invite the commanding officer—if he messes separately—to have a meal in the wardroom. The same courtesy is normally extended to the unit commander by the ship's mess president. The unit commander will appreciate an occasional invitation to a meal in the wardroom of the ships of his command—particularly the flagship. Included with the unit commander in all such invitations is generally the chief of staff (chief staff officer). In some cases, as appropriate and desired, the senior officers of the unit commander's staff are also invited.

It is customary for unit commanders and commanding officers, if maintaining a separate mess, to return such meals as opportunity permits. The difficulty of an all-inclusive return of such courtesies to each individual in a mess should, however, be appreciated.

SOCIAL ACTIVITY

There are many pleasurable ways that ship's spirit can be nurtured, all of which require the interest and participation of all hands and the example and direction of seniors. Included among these are:

- Mess nights—scheduled evenings when the mess members and their ladies and other guests gather aboard ship for dinner and/or entertainment (movies or smokers). Family night may similarly be held.
- Parties, picnics, and dances ashore at beaches and service clubs.
- Group participation in recreational and athletic opportunities.
- Various kinds and types of tournaments such as golf, tennis, bridge, chess, and cribbage.

It is one of the Navy's better customs to have a night (or more) each month designated aboard ship as "Guest Night," when the officers wear dress uniform and the "Number One" dinner is served. Mess members know that in bringing aboard their wives, their dates, or guests to whom they wish to pay special honor, the guests will receive the most favorable impression of the mess, the ship, and the Navy.

Such scheduled festive occasions are popular not only because they are fun, but because they convey the feeling of belonging to a close knit organization. Every wardroom mess should tender a formal dinner to the commanding officer at some convenient time soon after his assuming command. This should be a formal dinner with wives and ladies attending, and with all hands present.

In similar fashion, a farewell dinner should be held in honor of the commanding officer prior to his being detached. These two dinners may be held separately, or a combined "Hail and Farewell" party is appropriate.

Informal farewell dinners and welcome aboard dinners for new members are generally not feasible in large messes. Additions and detachments of officers in large messes are best cared for at the regular monthly formal mess dinners when the president makes a brief speech of introduction or farewell for members—and their wives—who are leaving or "coming aboard." These officers then make suitable short responses.

In small messes of a dozen members or less, the number of arriving and departing members are generally such that each occasion may well call for separate observance. Outside entertainments by the mess need not follow any set rule but are governed by the individual circumstances, and the collective desires of the mess members, and personal desires to do things as a group.

VISITS AND CALLS ABOARD SHIP

In the Armed Services, visits and calls are more or less required by custom and by courtesy. In Service life, the formal visit fulfills a very useful purpose: not only is this a matter of courtesy, but it permits the newcomer to become acquainted with those with whom he will be associated.

In addition to complying with official orders by reporting for duty, the officer is expected to make a visit of courtesy on his commanding officer within forty-eight hours after reporting to station.

A junior making an official call on the commanding officer in his cabin aboard ship may say, "Captain Jones, I wish to pay my respects." and to the orderly before entering the cabin, "Orderly, please tell the captain that Ensign Brown wishes to pay his respects."

You should always ask the executive officer when it will be convenient for you to call on the commanding officer. When you make your call, do so in the prescribed uniform, and be sure that your linen is clean, your uniform well-pressed, and that you look your best.

Official courtesy calls should last no longer than *ten minutes,* unless the caller is specifically requested to remain longer. It is important that you learn to make a quick but courteous exit, and you should not stand in extended comments or long conversations after it becomes evident that departure is imminent.

During these initial calls, seniors closely observe their juniors, and modesty in demeanor and restraint in conversation are recommended for the junior.

In years past, a senior in sending an oral communication to a junior, would use this form: "Rear Admiral Jones presents his compliments to Captain Smith and says, etc., etc.," Such a message was delivered by an orderly. Today a less formal address may be used, according to the desires of the officer, but it is still perfectly acceptable to use the more formal greeting which includes "presents his compliments, etc., etc." A junior, however, *never* presents his compliments to a senior.

CALLS ON FOREIGN SHIPS IN FOREIGN PORTS

When an American warship calls at a foreign naval activity, the visited country's senior officer present will probably send a liaison officer to call upon the visiting ship's commander to offer courtesies and to exchange information as appropriate. This liaison officer is usually invited to the wardroom after his visit with the commanding officer. He gives pertinent information and assistance to wardroom members who are planning excursions ashore as well as to those who wish pertinent information in general about the port of call. If security clearance and official approval for such an act are obtained, it is proper to make the liaison officer an honorary member of the mess, with an invitation to live aboard during the visit. It is also courteous to include his family in an invitation to be guests of the wardroom for a visit.

After the prescribed exchange of official calls by senior officers, it is appropriate and courteous for committees of the visiting ship's officers to make calls on the wardrooms of the other foreign ships in port, in the same order in which the respective commanding officers have exchanged visits. For this purpose the wardroom should have printed or engraved calling cards which are suitable for use in extending formal invitations for a meal, for movies in the mess, or for receptions.

The liaison officer may deliver to the wardroom guest cards or invitations to honorary membership in the port's officers' club, or country club, as well as invitations to social functions, such as cocktail parties or dances, etc. These invitations should be answered promptly and politely, in handwritten replies. If visiting officers are made honorary members of any club, they should be sure to visit the club and sign the guest register there.

When your ship is in a foreign port for several days, it is desirable that members of the mess give a dinner to their foreign hosts to repay the hospitality and kindnesses that have been extended to the ship. A buffet supper usually is the most practicable method of entertaining.

Thank-you notes for all courtesies received during a visit should be written promptly by the visiting ship's officers upon its departure from the port.

CALLS ON FOREIGN SHIPS IN U. S. PORTS

When a foreign ship visits your home port, special rules of good manners and courtesy apply. A committee is customarily sent to the visiting ship to ask if there is anything you can do to make their visit more pleasant —especially if you have recently visited the home country of the ship, or when your own ship is close aboard the visitor. In some ports, when foreign ships arrive, the nearest ship of the home Navy may be designated as the "host ship." It is then the host ship's specific responsibility to assist the visitor in any way possible. This usually includes—in addition to exchanges of visits and meals—a standing invitation for the movies and/or appropriate athletic and recreational events.

Generally, when more than one U. S. ship is present, the senior officer present designates a ship to send a committee; this action precludes too many visits.

RELATIONS WITH ENLISTED PERSONNEL

Officers' country (the wardroom, staterooms, washrooms, and heads assigned to officers) is out of bounds for enlisted personnel unless these are on official duty. The wardroom is normally not to be used as an office by any member, so contacts with enlisted personnel should be confined to their part of the ship or to the departmental office. On a small ship, this may be your stateroom.

RELATIONS WITH STEWARDSMEN

Every officer must always be civil and just in all his relations with stewardsmen. If you have a complaint, make it to the mess caterer or mess treasurer who has charge of the stewards.

The stewardsman is usually interested in his job of keeping your room ship-shape—but don't expect him to take any greater interest in its appearance than you do. He will usually keep things up to standard if you call his attention to each omission immediately after it happens.

There is a certain minimum of personal service which officers should require of the stewardsmen assigned them. This service consists of daily cleaning and straightening of rooms, the weekly duties assigned to them.

However, you must consider the number of stewardsmen available, how much work the stewardsman has to do elsewhere, and the time he has to do it.

In general, one word of praise is worth ten of censure in dealing with stewardsmen, and you accomplish most by keeping your tones cheerful. But remember—tipping of stewards is forbidden.

PAYMENT OF MESS BILL

Every officer attached to a ship belongs to one of the officers' messes in that ship, and he is required to pay to the mess treasurer the full amount of his mess bill monthly, and in advance. No officer is excused from such payment except as provided in Navy Regulations.

An officer ordered to detached duty, or sent to a hospital, is entitled to a rebate of the full amount of his mess bill for the period of his absence or as prescribed by his mess by-laws. An officer ordered temporarily to duty away from the ship to which he is attached, so that he does not avail himself of the privileges of the mess during such absence, is "ordered on detached duty" within the meaning of this paragraph, even though such duty is merely in addition to his duty aboard his regular ship.

An officer granted leave of absence for more than six days (including travel time) is normally entitled to a rebate of the amount of his mess bill for the period of his actual absence in excess of six days, but no rebate shall be allowed for the first six days of leave.

Officers and others in a transient or temporary duty status, who are not entitled to reimbursement for meals, shall be charged at a rate prescribed by the president of the mess. Officers in such status may become temporary members of the mess if their temporary duty becomes of an extended nature.

All of these above special cases are normally covered in the by-laws of each mess. Also, on small ships, and when the officer complement is too small to maintain a wardroom mess, the *Manual of the Bureau of Supplies and Accounts* provides for officers subsisting from the ship's general mess on a cost-per-meal basis. This provision is also applicable when ships are in the shipyard for overhaul and it is necessary to disband the organized mess.

During time of war, however, wardroom life cannot follow the pattern just described. Prolonged general quarters, additional watches, the disadvantages of concentrating officers in a single compartment of the ship— are all factors which modify peacetime conditions. The importance of the wardroom should not, however, decline; it is merely that each ship must alter her routine to fit the particular circumstances encountered.

The attitude and spirit of the wardroom permeate the entire ship. Unless the wardroom is more than just a place to eat, its influence can be neither positive nor advantageous. It must be an institution in its own right that unites the officers and creates among them the desire for cooperation and improvement. To achieve such a status, the wardroom must satisfy the interests and characteristics of many decidedly different individuals. All members must be considerate of each other, and willing to adhere to the customs and rules essential to the common good of the group.

CHAPTER 27

Etiquette of the Quarterdeck

PIPING IMPORTANT OFFICIAL VISITORS ALONGSIDE

Piping a boat alongside—following a gun salute, if any—commences at the discretion of the boatswain's mate, lasts about twenty seconds, and ends as the official visitor steps onto the lower gangway platform. Those on deck cannot see this but may ascertain the progress of the honored visitor by observing the boatswain's mate, who stands where he has a full view of the visitor's movements. Those on deck stand at attention but do not salute during this pipe, and you will observe that the boatswain's mate does not salute. The visitor coming aboard takes no outward note of this pipe, but proceeds smartly from boat to gangway and ascends to the upper platform.

PIPING ABOARD

As the "piping alongside" ends, there is a pause, during which time the boatswain's mate steps back one pace and waits for the honored guest to ascend the ladder until his head reaches the level of the deck. At this point the boatswain's mate salutes with his left hand and commences piping the visitor aboard. All hands in the quarterdeck area salute—and hold the salute for the full duration of this pipe, plus the ruffles and flourishes or music, whichever shall be the last rendered.

As this "piping aboard" commences, the visitor ascends to the upper gangway platform, pauses, faces aft, and salutes the colors. He then turns, salutes again, holds his salute, and proceeds through to the end of the line of sideboys; then he halts, holding his salute until the end of the music. If there is no music, he holds his salute until he reaches the end of the line of sideboys. Still holding the salute he looks at the officer of the deck or senior welcoming officer, and says, "Sir, may I have (or, Sir, I request) permission to come aboard?" He then completes the salute, the boatswain ends his piping, and all hands on the quarterdeck area complete their salute.

Senior officers and ranking dignitaries have personal variations of this salutation when coming aboard, since in most cases they are acquainted with the senior officer greeting them and naturally make their salutation a personal one.

All hands stand at attention during the greeting ceremonies, which will

281

frequently involve inspection of the guard, to be followed by introduction of the distinquished guest to certain principal officers on deck. During this personal greeting ceremony only those personally involved will salute, shake hands if appropriate, and be prepared for suitable short rejoiner if addressed. All others stand at attention until the visitor has left the quarterdeck and "carry-on" has been sounded.

Upon departure, notice is sent to the quarterdeck by the flag lieutenant, the sideboys are paraded, and all hands in the quarterdeck area act as follows:

Attention is sounded just prior to the arrival of the visitor on the quarterdeck. The visitor steps into the quarterdeck area, takes leave of the principal officers, turns, addresses the officer of the deck, and says, "Sir, may I have (or, Sir, I request) permission to leave the ship?" The visitor, holding his salute, proceeds through the line of sideboys, faces the national colors and pauses to terminate his salute, then proceeds down the gangway.

The boatswain's mate terminates his piping as the visitor's head passes below the level of the deck. All hands in the quarterdeck area terminate their salute and remain at attention when this pipe ends.

The boatswain's mate observes the visitor going down the gangway, and as the visitor steps into the boat, commences piping the boat away from the side. During this ceremony all hands in the quarterdeck area remain at attention but do not salute.

The gun salute is fired just before the boat comes alongside upon arrival, and as soon as the boat is clear upon departure. The visitor's boat lies to during the gun salute. All hands on deck stand at attention and salute during the gun salute.

The officer receiving the gun salute stands in his boat, faces the quarterdeck, and renders the hand salute from the first to the last gun.

It will be a high point in the junior officer's life when he receives side honors aboard ship. Therefore he should memorize the correct procedure so that he will not embarrass himself, his ship, or his country—because it might happen—that the first time he receives side honors might be aboard a foreign ship.

SALUTING ON THE QUARTERDECK

As already stated, all officers and men, whenever reaching the quarterdeck of a man-of-war, whether from a boat, a gangway, or from shore, shall salute the national ensign. And, as stated, in leaving the ship the same salutes shall be rendered in inverse order.

It was formerly customary for all hands to salute when coming into the quarterdeck area from any part of the ship. This custom is no longer strictly followed in some of the smaller ships, but is a custom that should be recognized.

In man-of-war routine today it is generally customary for all hands having no official business on the quarterdeck to keep clear. Those having official business approach the officer of the deck smartly and salute him and carry out their official conversation. Those having official reason to come on the quarterdeck, and whose business does not require that they address the officer of the deck, will generally approach the quarterdeck area in an alert manner, salute the officer of the deck if he is in the vicinity, and then speak to the quartermaster, or any other person with whom they have official business.

A person having entered the quarterdeck area while the officer of the deck is at the other gangway need not make a point of this initial salute until the officer of the deck has occasion to come near, at which time he should come to attention and render the salute.

The situation to bear in mind is that the quarterdeck is an official area, with very official responsibilities calling for a precise routine. This routine is governed by the officer of the deck, who is responsible. All strangers coming into this area, whether from off the ship or another part of the ship, should do so only for official reasons and should stay as short a time as possible and conduct themselves officially while in the prescribed quarterdeck area. Loitering in the area of the quarterdeck is never condoned.

LADY GUESTS ABOARD

When you bring a lady guest aboard, she will precede you. If this is her first time aboard, she may ask for detailed instructions. The following is the proper procedure:

When the lady reaches the quarterdeck she should step quickly aboard— and then step out of the way so that you (her officer escort) will be clear as you execute the ritual of saluting the colors aft, and then turning and saluting the officer of the deck. It is well for her to be careful *not* to stand between you and the officer of the deck as you exchange salutes. She should not distract either officer in their performance of this traditional ritual.

Following this brief salute, the lady should join her escort, who will then introduce her to the officer of the deck.

A lady may wish to make some recognition of the flag when coming aboard or leaving a ship. This is accomplished by the lady hesitating at the top of the gangway and glancing up for a moment at the flag. When women are not military personnel, they are not privileged to honor the flag with a salute. But such an act as described above is in good taste as well as being patriotic.

A woman member of the Armed Services renders the same salute and honors as her male counterparts.

CHAPTER 28

Salutes

Certain customs, traditions, and usage have from time immemorial been distinctive of the military forces. These customs are the hallmark of the Service officer and they contain certain little differences, often stemming back to glorious tradition, of which the officer has great reason to be proud. It is a mistake to think that these differences are stubbornly maintained by Service people just to be different. Just as your way of life in its connection with the Service is different from any other, so are your ways of doing things just enough different that a real military man is known by his manners.

There is a touch of saltiness in many naval customs, and even in their way of "thinking." But saltiness, rather becoming in Service language and in customs, should, by and large, remain in the Navy.

Various customs and traditions are covered in the regulations of the particular Service as well as in specific regulations of the Service Academy itself. With specific adaptations they are also covered in instructional material at the Academies and the various Reserve and officer training programs.

All groups should consult the regulations on this subject at their earliest opportunity. The rules for military etiquette are founded on custom and tradition and their strict observance forms an important factor in the maintenance of discipline. It must be understood that these evidences of respect and courtesy are observed equally by all officers and men of the Service, and the responsibility is a mutual one in which the junior accepts the role of initiating the act.

THE HAND SALUTE

The hand salute is required on military installations both on and off duty. At other places and times, it may be suspended by regulation or local order; however, it is important to remember that the salute is an act of military courtesy. When in doubt salute.

You will always salute the captain (or any flag officer) any time you meet him during the day. You should salute your other seniors the first time you meet them each day. Remember "Precept and Example"; those of less rank than you will imitate you, for better or for worse.

Saluting distance is that distance at which recognition is easy. Usually it does not exceed *thirty paces*. The salute is rendered when the person to be saluted is *six paces* distant, or at the nearest point of approach if it is apparent that he is not going to approach to within six paces. Twenty-five paces is not considered excessive. Hold the first position of the salute until the person saluted has passed or the salute is returned, then you execute the second movement of the hand salute.

A salute is rendered only at a halt or a walk. If running, a person comes to a walk before saluting.

Salutes are usually accompanied by an exchange of greetings, depending upon the time of day, such as: "Good morning, Sir," or "Good evening, Captain Blank." The customary greetings are:

- From early morning until noon: "Good morning—."
- From noon to sunset: " Good afternoon—."
- From sunset until turning in: "Good evening—."

When overtaking a senior, and the junior must pass him, the salute shall be given when the junior is abreast of the senior and the junior should ask, "By your leave, Sir?"

In the Army and Air Force, salutes are exchanged whether individuals are covered or uncovered. It is customary in the Air Force that when a senior officer on foot approaches a junior, the junior renders the salute *at or within twelve paces*. Should the junior be at double-time when he encounters the senior, the junior slows his pace to quick-time, renders the salute, then resumes double-time. Should the senior wish to speak to the junior, the junior salutes as the senior approaches and again when the conversation is terminated.

UNCOVERING

Navy protocol does not call for saluting when uncovered except for the return of uncovered salutes rendered first by Army or Air Force personnel. The Navy's exception in this case follows the general rule that *"Social customs or military courtesy should always be interpreted so as to prevent awkward situations."* Therefore, the Navy establishes an exception whereby any uncovered salute may be returned.

Individuals *under* arms uncover only when:

- Seated as a member of or in attendance on a court or board
- Entering places of divine worship
- Indoors and not on duty
- In attendance at an official reception
- When entering messing facilities during meal hours.

WHEN TO SALUTE

The salute is rendered but *once* if the senior remains in the immediate vicinity and no conversation takes place. If a conversation does take place, the junior again salutes the senior on departing or when the senior leaves.

In making reports, the person making the report salutes first, regardless of rank. An example of this is the case of a regimental commander making a report to the brigade adjutant during a ceremony or a commander head of department making a report to a lieutenant officer of the deck.

The saluting requirement varies upon various occasions, such as:

- If you are in the company of a junior officer and a senior approaches, you should make sure that the junior is aware of the senior's approach. This may be done by a pause in the conversation. When the junior officer salutes, you salute with him.
- If you are in the company of a senior officer and a junior approaches, you salute at the same time as the senior, and you hold your salute until after both officers have dropped theirs. If the senior is unaware of the junior's salute, do not interrupt him by rendering your salute to the junior.
- Customarily, you will salute with your right hand. If an injury prevents your doing so, render a left-hand salute.

Reporting to an Officer

The salute is always rendered by the junior on reporting to a senior. Juniors are expected to rise and stand at attention whenever a senior officer enters their room or an office in which they are present, and remain standing until the senior gives permission to carry on.

A junior shall stand at attention when formally addressed or when being addressed by a senior. If covered, the junior shall salute when first addressed and again upon the conclusion of the conversation. If uncovered, the junior stands at attention throughout the conversation unless otherwise directed.

Midshipmen, Cadets, and other officer candidates are subject to local regulations which generally require that when addressing an officer, during the salute and before entering upon any conversation, they give their names —as, for instance, "Midshipman Doe, Sir." It is customary to relax this procedure as officer candidates approach graduation and as they become known to their senior officers. This is a matter for the officer candidate's own good judgment. The word "Sir" shall always be added to statements by the very junior. Thus, "I report for duty, Sir." The "Sir" is a military expression which is always used in connection with "yes" or "no," whenever conversing with seniors.

Reporting indoors unarmed: When reporting to an officer in his office, a junior not wearing arms removes his hat, knocks, and enters when told to do so. Upon entering he should approach to within about two paces from the officer and stand at attention. While standing, a salutation such as "Good morning, Sir, I wish to make the daily magazine report," should be spoken. When the business has been terminated, he leaves promptly.

On shipboard, the salutation and the manner of conducting the following business will ordinarily follow prescribed lines of official informality as befits working shipboard life. Too rigid formality must be avoided. The respect due the senior officer is a most important factor of the situation and as long as this is shown in a sincere manner, proper shipboard procedure will not be a problem.

Reporting indoors, under arms: Ordinarily, in the Service reports are not made indoors under arms except in rare cases. In carrying a rifle, a junior enters with the rifle at the trail, halts, and renders the rifle salute at *order arms.* When wearing sidearms or duty belt, the hand salute is given and the hat is kept on.

Reporting outdoors: The procedure outdoors is the same as described in the foregoing two paragraphs. The hat is never removed outdoors, and the junior armed with the rifle may, in approaching the senior, carry it at the trail or at right shoulder arms. He executes the rifle salute at the order or at right shoulder arms.

It is improper to change the rifle position when addressing or being addressed by a senior except during a formal inspection. For example, if at right shoulder arms upon approaching or being approached by a senior, you render the salute at the position held. This avoids awkwardness which would result if the junior approached the senior at right shoulder arms, then came to the order—and then rendered the salute.

The term "outdoors" is construed to include such buildings as armories, gymnasiums, and other huge-roofed inclosures used for drills. Theater canopies, covered walks, and other shelters open on the sides to the weather, are also considered outdoors.

"Indoors" includes offices, corridors, etc. The expression "under arms" means carrying the arms, or having them attached to the person by sling, holster, or other means. In the absence of arms it refers to the equipment pertaining directly to the arms, such as cartridge belt, pistol holder, or automatic rifle belt.

SALUTING IN GROUPS

In formation: Individuals in formation do not salute or return salutes except at the command PRESENT ARMS. The individual in charge will salute and acknowledge salutes for the whole formation. Commanders of organizations or detachments which are not a part of a larger formation salute officers of higher grades by bringing the organization or detachment to attention before saluting.

An individual in formation *at ease* or *at rest* comes to attention when addressed by a person superior to him in rank. The group will remain at attention until directed by the senior to CARRY ON, at which time it is proper for the group to resume normal activity. The group will continue to be aware of the senior's presence during the time he is in conversation with members of the group, or whatever his business may be.

Not in formation: On the approach of an officer of higher rank, a group of individuals not in formation is called to attention by the first person noticing the senior officer, and all in the group come to attention and salute. Individuals participating in games, and members of details at work, do not salute. The individual in charge of a work detail—if not actively engaged —salutes or acknowledges salutes for the whole detail. A unit resting alongside a road does not come to attention upon the approach of an officer.

However, if the officer addresses an individual or group, they come to attention and remain at attention (unless otherwise ordered) until the termination of the conversation, at which time they salute the officer.

SALUTING IN AUTOMOBILES

Navy procedure in the case of military personnel in automobiles is generally more liberal than that of the Army or Air Force. When senior officers pass in an automobile, juniors should stand at attention and render the salute and have no concern whether the salute is returned by the senior officer in the car.

In some cases, it may be awkward (due to the presence of ladies or civilians in the car) for the senior officer to return the salute properly. He may then properly make recognition by a modified salute or a slight nod of the head. You salute only when the car is at a halt and the engine is not running. Salutes are not required in any case where it would adversely affect the driver's ability to operate the car safely.

Salutes are not exchanged between persons in different moving automobiles, or between persons in moving automobiles and pedestrians, except:

- When an automobile is clearly marked by methods prescribed in regulations to indicate the presence of a general officer
- When required as part of a ceremony.

In case a detail is riding in an automobile, the individual in charge will render the hand salute for the entire detail. At the Service Academies, Midshipmen and Cadets salute officers in moving automobiles—when they recognize the officers as such.

Juniors must be alert to notice the passing of automobiles from which the flag of a high ranking dignitary is displayed and, when such is observed, be punctilious in saluting the occupant of the car. These salutes shall be rendered at all times, day or night, on all occasions when meeting or passing near a senior officer, whether he be covered or not, except upon occasions of such informality that saluting might become continuous or awkward. In circumstances where local regulations prescribe special procedure, those regulations take precedence.

You should remember that officers of high rank, civilian leaders of the Defense Department, or foreign dignitaries riding in automobiles will have the insignia of the highest ranking passenger displayed on the automobile in either flag or plate form.

COURTESIES TO INDIVIDUALS

When an officer enters a room, Midshipmen, Cadets and other juniors present will uncover (if unarmed) and stand at attention until the officer directs otherwise or leaves the room. When more than one person is present, the first to see the officer commands "Attention!" in a sufficiently loud and clear tone.

When an officer enters a room used as an office, workshop or recreation room, those at work or play therein are not required to come to attention unless addressed by him. A junior, when addressed by a senior, comes to attention—except in the transaction of routine business between individuals at work.

A junior shall always answer "Sir" or "Here, Sir," when his name is called by an officer. However, it is preferable for the junior to call the senior by his title and name, such as "Captain Jones," rather than by the impersonal "Sir."

Juniors escorting young ladies will, on meeting their senior officers, render the customary salute. If seated, you should rise and salute. It is customary for the lady being escorted to remain seated. However, on both occasions, it is considered good form for her to look at the officer being saluted, during the period of the salute, and to that extent she will join in the recognition by her escort of the senior officer.

Midshipmen or Cadets are expected to salute their contemporaries on duty when addressed by or addressing them officially.

All officers must remember that personal likes and dislikes have nothing to do with salutes. Therefore, you salute those whom you like and those whom you do not like, without discrimination.

WHOM TO SALUTE

As a member of the Armed Services, you will salute all individuals who are senior to you in rank in any of the Armed Forces of the United States or of friendly foreign governments. In addition, there are certain appointed or elected civilian members of both our National and State governments who are so honored. Among the individuals of the United States you customarily salute are:

- President of the United States
- Vice President of the United States
- State Governors
- Secretary of Defense
- Senators and Congressmen of the United States
- Deputy Secretary of Defense
- Secretaries of the Navy, Air Force, and Army
- Assistant Secretaries of Defense
- Under Secretaries of the Navy, Air Force and Army
- Assistant Secretaries of the Navy, Air Force, and Army
- Officers, male and female, in any of the U. S. Armed Forces.

Among the members of the friendly foreign governments whom you salute are:

- Heads of State
- Ambassadors
- Ministers of Defense or other civilian leaders of Defense Establishments and their assistants at or above the level of the Assistant Secretary of the Navy, Air Force, and Army.
- Officers, male or female, in any of the Armed Forces.

WHEN NOT TO SALUTE

In some situations, the salute is not appropriate. In general, you do *not* salute when:

- Engaged in routine work if the salute would interfere.
- Indoors, except when reporting to a senior or when on duty as a sentinel or guard.
- Carrying articles with both hands or being otherwise so occupied as to make saluting impracticable.
- The rendition of the salute is obviously inappropriate.
- A prisoner (the guard does the saluting for the prisoner).
- Working as a member of a detail, or engaged in sports or social functions.
- You are the driver of a moving automobile. However, whenever practicable, you should return the salutes of others.
- In places of public assemblage such as theaters or churches, and in public conveyances.
- You are in the ranks of a formation. However, if at ease in a formation, you come to attention when addressed by a senior.

CHAPTER 29

Flag Etiquette

A military man is expected to be something of an expert upon the national flag, including its history, its etiquette, and the customs and conventions which govern its display and handling. But regardless of whether one is in military or civilian life, every loyal American citizen should know the history of his country's flag.

HISTORY

With the onset of the American Revolution each of the thirteen colonies created its own flag, frequently, several of them. They were symbolic of the country and the struggle, carrying a tree, anchor, rattlesnake, or beaver and a motto such as "HOPE," "LIBERTY," or "AN APPEAL TO HEAVEN." A noted one bore a coiled rattlesnake and the motto "DON'T TREAD ON ME." Each regiment raised had its own colors, and the naval vessels and privateers fitted out by each colony flew distinctive flags.

Clearly some standardization became necessary as the colonies drew closer together and the Revolution grew. On December 2, 1775, the Continental Congress approved the design of a flag to be flown by the ships departing to intercept British supply vessels. This flag was first hoisted the following day aboard the *Alfred,* at Philadelphia, by Lieutenant John Paul Jones. It consisted of thirteen red and white stripes and, on a canton, the British Union Jack with its crosses of St. George and St. Andrew.

On January 1, 1776, identical flags were displayed in the lines of the colonial forces besieging Boston, the same day that the new Continental Army came into being. This famous flag has been called the Continental flag and, later, the Grand Union flag. After the Declaration of Independence, continued use of the British Union Jack became inappropriate, and a new flag was created. The first Act of Congress establishing the Stars and Stripes, June 14, 1777, ordained the present arrangement of stripes but merely stated that the thirteen white stars would represent "a new constellation" on a union of blue.

It is not surprising that different arrangements should appear. The Continental Army adopted a design in which the thirteen stars were arranged in a circle so that no colony should take precedence. The first Navy version of the Stars and Stripes had the stars arranged in a staggered formation in alternate lines and rows of threes and twos, on a blue field. Even variations in the stripes continued, and privateers continued to use the superseded flag with its British Union Jack. But eventually order emerged from what must have been a chaotic condition.

Both stars and stripes continued to be added: after the admission of Kentucky and Vermont, a resolution was adopted by Congress on May 1, 1795, making the flag one of fifteen stars and fifteen stripes. This flag flew over Fort McHenry on the occasion of its bombardment by a British fleet and inspired Francis Scott Key to write "The Star-Spangled Banner," later to become our National Anthem. This resolution provided for the addition of a stripe and a star for each new state.

Realizing that the flag would soon become unwieldy, Captain Samuel C. Reid, U. S. Navy, who commanded the *General Armstrong* during the War of 1812, suggested to Congress that the stripes be fixed at thirteen in number to represent the original thirteen colonies that had struggled to found the nation and became its first states, and that a star be added to the blue field for every state coming into the Union. This suggestion became the text of a resolution by Congress, effective April 18, 1818, whereby the flag should contain thirteen alternate red and white stripes representing the thirteen original states, with a new star being added for each new state on the July 4th following its admission. The flag next ordered had twenty stars.

During the Mexican War the Stars and Stripes had twenty-eight and and twenty-nine stars; during the Civil War it had from thirty-three to thirty-five, no stars being removed because of the states which had seceded. In the Spanish-American War it had forty-five stars. During the first and second World Wars and the Korean conflict it had the familiar forty-eight stars. With the admission of Alaska as a state, a forty-ninth star was added to the flag.

The *jack,* a nautical device, corresponds in design to the blue field and its stars. It is flown from the jackstaff (in the bow) from government vessels while at anchor, provided that the National flag is being displayed. Another American flag frequently seen is the yachting ensign, displayed by privately owned craft, which consists of the thirteen red and white stripes and a blue field with thirteen stars arranged in a circle.

HOW TO DISPLAY THE FLAG

The National flag should be raised and lowered by hand. It should be displayed only from sunrise to sunset, or between such hours as may be designated by proper authority. You do not raise the flag while it is furled. Unfurl it, then hoist it quickly to the top of the staff. In lowering it, however, lower it slowly and with dignity. Place no objects on or over the flag. For instance, various articles are sometimes placed on a speaker's table covered with the flag. This practice should be avoided.

When displayed in the chancel or on a platform in a church, the flag should be placed on a staff at the clergyman's right, and all other flags at his left. If displayed in the body of the church, the flag should be at the congregation's right as they face the clergyman.

Do not use the flag as a portion of a costume or athletic uniform. Do not embroider it upon cushions or handkerchiefs, or print it on paper napkins or boxes.

Other miscellaneous rules are:

- When displayed over the middle of the street, the flag should be suspended vertically, with the union to the north in an east-and-west street, or the east in a north-and-south street.
- When displayed with another flag, from crossed staffs, the flag of the United States of America should be on the right (the flag's own right) and its staff should be in front of the staff of the other flag.
- When the flag is to be flown at half-mast, it should be hoisted to the peak for an instant, and then lowered to the half-mast position; but before being lowered for the day, it should again be raised to the peak. By "half mast" is meant hauling down the flag to one-half the distance between the top and the bottom of the staff. On Memorial Day the flag is displayed at half-mast until noon only, then it is hoisted to the top of the staff for the rest of the day.
- When flags of States or cities or pennants of societies are displayed on separate halyards, but from the same pole on which the flag of United States of America is being flown, the latter should always be hoisted first and lowered last.
- When the flag is suspended over a sidewalk from a rope, extending from house to pole at the edge of the sidewalk, the flag should be hoisted out from the building, toward the pole, union first.
- When the flag is displayed from a staff projecting horizontally or at any angle from the window sill, balcony, or front of a building, the union of the flag should go clear to the peak of the staff (unless the flag is to be displayed at half-mast).
- When the flag is used to cover a casket at funerals or ceremonies honoring a person deceased, it should be so placed that the union is at the head and over the left shoulder. The flag should not be lowered into the grave or allowed to touch the ground.
- When the flag is displayed in a manner other than by being flown from a staff, it should be displayed flat, whether indoors or out. When displayed either horizontally or vertically against a wall, the union should be uppermost and to the flag's own right; that is, to the observer's left. When displayed in a window, it should be

displayed in the same manner; that is, with the union or blue field to the left of the observer in the street. When festoons, rosettes, or drapings in the National Colors are desired, bunting of blue, white, and red should be used, but never the flag itself.

- In this country or in any parade of U. S. troops, when carried in a procession with another flag or flags, the Stars and Stripes should have the place of honor at the right; or, when there is a line of other flags, our National flag may be *in front* of the center of that line.
- International usage forbids the display of the flag of one nation above that of another nation in time of peace.
- When the flags of two or more nations are displayed, they should be flown from separate staffs of the same height, and the flags should be of approximately equal size.
- A federal law provides that a trademark cannot be registered which consists of, or comprises, among other things, "the flag, coat-of-arms, or other insignia of the United States, or any simulation thereof."
- At all times, every precaution should be taken to prevent the flag from becoming soiled. It should not be allowed to touch the ground or floor, or to brush against objects.
- When the flag is used at the unveiling of a statue or monument, it should not be used as a covering of the object to be unveiled. If it is displayed on such occasions, it should not be allowed to fall to the ground, but should be carried aloft to form a feature of the ceremony.
- The pledge to the flag is as follows: "I pledge allegiance to the flag of the United States of America and to the Republic for which it stands, one Nation, under God, indivisible, with Liberty and Justice for all."

APPROVED FLAG CUSTOMS

Laws have been written to govern the use of the flag and to insure a proper respect for the Stars and Stripes. Custom has decreed certain other observances in regard to its use.

All Services have precise regulations regarding the display of the national flag—when, where, and how it shall be hoisted or lowered.

When U. S. Naval vessels are at anchor in port, the flag is flown from the flagstaff daily from 8 A.M. to sunset. When other vessels are entering or leaving port, the flag is flown *prior* to 8 A.M. and *after* sunset.

When the ship is entering or leaving port, or is in sight of land or another vessel, the flag is flown during daylight from the gaff, if such is rigged; otherwise, it is flown from the flagstaff.

It is the custom at posts and stations to raise the flag every morning at 8 o'clock, and it remains flying until sunset.

Honors to the Colors should be rendered at the gangway by everyone when boarding or leaving a ship of the U. S. Navy. If in civilian clothing, you give the hand salute the same as if in uniform.

More than half a century ago, it was the custom to salute the National flag by uncovering; nowadays the hand salute is rendered by personnel of the Armed Services when in uniform and covered.

In the U. S. Navy, only one flag may be flown above the Stars and Stripes, and that is the Church Pennant, a dark blue cross on a white background. Code Signal Books of the Navy, which date back to the early 60's, state: "The Church Pennant will be hoisted immediately above the ensign (National flag) at the peak or flagstaff at the time of commencing and kept hoisted during the continuance of divine service on board all vessels of the Navy."

The flag can be displayed on all days when the weather permits; but it should especially be displayed on New Year's Day, January 1; Inauguration Day, January 20; Lincoln's Birthday, February 12; Washington's Birthday, February 22; Armed Forces Day, third Saturday in May; Memorial Day (halfstaff until noon), May 30; Flag Day, June 14; Independence Day, July 4; Labor Day, first Monday in September; Constitution Day, September 17; Columbus Day, October 12; Veterans Day, November 11; Thanksgiving Day, fourth Thursday in November; Christmas Day, December 25; and such other days as may be proclaimed by the President of the United States, as well as on the birthdays of States (the dates of their admission into the Union), and on State holidays.

If a Service man or woman dies while on active duty, the flag for the funeral ceremonies is provided by the Service to which he or she belonged. However, if he—or she—dies as an honorably discharged veteran, the flag is provided by the Veterans Administration, Washington, D.C., and may be procured from the nearest post office.

In filling out the application, the person signing for the flag must state whether he is the next of kin or, if of other kinship, he must state his relation. The flag must be presented to the next of kin at the proper time during the burial service. If there is no relative of the deceased or, if one cannot be located, the flag must be returned to the Veterans Administration in the franked container provided for that purpose.

Postmasters require proof of honorable discharge of a deceased Service member before issuing the flag for use at funeral ceremonies, but flags are issued promptly upon proper evidence being presented.

When the national flag is worn out, it should be disposed of with due reverence. According to an approved custom, the union is first cut from the flag; and then the two pieces, which now no longer form a flag, are cremated.

UNITED NATIONS FLAG REGULATIONS

The United Nations flag code prescribes that the United Nations flag may be displayed as follows:

- When the United Nations flag is displayed with one or more other flags, all flags so displayed should be displayed on the same level and should be of approximately equal size.
- On no occasion may any flag displayed with the UN flag be displayed on a higher level than the UN flag, nor on any occasion may a flag so displayed with the UN flag be larger than the UN flag.
- The UN flag may be displayed on either side of any flag without being considered to be subordinated to any other flag.
- The UN flag should normally only be displayed on buildings and on stationary flagstaffs from sunrise to sunset.
- The UN flag should not be displayed on days when the weather is inclement.
- The UN flag should never be carried flat or horizontal, but always aloft and free. It should never be used as a drapery of any sort and should never be festooned, drawn back, nor up in folds, but always allowed to fall free.

The United Nations flag will be used generally to demonstrate the support of the United Nations and to further its principles and purposes. It should be displayed on the following occasions:

- On all national and official holidays.
- On United Nations Day, October 24.
- On the occasion of any official event particularly in honor of the United Nations.

HONORS TO THE NATIONAL ANTHEM

Outdoors: The following rules are customarily observed whenever and wherever the National Anthem or "To the Color" is played (not in formation):

- At the first note, all dismounted personnel present will face the music, stand at attention, and render the prescribed salute—except at the "Escort of the Color" or at "Retreat" you face toward the color or flag. The position of salute will be retained until the last note of the music is sounded.
- Vehicles in motion will be brought to a halt. Persons riding in a

passenger car or on a motorcycle will dismount and salute as directed above. Occupants of other types of military vehicles remain seated at attention in the vehicle, the individual in charge of each vehicle dismounting and rendering the hand salute. Tank or armored car commanders salute from the vehicle.

- The above marks of respect are shown the National Anthem of any friendly country when played upon official occasions.

Indoors: When the National Anthem is played indoors at a formal gathering, individuals will stand at attention and face the flag (if one is present), otherwise, face the music. You do not salute, unless covered or under arms.

OTHER HONORS

To colors: Military personnel passing an uncased color (standard) salute at a distance of six paces and hold the salute until they have passed six paces beyond it. Similarly, when an uncased color (standard) passes by, you salute when it is six paces away and hold the salute until it has passed six paces beyond you. Small flags carried by individuals are not saluted.

Personal honors: When personal honors are rendered, military personnel present, not in uniform, salute at the first note of the music and hold the salute until the completion of the ruffles, flourishes, and march.

When a gun salute is rendered, military personnel being saluted, and other persons in the ceremonial party, will render the hand salute throughout the firing of the gun salute. Other persons in the vicinity of the ceremonial party will stand at attention.

Acknowledgment by persons in civilian dress may be made by standing at attention. A gun salute to the national flag requires no individual action. Other than standing at attention during dress parades—say, on the parade field at a Service Academy—all officers under the canopy are considered to be in the ceremonial party.

Military funerals: Military personnel will salute during the passing of a caisson or hearse bearing the remains in a funeral procession. Those attending a military funeral in their individual capacity or as honorary pallbearers will stand at attention, uncovered (except in cold or inclement weather), and hold the headdress over the left breast at any time when the casket is being moved by the pallbearers and during the service at the grave, including the firing of volleys and the sounding of Taps.

During the prayers, you will also bow your heads. In cold or inclement weather, you will remain covered and will execute the hand salute at any time when the casket is being moved by the pallbearers and during the firing of volleys and the sounding of Taps.

COLORS ASHORE

The flag ceremony at a Service Academy is typical of this ceremony at all post and station ceremonies, and its observance should be scrupulously correct.

"First call" is sounded by the bugler five minutes before "Colors." At the first note of "Colors," all traffic stops, and persons driving automobiles should draw up to the curb, stop, and remain quietly in the car. Pedestrians stop and face the flag, if they can see it, or face toward the sound of the bugle. All hands stand at attention, and men and women in uniform salute.

All men in civilian clothes remove their hats and with their left hand hold their hats over their hearts. All men and women in civilian clothes stand perfectly quiet, their hands free at their sides until the ceremony is ended. At the last note of the National Anthem, or of the sounding of "Carry on" by the bugler, all hands resume their normal activity.

SECTION IX

PERSONAL MATTERS IN EVERYDAY LIFE

CHAPTER 30

Your Religion

The religious beliefs of men have very much in common, regardless of formal religious affiliations. Notwithstanding the many different religious denominations and the great variety of individual attitudes toward religion, the student of theology is generally impressed by the similarities, rather than the differences, in the basic teachings of all religions.

When you understand these similarities, it becomes apparent how ill-mannered and foolish it is for any person to make light of another's beliefs, or to make derogatory remarks about the faith of another. A person who does so is violating a basic fundamental of both his own and the other's religion—*to love thy neighbor.*

Religious discussions in dissimilar groups are generally unwise because statements, seemingly innocent to the speaker, may seem offensive to a listener. This does not mean that you should refuse to state an opinion on a religious subject, or to enter into a discussion, but it does mean that you should be careful of the company in which a religious discussion is carried on. Unless the group is composed of men of good will, intelligence, and tolerance, such discussions tend to break down into heated arguments and end in violent wrangles.

It is not enough for an officer simply to understand and respect the beliefs of another. In the social observances of religious ceremonials there are many occasions in which individuals of different religions are brought together in a common participation. It is necessary that you know the proper behavior and procedures to be followed on such occasions, since they will become a part of your everyday living.

As you go about your daily social and official life, you will be called upon to take part in numerous religious ceremonies, in either an active or impassive role. In most cases, you will do no more than stand quietly, uncovered, and with bowed head, until the ceremony is concluded.

There are other occasions when you will take an active part in the ceremony, such as funerals, weddings, christenings, and services of thanksgiving. Simple benedictions by a chaplain in an outdoor ceremony mean that you will uncover and follow the motions of the chaplain.

Ceremonies in a church or chapel will require specific knowledge of procedure. A member of a wedding party or a funeral cortege will need to learn everything possible about his responsibilities before the ceremony. In

301

some cases, you will find yourself a participant in an unfamiliar church or synagogue, and it is advisable that you find out what to do ahead of time.

BLESSINGS AT THE TABLE

As a guest at a meal, you may be called upon to take part in a simple family observance of religious custom. These expressions of thanksgiving may help you:

Catholic: "Bless us, O Lord, and these, Thy gifts, which we are about to receive from Thy bounty. Through Christ our Lord. Amen."

Jewish: "Lift up your hands toward the sanctuary and bless the Lord. Blessed art Thou, O Lord our God, King of the universe, who bringest forth bread from the earth. Amen."

Protestant: "Bless, O Lord, this food to our use, and us to thy services, and make us ever mindful of the needs of others, in Jesus' name. Amen."

When you are a guest in a home of another religious affiliation, do not attempt to use a blessing of the host's religion unless you are familiar with it. Instead, use your own favorite grace and say it in your own sincere way.

CHAPTER 31

The Military Wedding

Throughout the course of your Service career you will be called upon to take part in weddings. You may be an usher or the best man. Perhaps the wedding will be your own. It is difficult, sometimes, for officers at sea or some remote station to obtain the correct and detailed information concerning wedding ceremonies, and what is expected of the groomsmen.

The military wedding is like other weddings—except that the officers in the bridal party are in uniform, and the bride and groom usually leave the chapel or church under the traditional arch of swords. The groom's sword will be used to cut the bride's first piece of cake at the wedding reception.

The uniform worn will be in accordance with the kind of wedding planned —formal or informal—and with the seasons of the year. Evening dress uniform may be worn at the very formal wedding, and dinner dress uniform at the less formal. Dress blues or whites will be worn at informal weddings. Boutonnieres are never worn with uniforms.

The arch of swords takes place immediately following the ceremony— preferably when the couple leaves the chapel or church, on the steps or walk. The arch may be formed inside the chapel or church, upon leaving the chancel, *but this depends upon the religious convictions of the officiating chaplain or clergyman.*

Since a church is a sanctuary, the arch is formed *with permission* inside Protestant churches, and is *never* formed in Roman Catholic churches. In case of bad weather, the arch may be formed in the chapel or church vestibule.

The following information as to June Week weddings at the U. S. Naval Academy Chapel is given for the particular information of Midshipmen:

The chapel is reserved on a first-come, first-served basis. Permission for its use should be obtained as soon as you can, in order to secure the desired date and hour for your wedding. Whenever possible, applications should be made in writing to the chaplain's office at least fifteen days in advance of the event—and should be made long before that.

There is no charge for the use of the chapel, but a donation to the Chapel Fund is accepted. The fund is for the maintenance of candles, flowers, marriage books, and many other supplies.

Although a chaplain never requests—and therefore does not expect— a couple, or any member of the bride or groom's families, to donate to the fund, it is a considerate gesture for them to do so. The cost of the average wedding decorations in the Naval Academy Chapel is *twenty dollars.*

Since June is the traditional month of weddings, it is advisable that wedding dates are made earlier than usual that month. June Week weddings are held in the Main Chapel and in the smaller St. Andrew's Chapel in the lower level, one on the hour and the other at the half-hour.

In order to schedule these many June Week weddings, forms are sent to all First Classmen at the Naval Academy early in November, to be filled out and returned to the chaplain's office. Drawings will be made for positions before Christmas leave. Before June Week, wedding rehearsals will be held at the convenience of the chaplain and the couple, with a mass rehearsal held for couples who cannot previously schedule individual rehearsals.

The first wedding ceremony in the chapel will be performed immediately after graduation. Ceremonies are also held in various churches in the Annapolis community. Photographers may take pictures *after* any chapel wedding, but never during the ceremony.

THE CHAPLAIN AT MILITARY WEDDINGS

As in the case of all weddings, it is important that the engaged couple visit their chaplain or clergyman before the wedding—a month or so, if possible. Where they are of mixed faith, or where the bride has been married previously—these facts must be brought to the attention of the chaplain or clergyman before the couple continue with their wedding plans.

Although most chaplains prefer to officiate at ceremonies held in the chapel to which they are assigned, a clergyman from the couple's home church may assist at the ceremony—if this is acceptable to the chaplain and is so arranged beforehand. The officiating chaplain will be in accordance with the religious preference of the couple. The chaplain, like the clergyman, is bound by his ordination vows to uphold the laws and regulations of his particular church regarding marriage.

Navy chaplains are of many faiths, and as commissioned officers, they are subject to transfer. Therefore, customs change in Navy chapels and what is customary in one may not be carried out in another.

Chaplains on active duty are paid by the Service which they represent, and will not accept a fee. However, it is customary to offer a civilian clergyman an honorarium, usually *ten dollars.* The bridegroom pays this fee, which is usually placed in an envelope and handed to the clergyman at some time before the ceremony by the best man.

THE MUSIC

Since wedding ceremonies are religious ceremonies, the organist will play traditional wedding music and selections from the library of sacred music available in the chapel or church. The couple may select the music they prefer.

In the case of Navy weddings, when the organist is attached to the station—such as the Naval Academy Chapel—he will receive no fee for his services. At the Navy Chapel in Washington, D.C., the organist is a civilian and receives a fee of *ten dollars* for the wedding, and an additional *five dollars* when he attends the rehearsal. If the organist accompanies a soloist, there is an additional fee of *two dollars*.

It is not necessary that the organist and soloist attend the wedding rehearsal, unless the couple so desires. The fees should be given to the organist and soloist at the rehearsal—or at some convenient time prior to the wedding. The bride's family pays these fees.

It is customary for the bridal chorus from Wagner's *Lohengrin* and the wedding march from Mendelssohn's *Midsummer Night's Dream* to be used in the chapels for the processional and recessional.

FLOWERS AND DECORATIONS

Rules for decorating the chapels vary throughout the nation. At the Naval Academy Chapel, flowers, candelabra, and white hangings are furnished by the Chapel Guild and are the same for all weddings.

Other chapels, including the Navy Chapel in Washington, D.C., do not furnish them and such decorations are paid for by the bride's family. Any decorations which require alterations to the chapel or church, or which are to be fastened to the pews, walls, or items of furniture, will not be permitted without the chaplain's or clergyman's approval.

PLANNING THE WEDDING

The bride's family always announces the engagement and sends out the wedding invitations and announcements—unless the parents cannot do so, or are deceased. In such cases, a close relative of the bride may act in this capacity, and sometimes the groom's family accepts this responsibility. (See Chapter 17, *Invitations and Replies*.)

The essentials of planning a wedding are: (1) religious ceremony; (2) a father (brother, uncle, or any male relative of age) to give the bride away; (3) a best man for the groom; (4) an attendant for the bride; (5) a bouquet or corsage for the bride; (6) rings for the bride and groom (when he desires one); (7) a reception—if no more than a wedding cake and punch, tea or coffee; (8) a wedding trip of at least a day or so.

Invitations should be ordered by the bride's family *six weeks* in advance of the wedding date, and mailed out by the bride's family *four weeks* before the day. Her family sends marriage announcements *after* the wedding takes place to those to whom invitations were not sent.

WEDDING EXPENSES

The bride's family carries out the plans and main expenses of the wedding since they are responsible for their daughter up to the moment of her marriage. *But the groom should help decide the size and style of his wedding.*

The *groom's expenses* include the engagement and wedding rings; marriage license; bride's bouquet (which she selects; the center of the bouquet may be removable and used for the going-away costume); usually the corsages for both mothers; the ties and gloves for the best man and ushers, and mementoes for each. Also, the clergyman's fee, if any—and, of course, the wedding trip.

If the ushers are in civilian dress, the groom pays for their boutonnieres. But the ushers and best man pay for their own clothes, other than their ties and gloves, and for their transportation to and from the city or place of the wedding. The groom, or members of his or the bride's family, will find places for the groom's attendants to stay, otherwise the groom pays for any hotel bills incurred by his attendants.

The groom gives his bride a gift on, or just before, the wedding day. The gift is something lasting, usually jewelry. He pays for his bachelor dinner, if he has one, which is held a few days before the wedding but *not* the night before. His gifts to the ushers are usually of gold or silver, such as cigarette cases or lighters, cuff links, etc., and should all be alike.

The *bride's family* pays for all expenses of the wedding—up to the moment she leaves their care. This includes the wedding invitations and/or announcements; bridal photographs before and during the event; trousseau; flowers for the church and reception and any other decorations not furnished by the chapel or church; fees for the organist, soloist, sexton, if any; bridesmaids' bouquets and present for each (which are presented by the bride and are usually jewelry, such as a bracelet); all reception expenses, and any car expenses to and from the wedding (and, frequently, the reception). The bridal gown and all accessories are of course paid for by the bride's parents, and they usually give the bride as nice a gift as possible for the new household.

WEDDING REHEARSAL

In order that a wedding ceremony may proceed smoothly, it is customary that a rehearsal be held in the chapel, or church at least a day or so in advance of the wedding.

It is also a violation of good manners to hold such rehearsals immediately after a cocktail party or a dinner because the over-indulgence of a member, or members, of a bridal party in intoxicating drink violates the solemnity of the chapel or church, as well as the occasion.

Although it is a growing custom to schedule the rehearsal the night before the wedding, it is important that the rehearsal be held *before* the dinner for the bridal party—which is usually given by the bride's parents.

The hour of rehearsal is set with the chaplain or clergyman, and at the convenience of all members of the bridal party *who are expected to attend.* No words of the ceremony are spoken during the rehearsal, but the chaplain or clergyman will indicate at what point each member takes his role. The actual wedding rings are not used, but the motion of placing the rings on the bride's and groom's fingers is practiced.

THE WEDDING RING OR RINGS

When you are the prospective bridegroom, you will go with your fiancee to the jeweler in plenty of time to select and order the wedding ring—or rings, if you also want one.

The modern wedding ring has little space for much engraving, so it is customary to inscribe only the initials and date, with the bride's initials coming first: "A.B.S. and M.W.J. 6 June 1958"; or the man's initials may be used first in this case: "M.W.J. to A.B.S.—"; or they may simply be inscribed: "A.B.S.-M.W.J." When the wedding band is wide and you desire an inscription, any personal phrase may be used.

After the ring is selected, the bride-elect will not see it again until the ring is placed on her finger during the ceremony. You will pay for her ring, and it will be delivered to you.

When you also want a wedding ring (in the double ring ceremony), yours will be a little wider and heavier than a woman's wedding ring. You will wear it on the fourth finger of your left hand, just as the bride will, and not on your little finger, as was customary in former years. Your ring will be a gift from the bride. She pays for it, and it is engraved in a similar way to her own.

TIME OF THE WEDDING

The date and time of the wedding will be decided by the couple and the bride's mother, but in the Services the time is frequently a matter of convenience for the bridegroom. At the Naval Academy, June Week weddings are held according to the time chosen by drawings.

The most favored hour for the wedding differs in various sections of the country, with evening weddings perhaps held more frequently in the southern and southwestern states (probably due to the weather), and afternoon weddings often held at four, half-past four, or five o'clock, in northern and eastern states.

A formal wedding may be held in the daytime or at eight or half-past eight o'clock of an evening. The most formal wedding is one held in a church or chapel, but a formal wedding may also be held at home. Weddings—formal or informal—are held at almost any convenient hour of the day or evening.

Couples of various religious faiths will always discuss the time, day, and hour of their weddings with their chaplains or clergymen, priests, or rabbis, with particular concern for the Lenten season and holy days.

WHAT TO WEAR

At a Navy wedding, officers will wear the uniform in accordance with the formality of the wedding. *Evening dress uniform* conforms to civilian *white tie* or *tails. Dinner dress uniform* is in accordance with *black tie. Service blues* or *whites* compare to a dark blue or conservative business suit or a cutaway. Any male member of the bridal party not in uniform will dress accordingly. (See Chapter 2, *Service and Civilian Dress.*)

In Service weddings, the uniforms of the groom, best man, and ushers will be alike. In civilian ceremonies, the groom and best man will be dressed alike, but the ushers may be dressed like the groom and best man, or there may be slight differences in their shirts and ties. The fathers usually dress like the groom except that their ties need not match.

At Service weddings, formal or informal, the groom will carry white gloves but not wear them. The ushers wear white gloves throughout the ceremony. At civilian weddings, the groom and best man usually carry gloves, but these need not be carried at informal weddings.

When you are a member of a civilian wedding party, you will want to known the general dress for formal and informal, daytime or evening ceremonies:

Formal Daytime

The groom, best man, and ushers will wear cutaways complete with stiff collars and ascots, and boutonnieres.

The groom and best man may wear stiff collars and ascots, with the ushers wearing soft collars and ties. All ushers must be dressed alike.

Formal Evening

"White tie" or "tails" will be worn by all men in the bridal party, with different boutonnieres the only distinguishing mark between them.

"Black tie," or dinner jackets, are worn at the less formal wedding—but not before 6 P.M.

Summer formal evening weddings call for dinner jackets, usually white, since tails are not customarily worn during summer months.

Informal Daytime

Dark blue or gray business suits, white shirts, black shoes, boutonnieres for all; the bride will wear a long gown or short dress.

Summertime: white suits, white flannels with a dark coat, or any conservative summer suit. (The bride dresses the same as for informal daytime.)

Informal Evening

When bride wears long bridal gown, the groom, best man, ushers wear dinner jackets.

When bride wears short dress, all men in the bridal party wear the same as stated in Informal Daytime.

PARENTS OF THE COUPLE

While the fathers dress similarly to the groom at a civilian wedding, the mothers of the couple will wear street-length dresses for any daytime wedding and usually a dinner dress for an evening or night wedding. They will wear something on their heads—a small hat or a veiling with flowers, etc.—and long gloves, but *never* a black dress or black gloves. The fathers will wear boutonnieres and the mothers will wear corsages.

GUESTS

Officers will wear Service blues or whites at an informal wedding, or a dark blue business suit or any conservative suit according to the season. The same type of dress is worn at a formal daytime wedding, since cutaways are almost extinct for any man except those in the wedding party.

For a formal evening wedding, you will wear dinner dress uniform or a dinner jacket, but if you are a relative you may wear evening dress uniform or "tails" at a very formal wedding. Women wear long dinner dresses, with a small hat or veiling, and gloves. Children wear their best party clothes.

BRIDAL ATTENDANTS

The bride and groom may have only one attendant each; at a chapel or home wedding these would be the best man and maid or matron of honor. Usually, there are a maid or matron of honor and from two to six bridesmaids at the average wedding.

The bride will ask a sister or very close relative, or an intimate friend, to be her maid or matron of honor. The bridesmaids are close friends of the bride and usually include a sister or relative of the bridegroom.

Ushers and bridesmaids may be married or single, and they may be in the bridal party together. However, it is *not* necessary to ask a husband or wife to be a member of the wedding party when only one or the other is a close friend of the bride or groom. The husband or wife not included in the wedding party would be included in any pre-nuptial parties, but need not be invited to sit at the bridal table at the reception unless the bride and groom so desire.

At a very large wedding, there may be both a maid and matron of honor and as many as eight or ten bridesmaids, as well as junior bridesmaids (7 to 14 years of age), flower girls, pages, train bearers, and a ring bearer. Normally, this is not the case, however, since it would be overwhelming.

Frequently, the bride gives a dinner for her bridesmaids on the night that the groom gives his bachelor dinner. When such a dinner is given, this is the time for the bride to give the bridesmaids their presents, such as bracelets, or earrings, etc.

THE BEST MAN

The groom chooses his best man and ushers from among his closest friends and relatives. His best man may be a brother or intimate friend, and occasionally is his father.

The best man is the bridegroom's aide. It is his duty to carry on, regardless of what arises. In order to instill calmness in members of the bridal party, he must maintain it himself.

Before the ceremony, the best man checks on the groom's uniform, gloves, marriage license, wedding ring, sword—and if the ceremony is held in a church, he takes care of the clergyman's fee. He has notified the ushers to be at the chapel or church approximately forty-five minutes before the ceremony, and he will arrive with the groom to be sure that the latter is not late and that he is properly dressed.

Following the couple's vows, the best man joins in the recessional, in which he customarily escorts the maid or matron of honor. Afterwards, he may wish to hurry on to the place of reception and check on details—such as stowing the bridal luggage in the going-away car. He does not stand in the receiving line at the reception, but is near at hand to the groom to be of further help. His is the first toast to the bride and groom at the bridal table.

THE USHERS

The ushers represent not only the groom but the families of the bride and groom as well. They act as unofficial hosts, greeting the guests in a pleasant manner, and are escorts to the bridesmaids. Ushers will give the couple individual gifts, or they may prefer to give a major gift together.

The number of ushers depends on the size of the wedding. An average-sized chapel wedding may be well handled by four to six ushers, with more serving at a large formal wedding. When the wedding is very small, no ushers may be needed. It is not necessary to have an equal number of ushers and bridesmaids. Usually, there are more ushers than bridesmaids since they have definite duties to perform.

The main duty of the ushers is to seat guests in the chapel, church, or home. In accordance with the chaplain's faith, ushers may—or may not—wear swords while ushering. If not, the swords are left at a place convenient for the arch of swords ceremony.

At the Naval Academy Chapel, swords are not worn while ushering. They are hooked on by the ushers taking part in the wedding procession just before the Wedding March is played. The swords are thus in position for the arch of swords ceremony.

When guests arrive at the chapel, church, or home, ushers ask if they wish to be seated on the bride's side or on the groom's side, or they may ask, "Are you a relative (or friend) of the bride or groom?" Guests are seated accordingly—on the *left* of the chapel facing the altar for the bride's friends, on the *right* for the groom's.

However, when one side of the church is rapidly filling while the other side remains empty—as may happen when the groom's relatives and friends cannot go a distance to the bride's home town—then the ushers may ask late-arriving guests to sit on the groom's side of the church, regardless of whose friends they are.

When the chapel or church has two center aisles, you may select one aisle and run the entire wedding as though that were the only one in the building, and with only those aisle posts decorated.

USHERING

A woman who arrives with her husband or other male guest will be escorted to the proper pew, the man following behind. Children will follow their parents. A man attending alone walks beside the usher—who does not offer his arm.

Each woman is escorted to a pew separately unless there are many guests waiting to be escorted. Then, the usher may offer the oldest woman his arm and request the others in the party to follow. He may make appropriate remarks while escorting, but quietly, and in keeping with the dignity and reverence accorded a sanctuary. Guests should not be hurried to their seats, but the seating must be done with a minimum of delay and confusion.

Guests who arrive first are given the choice aisle seats, and later arrivals will take the inner seats. In a large wedding, the head usher may be given a typed alphabetical list of guests and the seating arrangement.

The commanding officer of the groom, and his wife, may be invited to sit in the front pew on the right if the parents of the groom are unable to attend. Where the groom's parents are in attendance, the commanding officer and his wife may be accorded courteous recognition by being seated with the groom's immediate family.

Flag officers and other commanding officers may be seated in accordance with rank just behind the families of the couple, but rigid protocol is not adhered to at weddings.

The head ushers are so designated by the groom. One usher will escort the groom's mother to her pew on the right. Just before the ceremony is to start, the head usher will escort the bride's mother to her pew on the left— and she will be the *last* person to be seated. The chapel doors will then be closed, but if they are not locked the late-comer may seat himself in the back of the chapel. *But guests are not expected to be late.*

CHAPEL OR CHURCH PEWS

It is customary that the members of the bride's family sit at the left side of a center aisle, facing the altar. Relatives and friends of the family will sit behind them. The members of the groom's family, their relatives and friends, will sit at the right side of the aisle.

When there is no central aisle, the bride's family and friends will sit at the left side of the right-hand aisle, and the family of the groom and their friends will sit at the right of the left aisle.

When there is no central aisle, the right aisle may be used for the procession to the altar, and the left aisle for the recessional—or one aisle only may be used for both the processional and recessional.

All guests are expected to be on time at a wedding. The bride and her party should be in the chapel or church about fifteen or twenty minutes before the designated hour, and should go directly to the dressing room where they make final preparation. *It is inexcusable for the bridal party to be late.*

The groom and best man should also arrive at the chapel or church about twenty minutes before the time of the ceremony, and ushers should arrive forty-five minutes before the hour of the wedding, in plenty of time to seat early-arriving guests.

When the center aisle of the chapel or church is banked by candelabra, two ushers will light the candles some fifteen minutes before the hour of the ceremony. They will proceed to the front of the chapel or church, with each usher lighting the candles on his side with the aid of tapers provided for that purpose. The pews are frequently marked by ribbons or sprays of flowers at the pew ends.

Runners are not used at the Naval Academy Chapel. When they are used in a chapel or church, two ushers will march in step to the front of the chapel where they will grasp the runner, face the back of the chapel or church, and keep walking until the runner is stretched as far as it will go.

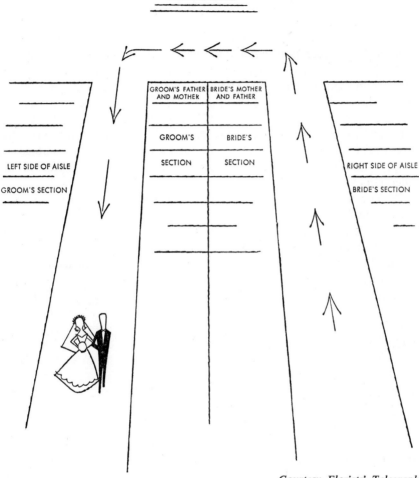

ALTAR

GROOM'S FATHER AND MOTHER · BRIDE'S MOTHER AND FATHER

GROOM'S SECTION · BRIDE'S SECTION

LEFT SIDE OF AISLE · RIGHT SIDE OF AISLE

GROOM'S SECTION · BRIDE'S SECTION

*Courtesy Florists' Telegraph
Delivery Association*

Church with two center aisles.

THE WEDDING CEREMONY

The Processional

Since the Naval Academy Chapel is the heart of the Naval Service, the following procedure, used in wedding ceremonies there, is selected as representative of Navy weddings in general.

The procession forms upon the completion of the usher's duties, with the ushers taking their places at the head of the procession in the vestibule.

The first note of the wedding march is the signal that the ceremony is about to begin. By this time, everything is in order, with everyone in his or her place.

The order of procedure is:

A. The chaplain enters from a side door, faces the altar in a quiet moment of prayer, then turns left and advances toward the congregation.

B. The groom enters, followed at about two paces by the best man, and both are in the same marching step as paced by the chaplain. As they approach the altar area, they pause in a moment of prayer, then turn left and face the congregation and the direction from which the bride will enter.

C. Simultaneously with the appearance of the groom and best man, the first ushers start forward *in pairs*. The pairs of ushers are separated by *six pew spaces*. Ushers are paired so that the shorter ones precede the taller. (In other chapels and churches the ushers may walk singly.)

D. The ushers face the altar until all are in position, then they turn together and face the approaching bride.

E. The bridesmaids follow the ushers, walking *singly* in order that their loveliness may be observed by all guests. They are also *six pew spaces apart*. The bridesmaids face the altar until the arrival of the maid of honor. (The bridesmaids may also walk in pairs.)

F. The maid or matron of honor is *eight pew spaces* behind the bridesmaids. She will also face the altar, then she and the bridesmaids *together turn right* and face the bride.

G. When there are a ring bearer and flower girl (in that order), they will walk *ten pew spaces* between the maid or matron of honor and the bride —or, five pew spaces behind the maid or matron of honor, and five pew spaces in front of the bride. (A ring bearer and/or flower girl may walk singly or in pairs. They are not used as frequently as in former years.)

H. The bride approaches on the *right* arm of her father.* The members

* Although the bride customarily enters upon the right arm of her father, it may be advisable that the bride approach the altar on the left arm of her father because: (a) it is less awkward at a certain point in the ceremony. When the father (or whoever gives the bride in marriage) is asked, "Who giveth this woman to be married to this man?" his answer, "I do" or "Her mother and I do," means that the bride is nearer the pew where the mother is seated. (b) At the time when the father places his daughter's right hand in the hand of the groom, if the daughter's right arm is in the father's left arm, this means that the passing of her hand to the hand of her husband-to-be is quite simple. (c) Moreover, when the father is on the left side of his daughter, he then must make a choice of crossing in front of her and taking her right hand and placing it in the groom's, or going around her train and coming up between the bride and groom, taking her hand and crossing it over. (d) Since the bride's mother is sitting at the left side of the chapel or church, it is symbolic of the bride's devotion to both parents that she pass between her mother and father on her way to the altar—which she cannot do when she is on the right arm of her father.

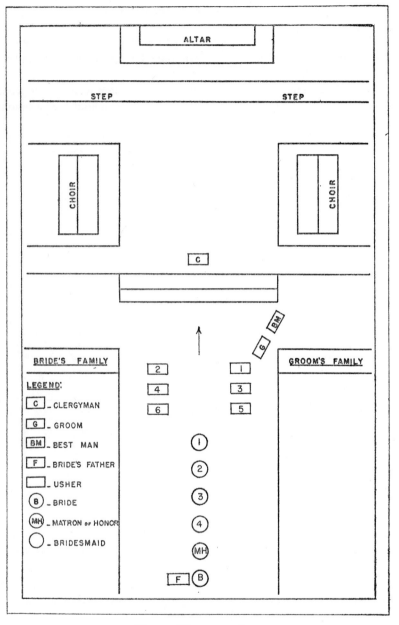

The wedding procession.

of the bridal party are now facing toward the chaplain, and the congregation is facing the altar.

I. When the bride reaches a point about three paces from the groom, the groom advances to meet her—at which time her father pauses, and she takes the *groom's* left arm.

J. Before the ceremony, the bride will tell the chaplain whether she would like the guests to be seated or to remain standing throughout the ceremony.

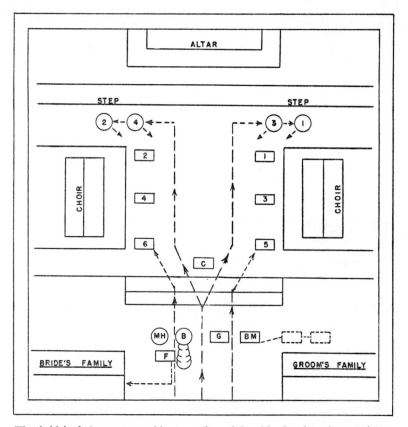

The bride's father goes to his seat after giving his daughter in marriage.

When guests are to be seated, the chaplain says, "At the request of the bride, all guests will now be seated." The father of the bride then gives his daughter in marriage, and goes to his seat.

K. The chaplain leads the way to the altar and the wedding ceremony now takes place. Upon reaching the altar steps, the bride hands her bouquet or Bible to the maid or matron of honor, and at the appropriate time the best man gives the groom the wedding ring. If the groom will also wear a

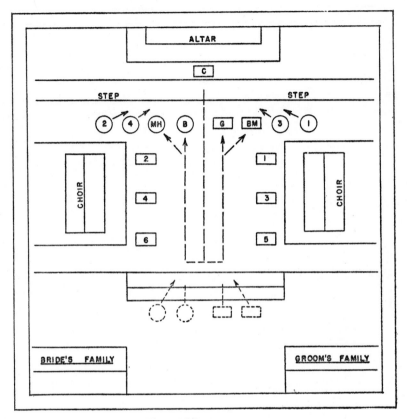

The wedding ceremony.

wedding ring, the bride at the same time receives it from the maid or matron of honor.

L. At the conclusion of the ceremony, the bride and groom are congratulated by the chaplain, and the groom may now kiss his bride. She receives her bridal bouquet or Bible from the maid or matron of honor, and holds it in her right arm during the recessional.

The Recessional

The bride and groom are the first to leave the chancel, with the bride on the *right arm* of the groom. The maid or matron of honor and the best man walk out together, followed by the bridesmaids and ushers in pairs. *(See illustration on next page.)*

When there are two more ushers than bridesmaids—as shown in the above diagrams—the fifth and sixth ushers act as escorts to the bride's and groom's mothers, who are the first (in that order) to leave the chapel. *(Illustrated on page 319.)*

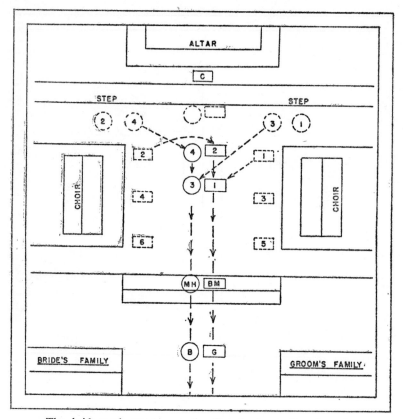

The bride and groom are the first to leave the chancel.

There is no effort made to keep step with the music during the recessional, but everyone walks with a natural, smooth gait—neither hurried nor slow. Following the families' departure, the guests leave in no precedence of departure.

It is important when a wedding reception follows elsewhere, that the bride and groom go immediately to an anteroom, or any secluded area, after they reach the vestibule in order that they are not immediately extended congratulations and best wishes by the guests.

It is the duty of the ushers (in fair weather) to see that all guests go outdoors immediately after the wedding for the arch of swords ceremony. An usher may clearly—and courteously—request that guests "Please proceed to the chapel steps."

Members of the bridal party usually stand at either or both sides of the outer door of the chapel, with guests standing at any convenient place along the steps or walk.

When the ushers have taken their positions on the steps or walk, the

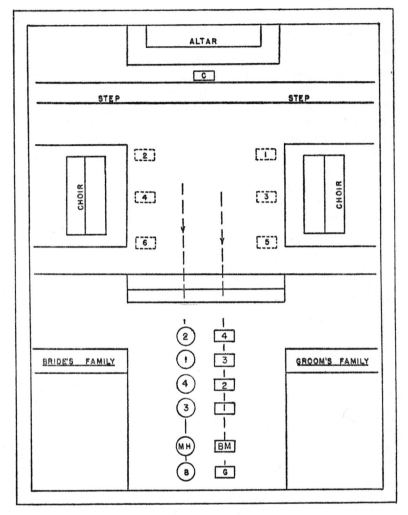

The recessional.

best man will notify the bride and groom that the arch of swords ceremony can proceed.

Arch of Swords Ceremony

Although the ushers usually act as sword bearers, other officers may be designated as sword bearers—which would accelerate the arch of swords ceremony following the wedding ceremony. In the main chapel of the Naval Academy, it is customary that six or eight ushers (or designated sword bearers) take part in the ceremony; in the smaller St. Andrews Chapel, it is customary that six ushers take part in the ceremony.

If they have removed them, the ushers hook on their swords, and proceed down the steps of the chapel where they form, facing each other in equal numbers.

The head usher gives the command, "Officers, DRAW SWORDS," which is done in one continuous motion. The bride and groom pass under the arch —*and only they may do so*—then they pause for a moment. The head usher gives the command, "Officers, RETURN (swords brought to the position of 'present arms') SWORDS."

Swords are returned to the scabbard for all but about *three or four inches* of their length. The final inches of travel are completed in unison, the swords returning home with a single click.

In *bad weather only*—when the arch of swords ceremony cannot take place outdoors, this ceremony may be held just as the couple arises after receiving the blessing. All members of the bridal party wait until the usher's swords are returned to their scabbards before the recessional proceeds.

WEDDING RECEPTIONS

The type of reception planned will depend upon the type of wedding— formal or informal—as well as the number of guests to be invited, and the time of day the wedding will take place.

A wedding may be large or small, simple or elaborate, and the reception will be in keeping with these points. A reception may be held at home, in a club or hotel, or in the church parlors.

RECEIVING LINE

At a comparatively large reception, such as one held at an Officers' Club, the mother of the bride customarily stands just inside the door, with the groom's mother standing next to her. The bride's mother greets the guests and introduces them to the groom's mother, then each guest will move on to greet each member of the bridal party, with the line formed a little apart from the mothers.

The fathers of the bride and groom may stand with the mothers for a time, but usually they prefer to be nearby and to mix with the guests. The best man and ushers never stand in the line; the best man will be near the groom, however, ready to help in any way possible, while the ushers act as unofficial hosts.

The bride and groom always stand together, and the bride is always on *the groom's right*. Next in order will be the maid or matron of honor, then the bridesmaids. If a flower girl stands in the line for a while (she usually is seven or under), she will stand on the groom's left. When sisters are bridesmaids, the older sister will precede the younger. The line will remain intact until all guests have been greeted.

If you are a guest at a reception and there is no one to announce you

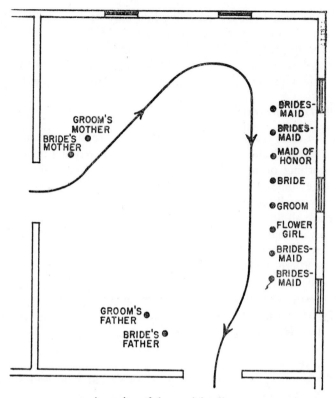

A version of the receiving line.

as you approach the line, you announce yourself. You would say to the bride's mother (who will extend her hand first), "I'm John Jones, Mrs. Smith. Such a lovely wedding." You will shake hands briefly, but you will not linger in the line even though you may be a longtime friend.

When you greet the bridal party, you offer *best wishes to the bride* and *congratulations to the bridegroom.* You *never* congratulate the bride. You will say a few words to the groom about how lovely his bride is, and he may answer, "Thank you so much," and agree that she is lovely as he passes you along with a "Here is John, Mary," or a more personal remark if there is a close friendship. Otherwise, he may say, "Mary, this is Commander Jones."

The simplest form of reception is one where the bride's mother and father greet the guests and introduce them to the groom's parents, with the guests going over to the bride and groom standing together and wishing them well.

At a small reception, the mothers of the bride and groom may stand in a continuous line with the bride and groom and the maid or matron of honor.

At a large reception, the receiving line may be in this order: half the bridesmaids, the maid or matron of honor, the bride, the groom, the flower girl, and the rest of the bridesmaids. The mothers of the bride and groom will be standing in the customary position near the door to the reception room, and the fathers will be standing nearby and/or mixing with the guests.

RECEPTION FOOD

There are three main types of food served at wedding receptions: a light buffet tea at small and informal receptions; or a wedding breakfast, which follows morning or noon weddings; or a buffet supper served following evening ceremonies.

At a very small reception, a wedding cake and punch with which to toast the bride are all that need be offered. It is customary at an afternoon reception, however, that a buffet tea include tea and coffee, thin sandwiches, small cakes, and punch or champagne.

At a late afternoon reception, the menu could be a seafood salad (shrimp, lobster, crab), ice cream molds, tea, coffee, and cakes. The menu could also be cold turkey or chicken, salad, ice cream or sherbet, tea, coffee, and cakes. By adding a hot soup and omitting the tea, either menu could be used for a buffet breakfast.

The menu for the wedding breakfast could be breast of chicken, tomato aspic, biscuits, ice cream or sherbet, wedding cake and champagne or punch. Creamed sweetbreads and peas, or baked ham and salads, little cakes, demitasse, and champagne or punch are frequently served.

A menu often served to guests who will eat standing up is: creamed chicken bordered by peas, salad, ice cream molds or meringues, cakes, coffee, and champagne or punch.

The buffet menu may be roast turkey, ham, or beef—or all three, if the reception is very large. Any wedding breakfast, luncheon, or supper may be served to guests seated at tables, but customarily is served buffet style, with the food and plates on a long table or tables, and with guests serving themselves and eating standing up.

SEATING ARRANGEMENTS

At a seated wedding breakfast or supper, there are usually two tables, one for the bride and groom and bridal party, the other for the parents and their intimate friends. The bride's table is always covered with a white cloth, and the wedding cake is placed in the center of the table. At a large table white flowers may be placed on either side of the cake.

The bride and groom will sit together at one end or at the center of the table, with the bride on the groom's right. The best man will be at the right of the bride, and the maid or matron of honor will sit at the left of the groom. The bridesmaids and ushers will alternate around the table.

The parents' table is set with a white cloth and bowl of flowers, and the parents of the bride will sit across from each other as they would in their own home.

The father of the groom will sit at the right of the bride's mother, and the chaplain or clergyman will sit at her left. The mother of the groom will sit at the right of the bride's father, and the wife of the chaplain or clergyman will sit at his left. Members of both immediate families, with intimate friends, will sit at the table. All other guests will be seated at small tables, for four or six each.

At smaller weddings, the bride's table and the parents' table are combined. Such an arrangement could be:

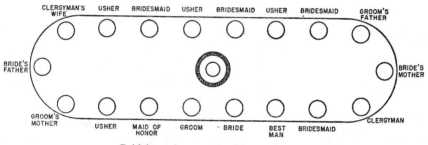

Bride's and parents' table combined.

At a buffet table, the food will be placed in convenient sequence together with stacks of plates, rows of silver, and napkins, with guests serving themselves at the table. The cake will be the centerpiece, or it may be placed on a smaller table, with guests coming to the table for a serving.

Champagne or punch is always placed on a table by itself except at a very small wedding, when it may be set on the main buffet table. There is usually a non-alcoholic drink served in addition to the champagne or punch—hot tea or coffee in winter, and iced tea or fruit juice in summer.

At the bridal table, the groom will unsheath his sword and hand it to the bride, and she will cut the first piece of cake with his hand over hers. Whether or not there is a seated bride's table, the first toast is always proposed by the best man to the bride. (See Chapter 9, *Toasts*.)

Other toasts may be to the bride's mother, proposed by the groom; then toasts to the bridesmaids, etc. When dancing follows, the bride and groom will dance the first dance together. The guests all join in the dancing, with the father of the bride dancing first with the groom's mother, and the bride's mother with the groom's father. The dancing may continue for an hour or so.

RECEIVING LINE AT THE CHAPEL

When a small reception is planned, to which it is impossible to invite all the guests who may have come to the wedding, a receiving line may be held in the foyer of the chapel—for example, the Navy Chapel in Washington, D.C.—immediately after the recessional. Such receiving lines may be formed in other chapels and churches throughout the country, but information concerning this must be obtained from the chaplain or clergyman.

The purpose of this type of receiving line is that a friendly and thoughtful way of receiving the congratulations of the congregation is offered. Guests who may have come from a distance and at some personal inconvenience will thus have the opportunity to speak to the bride and groom and to wish them happiness.

When such a receiving line is formed at the chapel, the same procedure is followed at the reception. The bride stands on the groom's right and the maid of honor at the right of the bride. The bridesmaids usually stand at the right of the maid of honor.

The bride's mother customarily receives alone at the door, but she may be accompanied by the groom's mother. The fathers of the bride and groom stand beside their wives, if they choose, or they may walk about among the guests. The ushers and best man are not in the receiving line.

GOING AWAY

It is a tradition that the bride throws her bouquet to her bridesmaids standing in a group, either from the stairs or in the doorway of an apartment or one-floor building. The bride will then change her clothes, and the groom will also change into traveling clothes, while the guests wait to see the couple off.

The parents will tell the bride and groom goodbye, in private, then the couple will go outdoors to a car that is waiting at the door while the guests traditionally throw confetti and rice on the couple. The destination of the wedding trip, and its duration, are strictly up to the couple—and the length of time the groom may have on leave, or between duty stations.

A HOUSE WEDDING

A couple may be married at home if they so desire. And in some cases, church regulations may prohibit a church ceremony between two persons of different faiths, or in the case of a divorced couple.

A wedding at home can be as large and as elaborate as a church wedding. The room where the wedding will take place should be emptied of as much heavy furniture as possible, with chairs and sofas placed along the walls.

The room farthest away from the door is usually the best place for the ceremony. A screen may be placed in front of a fire-place, and vases of white flowers may be effectively used. A long narrow table or altar will be placed in front of the screen, and here is where the bride and groom will stand. The arrangement of the altar should be according to the direction of the chaplain or clergyman, and the chairs will be placed in the room to form an aisle.

The immediate families of the bride and groom will sit in the first rows of chairs placed to the left and right, respectively, of the aisle. The first chair at the left side of the aisle is for the bride's father, or whoever gives her away. There will be other chairs, but some—or most—guests will stand. The ushers will not have lists, but they will stand near the front door and tell guests where they should go.

As soon as all guests have arrived, the groom's mother goes up the aisle with her husband. The bride's mother will be the last to be seated; she is escorted by a male relative or the No. 1 usher.

The chaplain or clergyman, the groom and best man, will take their places as they would in church. The groom and best man stand near the altar, at the right side of the aisle, with the best man just behind and at the right of the groom. The bride's mother rises at the first note of the Wedding March, and the procession follows the same form as in the chapel or church —except that ushers are *not* included.

The bridesmaids will enter the room first, then the bride and her father. When the ceremony is over, the bride and groom usually stand at the altar, with guests coming up to extend their best wishes and congratulations. The groom will kiss his bride at the altar—since he is always the first to kiss the bride after the ceremony.

The couple will go directly to the place of the reception, with the guests following. There is usually no seated bride's table, and the reception may be as elaborate or simple as desired.

At a very small afternoon wedding at home, with only members of the immediate families and intimate friends attending, the bride may wear a long bridal gown or she may wear a pastel colored or white afternoon dress or suit, with a corsage.

The parents of the bride and groom, and the couple, will stand a little apart to greet guests. A buffet tea may be served, with a wedding cake centering the table. Punch, tea, and sandwiches would be placed in convenient sequence around the table. Invitations to such a small wedding may be handwritten, with wedding announcements sent out after the ceremony. (See Chapter 17, *Invitations and Replies.*)

At a formal evening wedding (usually held at eight o'clock or half after eight) the members of the bridal party may be in full evening dress, with men in dinner dress or evening dress uniform or in "black" or "white tie." The women guests will wear evening dress, with their heads covered somewhat; the mothers of the bride and groom, and older women guests, usually wear long dresses with matching jackets or stoles, with the heads and arms covered.

Men, other than members of the bridal party, do *not* wear any form of evening dress during the daylight hours, even for a wedding. Evening dress is never worn before six o'clock.

Although a Protestant is not expected to make the Sign of the Cross at a Catholic wedding, a Christian man at an Orthodox or Conservative Jewish wedding must wear a hat. You must go as far as your own religious customs permit, when attending a ceremony foreign to you; you may bow your head when others kneel, but you should stand and sit when others do the same.

VARIATIONS IN THE PROCEDURE

There are variations in the traditional wedding procedures—such as when the bride's parents are divorced, when one or the other of the parents has remarried, or when the bride's father or mother is dead. There is also a variation in the procedure when the bride is a divorcée or a widow.

When the bride's parents are divorced, the mother customarily gives the wedding and the reception. The bride's father may give her in marriage, but he may—or may not—go to the wedding reception.

On the day of the wedding, the father will call for the bride just before the ceremony. He usually waits in the car, and sends word to the door that he is there.

Sometimes, the mother gives the wedding and the father gives the wedding reception. In this case, when the father has remarried, his *present* wife will act as hostess; if his *first* wife (the bride's mother) attends, she will attend as an important guest.

If the father has not remarried and he and his former wife are friendly, he may ask her to stand in the receiving line with him at the reception (regardless of whether she has remarried)—but *he* may precede her in the line since this is his home, not hers. If he has not remarried, he may also receive guests by himself.

At the chapel or church, the father will sit in the second pew during the ceremony; if he has remarried, he will sit in the third pew on the left with his present wife—if she attends. If the relations are pleasant, the father—and his present wife, if the relationship is truly congenial—will attend the reception.

When the bride's mother has remarried, her present husband sits with her during the ceremony in the first pew at the left of the aisle. At the wedding reception, he will act as host. When the relationship with a stepfather has been a happy one, and the father of the bride is at a distance or cannot attend the ceremony, the stepfather may give the bride in marriage.

When the *bride's father is deceased*, a brother, uncle, cousin, or a male relative of suitable age (about 21 years old) may give the bride away. A classmate of the father, or close friend, may give the bride in marriage. It is not proper for a bride to be given in marriage *by her mother or any other woman*.

When the *bride's mother is deceased*, and the father has remarried, the stepmother may be in charge of the wedding plans. If the bride prefers, an aunt, grandmother, or close friend of the family, may act in this capacity.

At a *double wedding*, when two sisters are being married, the elder takes precedence over the younger throughout the ceremony. The elder sister will walk up the aisle with her father, and the second sister will walk with a brother, uncle, or other male relative or older intimate male friend of the family. The father will give both daughters away—the elder daughter first, then the younger.

The bridegrooms will stand at the head of the aisle, with their best men behind them, the bridegroom of the elder sister nearer the congregation. The elder sister is at the left and the younger at the right during the ceremony, with the vows repeated separately. The elder sister goes down the aisle *first* when the ceremony is over.

Usually, the sisters have the same bridesmaids, half of whom each sister selects. The ushers are also divided in this way, but each bride should have her own maid or matron of honor, and each groom should have his own best man. In the wedding precession, the maid or matron of honor would directly precede each bride, with the ushers, bridesmaids, etc., preceding the entire bridal party.

The family of both grooms may share the first pew at the right of the chapel or church, or the family of the groom of the elder sister will sit in the first pew, and the family of the groom of the second sister will sit in the second pew.

At the wedding reception the elder sister stands before the younger sister, with the traditional order followed thereon. The mother of the brides will stand at the door to greet guests, with the mother of the elder daughter's husband next to her, then the mother of the other groom beyond.

When the brides are not sisters at a double wedding, the older girl, or the highest ranking of the brides' fathers, or the highest ranking bridegroom may decide the question of which bride precedes the other. Sometimes the question is settled by alphabetical order of the brides' names. The same precedence would follow at the reception.

At the *second marriage* of a woman who has been married before, the bride *never* wears a wedding veil, and does not wear the traditional long white wedding gown. She may wear a long dress of pastel color, with a flower arrangement in her hair or a small hat, with a corsage instead of a bridal bouquet.

The remarriage of a divorced or widowed woman is *always* less elaborate than a first marriage, with the wedding of a divorcée less elaborate than that of a young widow. The reception may be as large as the couple chooses, but a smaller reception is more appropriate and a small wedding *is required*.

When the bride is a young widow, an engagement announcement is proper in a newspaper. She may also send engraved wedding invitations and/or announcements. An older widow or divorced woman customarily sends out engraved wedding announcements only. (See Chapter 17, *Invitations and Replies*.)

A second marriage for a man does not affect the ceremony. When either a man or woman is widowed or divorced, however, this fact *must* be brought to the attention of the chaplain or clergyman when plans are discussed for the wedding.

ENGAGEMENT ANNOUNCEMENT

A formal engagement is announced by the bride-elect's parents, or closest relative, usually between six weeks and six months before the wedding date (the future groom's orders often determine the length of the engagement). The groom's gifts to the girl *before the engagement* should be relatively impersonal—never expensive.

When the announcement is sent to a newspaper to be printed by a certain date—but not before that date—then state the date of release at the top left of the announcement, FOR RELEASE MONDAY, MARCH 15. If for a Sunday edition, the announcement should be on the society editor's desk the first of the week, preferably a week or so in advance. The account should be brief, and factual, with full names rather than initials: For example:

Capt. John James Smith, USN (Ret.) and Mrs. Smith of Arlington, Va. announce the engagement of their daughter, Mary Ann, to Ens. Donald James Adams, USN, son of Mr. and Mrs. William Claton Adams of St. Louis, Mo.

Miss Smith was graduated from Wellesley College, and made her debut at the Bachelors Cotillon in Baltimore in 1957. Ensign Adams attended Gilman School, and was graduated from the Naval Academy, Class of 1958. He is in flight training at Pensacola, Fla. The wedding will take place in June.

PUBLISHED WEDDING ANNOUNCEMENT

Wedding accounts for publication in metropolitan newspapers should be sent to the society editor of the paper, in advance of the wedding day. A Sunday edition is customarily set up almost a week in advance of the day of issue, and out-of-town items should be on the editor's desk by the first of the preceding week.

The account should include all the pertinent information in the engagement announcement, plus accurate information such as: the date and time of the wedding, the name of the officiating chaplain or clergyman, the church or chapel, and the place of the reception. It is of interest to mention the new address of the couple or the duty station of the bridegroom. When either one is from a very old or distinguished family, such a fact may be included in the account.

A home-town paper will include additional information: the names and home-towns of the entire bridal party, as well as descriptions of the bridal gown and bouquet and, usually, that of the bridesmaids' and mothers' gowns and corsages as well.

When space permits, a newspaper will carry a list of distinguished or out-of-town guests and relatives, but a complete list of guests is never published. When you are the groom you may wish to send a brief account to your alumni magazine or Service paper, if such news is used by these publications.

WEDDING PRESENTS

When you have been invited to a wedding, you should be aware of the customary rules for giving wedding presents. These are as follows:

- You send presents to friends and relatives when they are close to you—but you are not obligated to send a present to everyone who sends you a wedding invitation or announcement.
- You do not send more than you can afford—but you should always remember that quality is superior to quantity.
- It is customary to send a wedding present when you are invited to both the ceremony and reception—but when you receive many invitations (such as the innumerable June Week weddings at the Naval Academy), you send presents only to those classmates or friends close to you, whether you attend the ceremony or not.
- When you are invited to the ceremony, but not the reception, you are not obligated to send a present—but you may, if you so desire.
- When there is no reception, an invitation to the wedding takes its

place and you may send a present, depending upon your friendship with the couple.

- When there are no invitations or announcements, you send a present to the couple according to your friendship with them. Every young couple enjoys a wedding present, and will always treasure it. If you prefer, you may take or send the couple a house-warming present.

Wedding presents are sent to the bride-elect's home before the wedding. After the wedding, presents are sent to the couple at their new address. It is the duty of the bride, within two or three weeks after a gift is received, to write thank-you notes to each person or family sending the gift.

Although writing many thank-you notes is a chore, a thoughtful bride will *always* include in each note some mention of the gift itself. Therefore, she must keep a list of each person or family sending a gift and a notation concerning the nature of the gift.

Ushers customarily give individual or joint gifts to the couple before the wedding. It is a growing custom that a joint gift is selected because a handsomer present can be given. Bridesmaids also give individual or joint gifts to the couple.

It is always better to give a small but choice gift rather than a larger—but cheaper—present. Most jewelry stores in smaller cities where weddings are to take place have a list previously given them by the bride, with information as to her choice of silver, china, and glass. In such cases, one or two cups and saucers, a single piece of silver, or a handsome goblet would be much more appropriate than a dozen inexpensive iced tea glasses. Usually it is perfectly proper for a bride to exchange duplicate presents.

MARRIAGE FINANCES

When you are the groom, you should have your financial house in order before marriage—with finances to cover the wedding trip, regardless of how short or extended the trip may be. A wedding trip may be en route to a new duty station, and in this case motel or hotel reservations should be made in advance.

You also must have finances to cover the establishing of your new household, which may be in a town or at a base unfamiliar to you. A classmate or friend stationed there frequently is of assistance in helping you find temporary quarters.

Sometimes the family of the bride and/or the groom give the young couple a check as a wedding gift, and financial problems are of no immediate concern. But a young couple should work as a team in household finances, with both the bride and groom fully understanding the limitations of a paycheck.

Since you are a naval officer and are subject to duty at sea, someone must handle your household and other financial obligations while you are gone. A young wife can contribute much to the success of a new marriage by her ability to handle capably these financial obligations. A household budget should be worked out, and thoroughly understood by *both* of you, before the hour of sailing.*

* For such information invaluable to a new bride in the Service, the book *Welcome Aboard,* a manual for the Naval officer's wife, published by the U. S. Naval Institute, will be an invaluable gift to any young Navy bride.

CHAPTER 32

Hospital Manners

Nothing is more exhausting to a hospital patient than to have a visitor who comes too soon after surgery or a painful illness, or who stays too long, or talks too loudly. If the patient were in good health and feeling fine, he would not be in the hospital. Some visitors, however, seem to regard a hospital room as a fine place for a social hour.

Any visitor in a hospital should observe the following rules:

- Walk quietly in hospital corridors, and talk quietly. Women particularly should guard against high heels clacking on tiled floors.
- The length of time of your visit depends upon the patient's condition, and how he is momentarily feeling. Five minutes may be too long. Fifteen minutes is generally long enough, unless you are a relative or *very* close friend, and even then the patient may not care to see anyone. Twenty minutes to half an hour is plenty of time for any visit.
- There are definite visiting hours in any hospital, and visitors should check them before going there. Make sure in advance that a patient wants visitors, by telephoning to the hospital or the patient's home.
- Visitors should not sit on the patient's bed and should avoid jostling the bed. Do not scrape the floor by moving your feet or chair in a noisy manner. Do not pace restlessly about the room.
- Do not visit anyone in the hospital when you have a cold. Sick persons are apt to be more susceptible to contagious diseases.
- Do not ask embarrassing questions concerning the patient's illness or surgery. He will tell you about it if he cares to.

When you are visiting in a hospital, do remember these *do's* and *don'ts*:

- When there are several other visitors ahead of you in the room, you should wait outside until some leave. If the patient has many visitors, he may be getting weary, so cut your own stay—unless he urges you to remain.
- *Don't* smoke in a hospital room unless the patient is smoking, or doesn't mind if you do. But find out about it first.
- *Don't* visit anyone immediately after surgery or a very painful illness, unless the patient is your mother or your wife, or a very dear relative or friend.

- *Do not* visit a new mother too soon after the event—unless it is your wife! You may always see the new baby by looking through the glass door of the nursery.
- When you wish to help the patient in some small way, you may change the water in flower vases, crank a bed up or down when necessary, write or mail letters, or remove unwanted objects cluttering the room.
- When you want to take the patient a small gift, flowers are always nice—but *don't* overdo it: too many flowers remind some persons of funerals. When a patient is to be in the hospital for some time, a potted plant is always nice. You may wish to take a small bottle of perfume to a woman. Men usually like to read books or magazines, and they always want a daily newspaper. Newspapers are usually delivered at most hospitals, but a visitor may care to do this for a friend.

When you are the patient in a hospital, there are some *do's* and *don't's* for you:

- *Do* be considerate of your nurse or corpsman—they are there to help you, not to wait on you. A nurse or corpsman is a professional man or woman—not a servant.
- *Do* cooperate with hospital rules, and *don't* make too much of a fuss concerning pills, needles, etc.
- In a private room, you can suit yourself (within reason) concerning the volume of your radio or TV, air conditioner, etc., and you may smoke with the doctor's permission. *But* in a semiprivate room or a ward, you must be considerate of your fellow patient or patients. Smoke can be disagreeable to another patient and your radio may drive him wild.
- *Do not* give orders to your nurse, and *do* call her by name: "Miss Smith," or "Mrs. Lee." Otherwise, call her "Nurse," but never "Miss." When the nurse doesn't tell you her name, you may properly ask her what it is. You *do not* ask her the details of your illness—you ask your doctor.
- Patients *do not* tip a trained nurse or a corpsman. You may give them a gift when you leave. In this case, it is proper to give the floor nurse a box of candy and the head corpsman a carton of cigarettes which may be divided among all the attendants on the floor.
- In a civilian hospital, you may tip the maid who has cleaned your room, or a porter who has served you. Ward patients *do not* tip.

CHAPTER 33

Accident or Death

When there has been an accident or the death of an officer while on leave or en route to a new station, such information should be immediately telephoned or wired to the commanding officer of the nearest Armed Forces activity. Any authorized person may send the message. The following information should be given:

- The officer's full name, rank, and service number.
- Where the death or accident (or illness) took place; the extent of the injury and present condition—if living; the name and address of the physician in charge; the name and address of the hospital or place where the patient or deceased is at that time; and the address where the person giving the information can be reached.

The person telephoning or wiring the information should ask for instructions, and then carry them out meticulously. A military officer will be assigned to check on the accident or illness. In case of an automobile accident, for example, it is necessary to have verification that the accident was not the fault of the deceased or injured, and that no negligence or carelessness on the part of the deceased or injured was involved—otherwise the wife or family may not receive all forthcoming benefits.

A member of the deceased or injured officer's or enlisted man's family can always obtain help from the commanding officer of the Armed Forces activity and its chaplain. All Services handle funeral arrangements for the widow, and legal advice is available without the services of a private lawyer. Service personnel, whether officer or enlisted, will receive emergency medical treatment at any government hospital or, when none is available, at a civilian hospital.

MESSAGES OF CONDOLENCE

The purpose of the message of condolence is to express your sympathy to the closest member, or members, of the deceased person's family. The brief note, letter, telegram, or telephone call should be taken care of immediately upon your receipt of the news of the death. (See Chapter 16, *Correspondence*.)

You may find a letter of condolence difficult to write—many people do. But when you realize how important it is for the bereaved person or persons to receive a message of sympathy, then you will immediately write or send it, when necessary.

When writing or sending the message, you may address it to the nearest living relative—whether you know him or her, or not. On the death of a male friend, you send the message to his wife, if he was married, or to his parents, if he was single. If there are no surviving parents, the message should be addressed to a brother or sister, or any near relative.

Letters of condolence are always written by hand, usually on plain white paper of the more formal type. Your letter should be short and simple—but sincere. Since you desire to express comfort to the bereaved, do not dwell on the illness or manner of death.

It is better to avoid Biblical quotations—not only in the interest of brevity, but because such a quotation may prove offensive in cases where the religious faith of the deceased's family is incorrectly judged. Most people prefer to grant to the chaplain or family minister the privilege of interpreting the Bible.

The words *died, death,* and *killed* are used only when absolutely necessary. It is frequently difficult to be sincere in expressing your feelings without occasionally using such words, but they should be used as infrequently as possible. However, it is better to use these words than such trite expressions as "John's untimely passing," or, "Now that Fred has left us."

FLORAL OFFERING OR CHARITY CONTRIBUTIONS

In sending flowers to a funeral, they should be sent to the nearest relative—*but never to the deceased.* If the services are to be held in a home, the flowers should be sent to the nearest relative. When services are to be held in a funeral home, then they should be sent there, addressed to "The funeral of Mr. Smith Jones." You write your full name on the card enclosed with the flowers. If the relationship with the bereaved is a close one, then sign your name "John Doe" or "Ann and John Doe." Do not write "Ann and John." You may sign "Captain and Mrs. John Doe" or enclose your personal card or joint card.

When the obituary notice states "Please omit flowers," then you omit them. If the notice states that contributions may be sent to a charity in lieu of flowers, you may send a check to the charity enclosed with a note stating that the check is in memory of the deceased.

You may send your personal card to the family saying that you have done this, but of course you never mention the amount sent to the charity.

CALLS ON THE BEREAVED

When you live near the bereaved person or persons, you will want to call on him or her—if they are close friends or relatives. The purpose of such a call is to give comfort and sympathy to the bereaved, but sometimes a call of condolence can bring more distress than comfort.

Whether you can be of assistance or are invading a family's privacy depends upon how well you know the bereaved. Your own good sense should give you the answer. When you cannot be of assistance, all calls should be brief.

In some cases, a family may urgently need assistance—as well as sympathy—whether you know them well or not. Such a case may follow an accident and death, which are always a shock to a family. Then, you may be able to help out with tact, thoughtfulness, and consideration of others' feelings.

If you are married, you and your wife may care for any children in the bereaved family for a day or two. Perhaps you may best help by wiring or telephoning friends of the family who are at a distance. Someone is usually needed in a bereaved house to answer telephone calls or to do whatever generally is necessary.

You should never take offense if you should call on a bereaved family and whoever answers the door says that the family is not receiving visitors. (Such calls, of course, are never returned.) You may leave your personal card with the phrase, "Deepest sympathy," written across it.

When making a call, remember to try not to become over-emotional, for such actions will be adding to the bereaved's distress rather than comfort. Friends less close to the bereaved family may call at the funeral home, rather than at the house.

GENERAL BEHAVIOR

When a death notice states "Funeral Private," you do not attend the funeral—unless you are a close friend and have been notified by the family beforehand.When services are open to the public but the "interment private," you will attend the services but do not go to the cemetery.

Mourners attending the funeral services (other than members of the family) will dress conservatively, but black clothes are not necessary.

IN MOURNING

During the past quarter of a century, there have been many changes made in the conventions of mourning—particularly in the matter of dress. Most people feel that grief is a private thing, and that the public appearance of an individual *after the funeral* is not now as important as it was a number of years ago.

It is traditional that all members of the family wear mourning at the funeral, but it is not necessary to wear mourning clothes for a long length of time following the funeral—unless you so choose.

However, customs vary throughout the nation, and the conventional mourning customs are observed in certain sections. But whatever the length of mourning, the transition from black to colors should be gradual, for women, with the black usually being relieved with a gray, a lavender, or a white dress. A girl does not wear mourning for her fiance. Usually, men wear a black band around the left sleeves of civilian coats and jackets that may not be black, and black studs and ties are sufficient indications of mourning.

The customary period of mourning may be observed if the individuals concerned care to or they may not be observed at all following the funeral. The general rules are:

- All members of the family wear mourning at the funeral.
- Mourning may be worn for six months to a year following the death of a husband, wife, son or daughter, or parent.
- Mourning may be worn for three to six months for a grandparent, a brother, or sister.
- Half-mourning may be worn for one to two months for all other close relatives.

How long a person should stay in social seclusion following a bereavement is a personal matter. It is proper that the bereaved attends the theater, concert, movies, and small quiet gatherings not too long after the loss—in many cases it is desirable that a bereaved person does not stay in seclusion.

Wedding invitations may be sent to those in mourning, and it is correct for the bereaved to accept such an invitation if he so chooses. Small weddings for members of the immediate families may continue, after being scheduled, during a time of mourning.

Generally, the gaiety of the occasion will determine whether a bereaved person attends a social function within several months after a death in the immediate family. Men usually do not resume their social life for at least two months afterwards, and a widow usually does not go to large formal functions—such as dances, balls, etc.—for a year.

Bibliography

Annapolis Today by Kendall Banning, revised by A. Stuart Pitt. Annapolis, Md.: U. S. Naval Institute, 1957.

The Bluejackets' Manual by CAPT John V. Noel, Jr., USN. Annapolis, Md.: U. S. Naval Institute, 1957.

Complete Book of Etiquette by Amy Vanderbilt. Garden City, N.Y.: Doubleday & Co. Inc., 1954.

Complete Etiquette by Frances Benton. New York, N.Y.: Random House, 1956.

Esquire Etiquette by Esquire Inc. Philadelphia, Penna.: J. B. Lippincott Co., 1953.

Etiquette by Emily Post. New York, N.Y.: Funk & Wagnalls, 1952.

Etiquette and Protocol by I. Monte Radlovic. New York: Harcourt, Brace and Co., 1956.

The Marine Officer's Guide by GEN G. C. Thomas, USMC, COL R. D. Heinl, Jr., USMC, RADM A. A. Ageton, USN (Ret.). Annapolis, Md.: U. S. Naval Institute, 1956.

Naval Customs, Traditions, and Usage by LCDR Leland P. Lovette, USN. Annapolis, Md.: U. S. Naval Institute, 1939.

The Navy Wife by Anne Briscoe Pye and Nancy Shea. New York: Harper and Brothers, 1955.

Rules of Order, Revised by Henry M. Robert. Watkins Glen, N. Y.: Century House, 1957.

The Serviceman's Wife by Elizabeth Land and LTCOL Carrol V. Glines, Jr., USA. Boston, Mass.: Houghton Mifflin Co., 1956.

Vogue's Book of Etiquette by Millicent Fenwick. New York: Simon and Schuster, Inc., 1948.

Welcome Aboard by Florence Ridgely Johnson. Annapolis, Md.: U. S. Naval Institute, 1958.

Index

Index

TRIMMED SIZE: 6 × 9 inches
TYPE PAGE: 27 × 44½ picas
TYPE FACE: Linotype Times Roman
TYPE SIZE: 10 point on 12
CHAPTER TITLE: 24 point Intertype Baskerville
PAPER: 50 lb. White Warren's Olde Style Wove
CLOTH: Bancroft's Linen Finish 4460